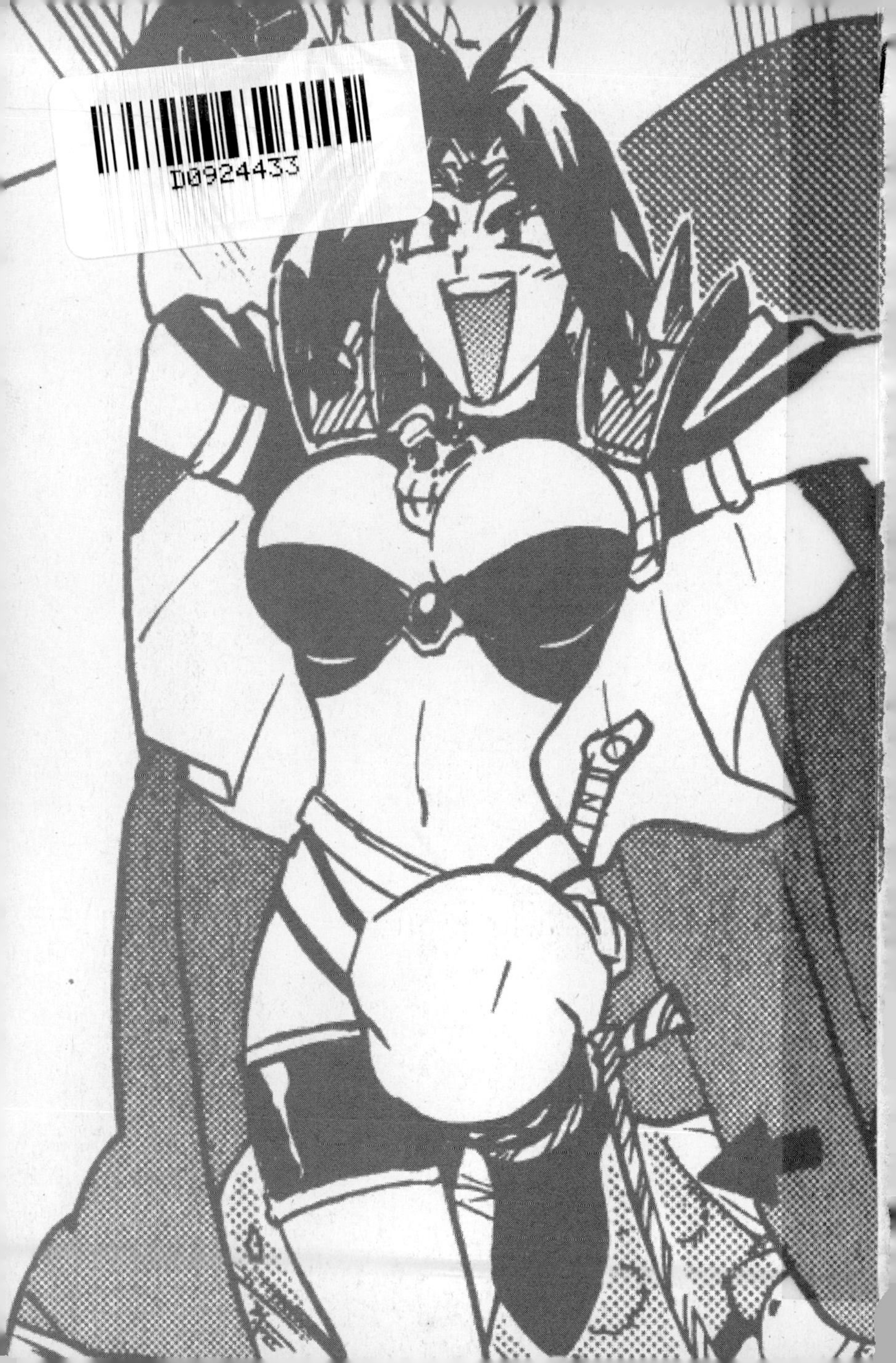

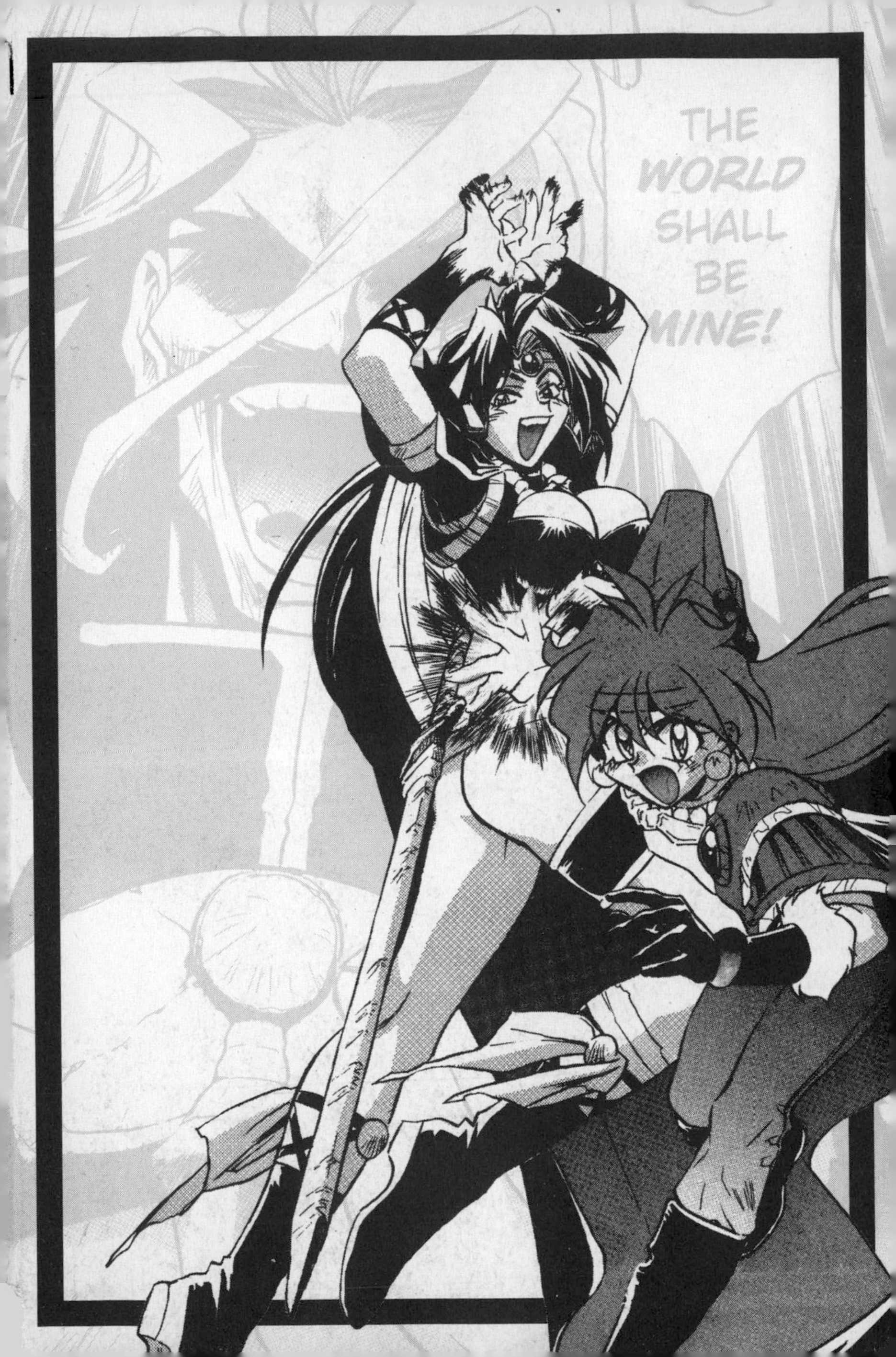
THE WORLD SHALL BE MINE!

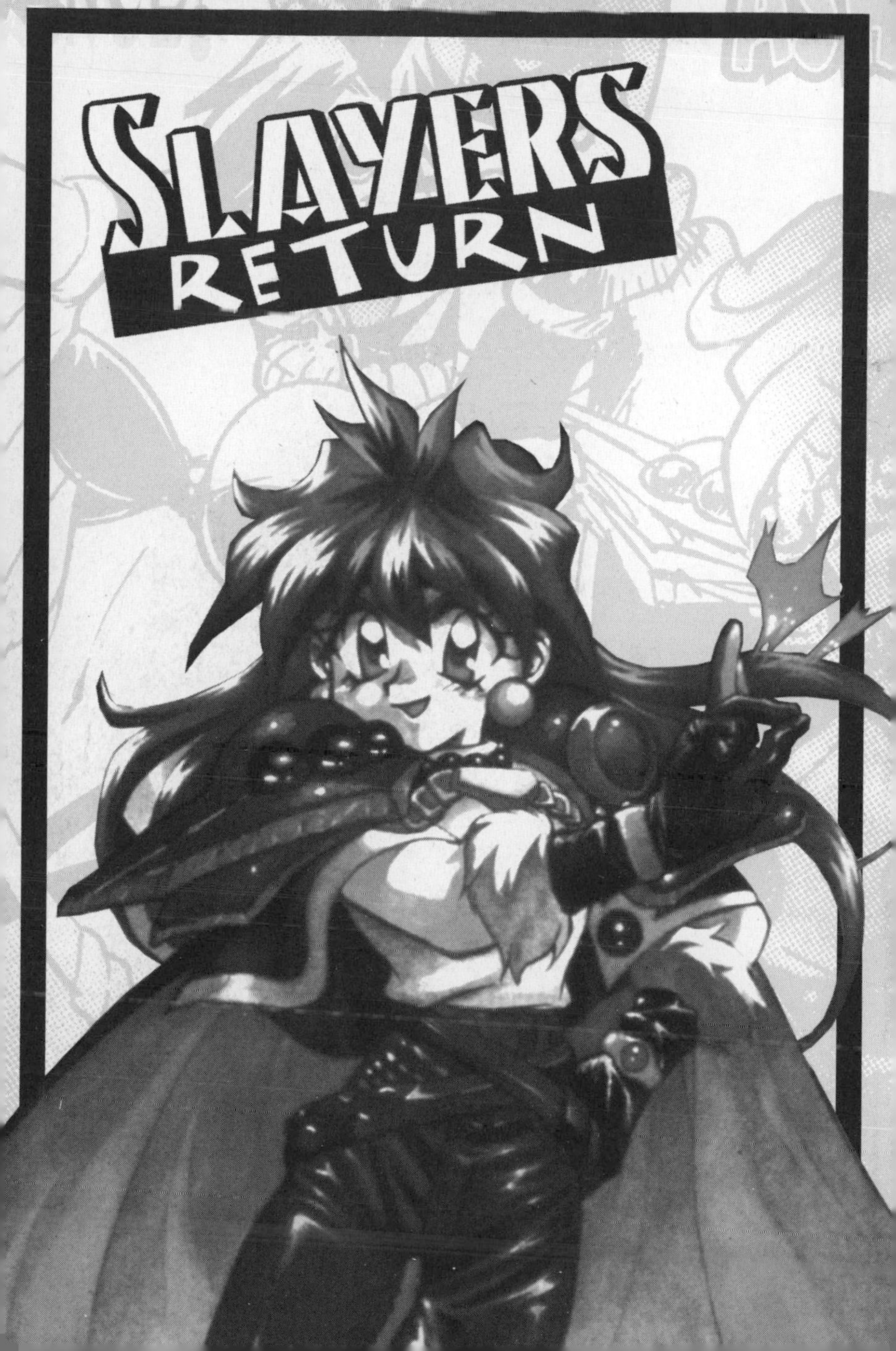

SLAYERS
RETURN

MAYUMI KOBAYASHI
Translation

MARK GRIFFIN
Retouch and Lettering

VANESSA SATONE
Designer

STEPHEN PAKULA
Production Supervisor

MIKE LACKEY
Print Production Manager

STEPHANIE SHALOFSKY
Vice President, Production

JOHN O'DONNELL
Publisher

World Peace Through
Shared Popular Culture™
centralparkmedia.com
cpmmanga.com

Slayers Return. Published by CPM Manga, a division of Central Park Media Corporation. Office of Publication – 250 West 57th Street, Suite 317, New York, NY 10107. Original Japanese version "CHOUBAKUMADOUDEN SLAYERS volume 4" © HAJIME KANZAKA/RUI ARAIZUMI/SHOKO YOSHINAKA 1997. Originally published in Japan in 1997 by KADOKAWA SHOTEN PUBLISHING Co., Ltd. English translation rights arranged with KADOKAWA SHOTEN PUBLISHING Co., Ltd., Tokyo through TOHAN CORPORATION, TOKYO. English version ©2003 Central Park Media Corporation. CPM Manga and logo are registered trademarks of Central Park Media Corporation. Original Manga and logo are trademarks of Central Park Media Corporation. Original Manga is a trademark of Central Park Media Corporation. All rights reserved. Price per copy $9.99, price in Canada may vary. ISBN: 1-58664-914-0. Catalog number: CMX 64604G. UPC: 7-19987-00646-1-00411. Printed in Canada.

SLAYERS RETURN

HAJIME KANZAKA
Writer

SHOKO YOSHINAKA
Artist

RUI ARAIZUMI
Character Design

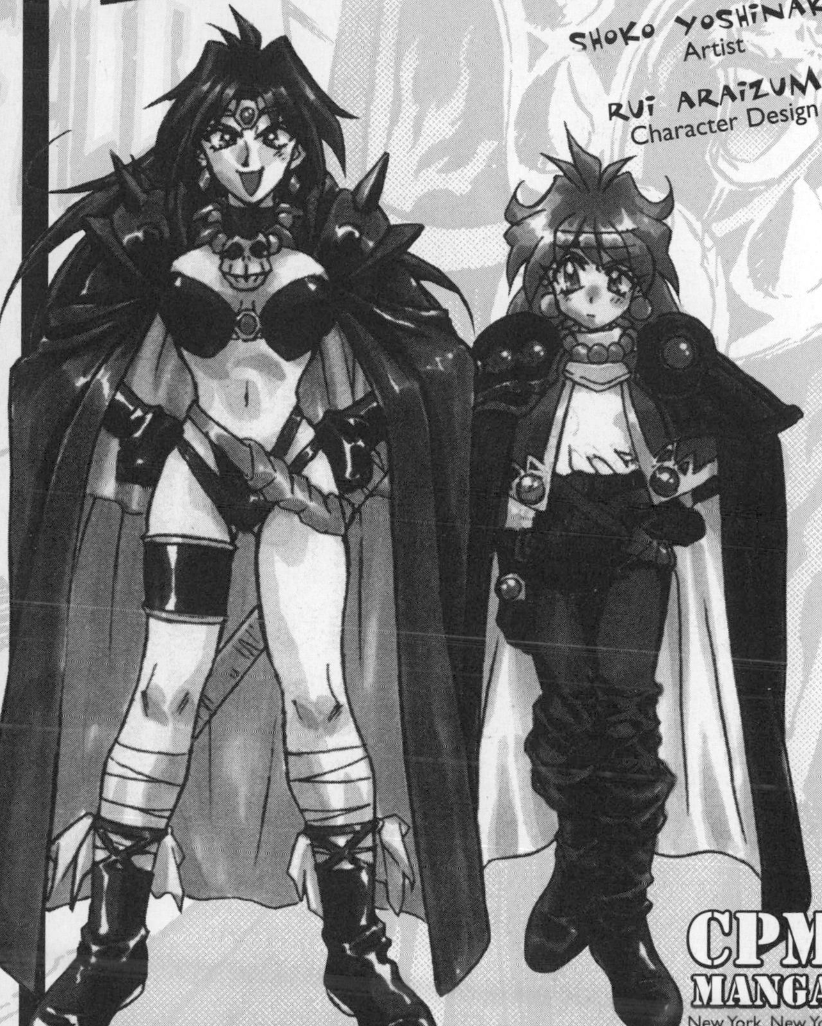

CPM® MANGA
New York, New York

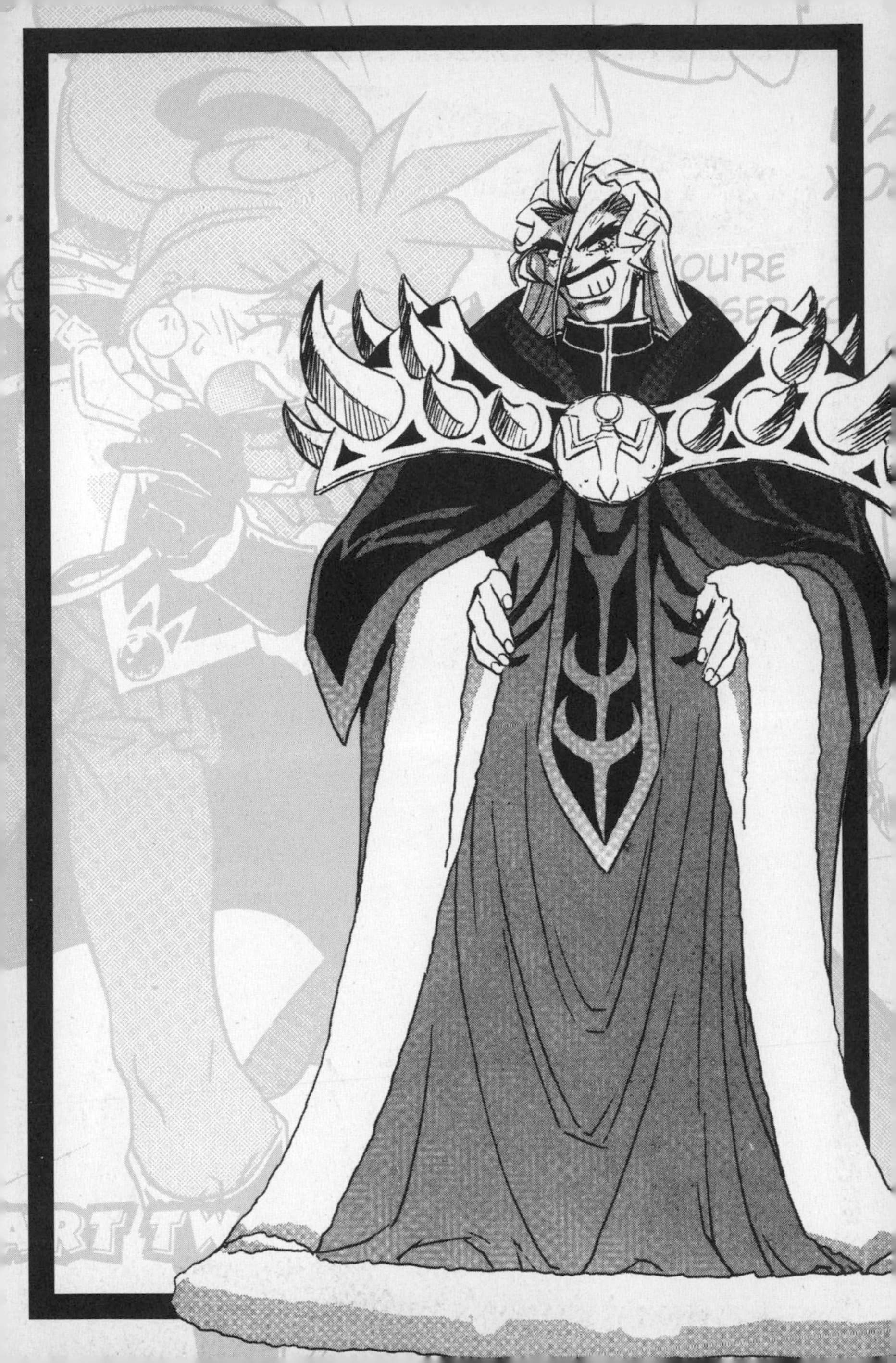
YOU'RE

CONTENTS

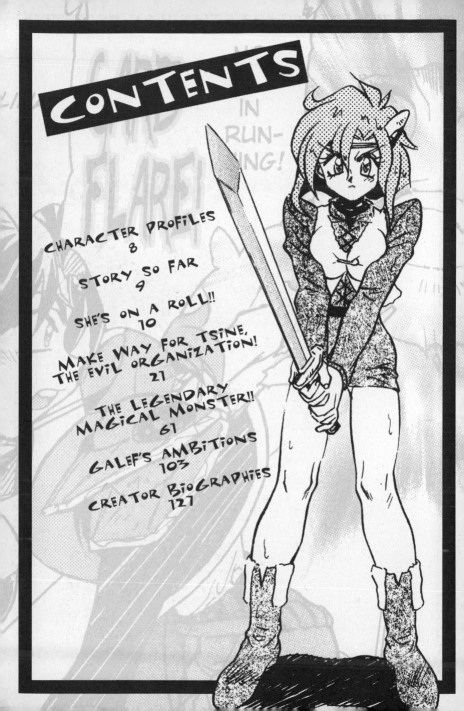

LINA INVERSE

Lina is a powerful sorceress with a short temper. Though still in her early teens, she's already mastered the incredibly powerful and destructive Dragon Slave...a spell powerful enough to kill a dragon in one blow! She wanders the countryside in search of adventure, treasure, and most importantly...good food.

YOU DEAL WITH IT.

FIREBALL!

OH YEAH... AND BECKER TOO.

NAGA THE WHITE SERPENT

Naga is quite the conjurer herself. She's bold, buxom, brash, and knows all kinds of frosty charms that cause great harm. She's not the most brilliant serpent in the world, but she's probably the most poisonous.

MEGA

VA O

VALAIMA

!!

CHARACTER PROFILES

STORY SO FAR

This is a story of the early days of Lina Inverse, when she first set out on her journeys of adventure, discovery, and gourmet food. It takes place before she met Gourry, Zelgadis or Rezo the Red Priest (as chronicled in SLAYERS SUPER-EXPLOSIVE DEMON STORY Books One -Three).

Accompanying Lina on this tale is her self-proclaimed rival and favorite target, Naga the White Serpent. Can these two powerful and skilled women successfully travel the lands seeking treasure and escapades without killing each other?

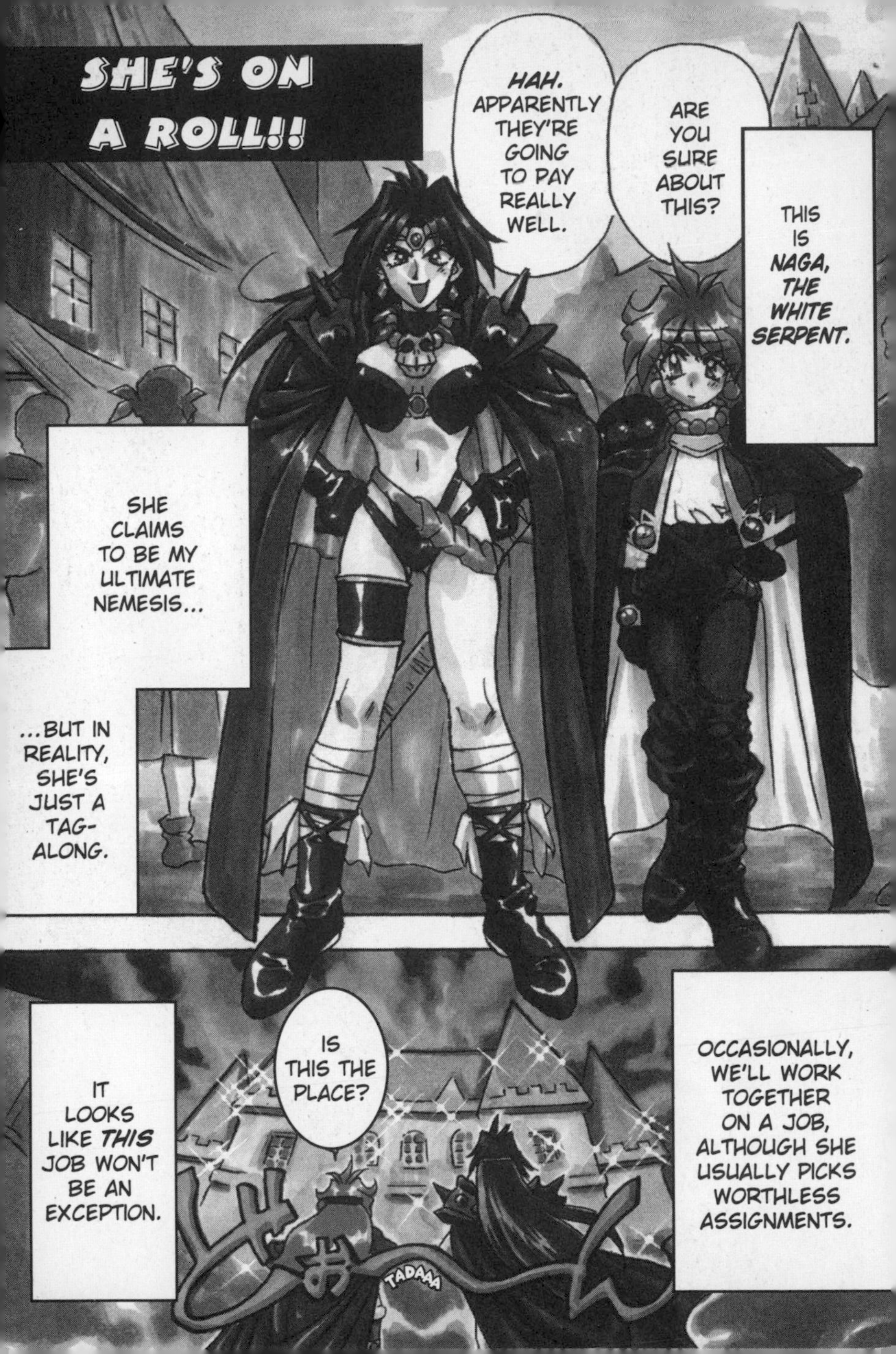

SHE'S ON A ROLL!!
ARE YOU SURE ABOUT THIS?
HAH. APPARENTLY THEY'RE GOING TO PAY REALLY WELL.
THIS IS NAGA, THE WHITE SERPENT.
SHE CLAIMS TO BE MY ULTIMATE NEMESIS...
...BUT IN REALITY, SHE'S JUST A TAG-ALONG.
OCCASIONALLY, WE'LL WORK TOGETHER ON A JOB, ALTHOUGH SHE USUALLY PICKS WORTHLESS ASSIGNMENTS.
IS THIS THE PLACE?
IT LOOKS LIKE THIS JOB WON'T BE AN EXCEPTION.
TADAAA

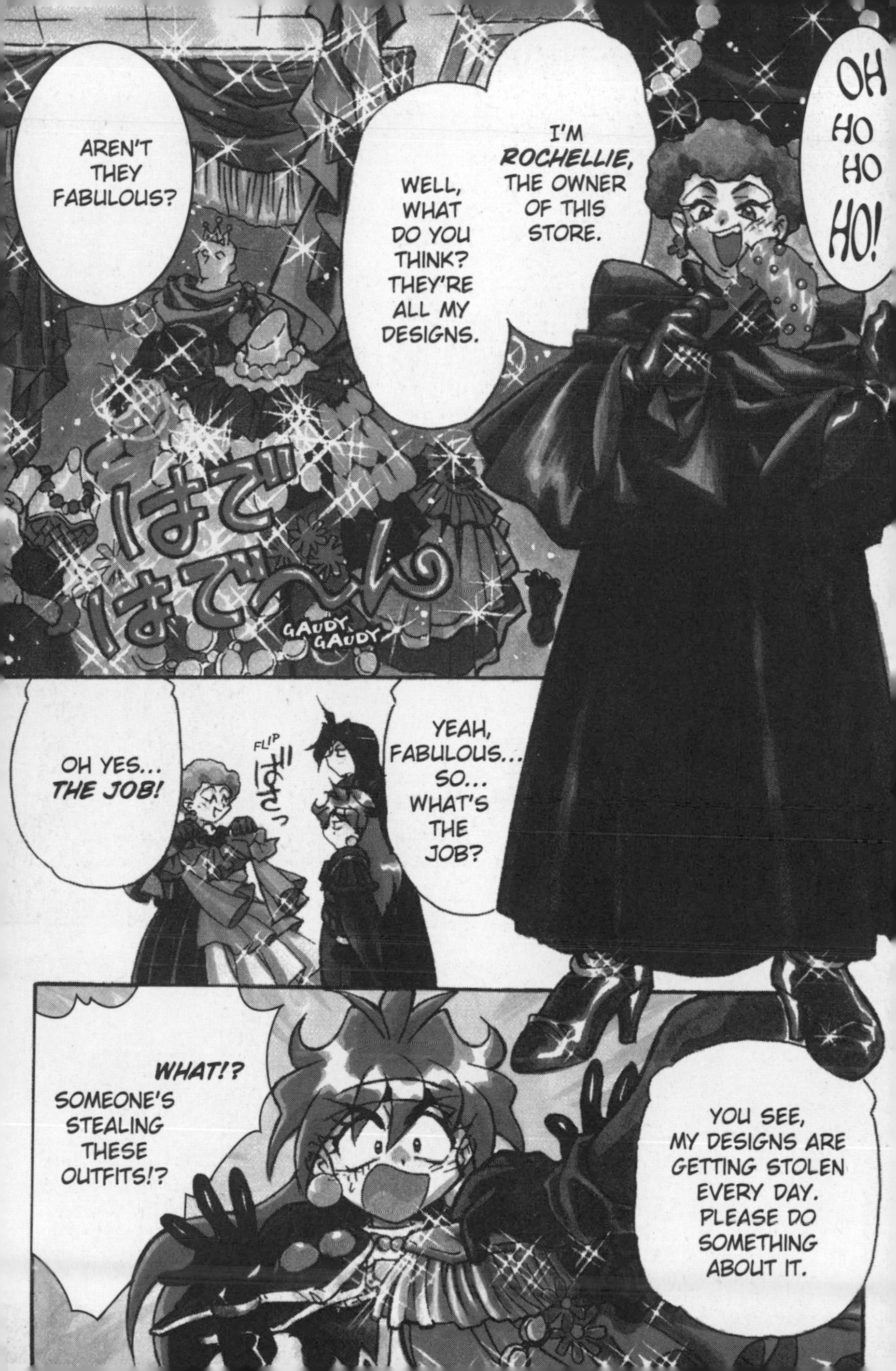
OH HO HO HO!
I'M ROCHELLIE, THE OWNER OF THIS STORE.
WELL, WHAT DO YOU THINK? THEY'RE ALL MY DESIGNS.
AREN'T THEY FABULOUS?
はで はでーん
GAUDY GAUDY
YEAH, FABULOUS... SO... WHAT'S THE JOB?
FLIP
OH YES... THE JOB!
YOU SEE, MY DESIGNS ARE GETTING STOLEN EVERY DAY. PLEASE DO SOMETHING ABOUT IT.
WHAT!? SOMEONE'S STEALING THESE OUTFITS!?

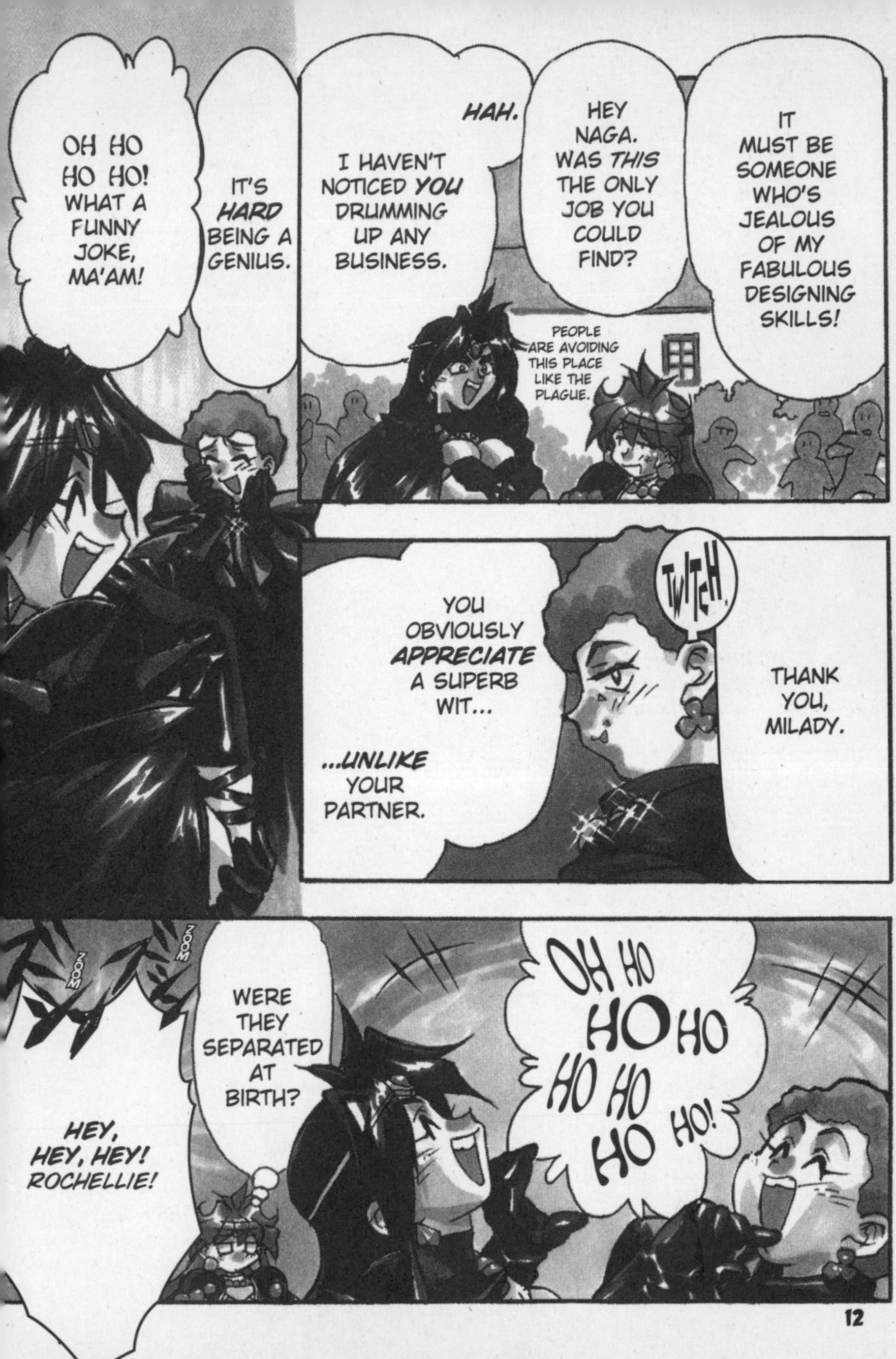

IT MUST BE SOMEONE WHO'S JEALOUS OF MY FABULOUS DESIGNING SKILLS!
HEY NAGA. WAS *THIS* THE ONLY JOB YOU COULD FIND?
HAH. I HAVEN'T NOTICED ***YOU*** DRUMMING UP ANY BUSINESS.
PEOPLE ARE AVOIDING THIS PLACE LIKE THE PLAGUE.
THANK YOU, MILADY.
TWITCH
YOU OBVIOUSLY ***APPRECIATE*** A SUPERB WIT...
...UNLIKE YOUR PARTNER.
IT'S ***HARD*** BEING A GENIUS.
OH HO HO HO! WHAT A FUNNY JOKE, MA'AM!
OH HO HO HO HO HO HO HO HO!
WERE THEY SEPARATED AT BIRTH?
HEY, HEY, HEY! ROCHELLIE!
ZOOM
ZOOM

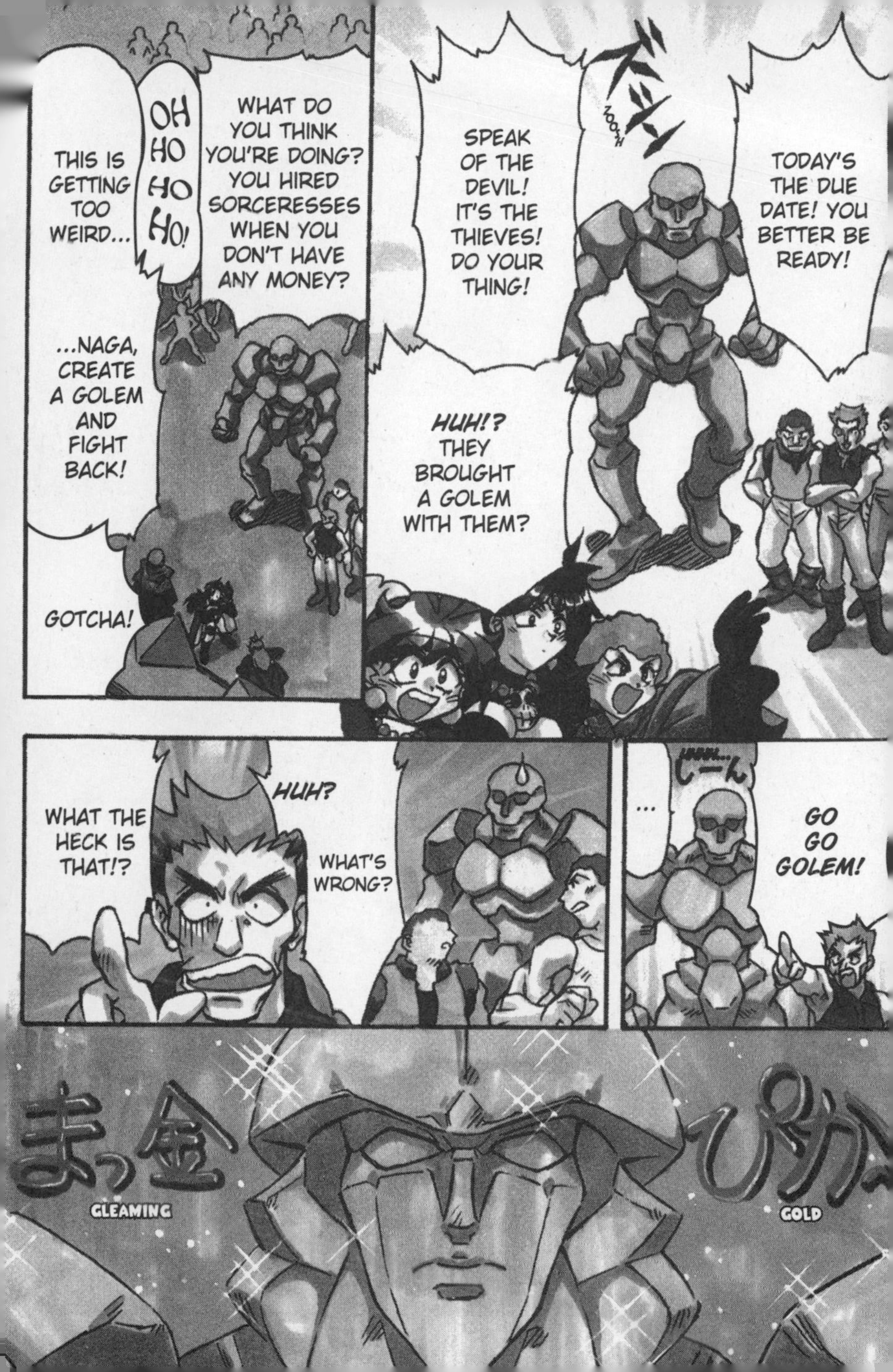
TODAY'S THE DUE DATE! YOU BETTER BE READY!
ズシン
WHOOSH
SPEAK OF THE DEVIL! IT'S THE THIEVES! DO YOUR THING!
HUH!? THEY BROUGHT A GOLEM WITH THEM?
WHAT DO YOU THINK YOU'RE DOING? YOU HIRED SORCERESSES WHEN YOU DON'T HAVE ANY MONEY?
OH HO HO HO!
THIS IS GETTING TOO WEIRD...
...NAGA, CREATE A GOLEM AND FIGHT BACK!
GOTCHA!
GO GO GOLEM!
じーん
...
WHAT'S WRONG?
HUH?
WHAT THE HECK IS THAT!?
まっ金
GLEAMING
ぴか
GOLD

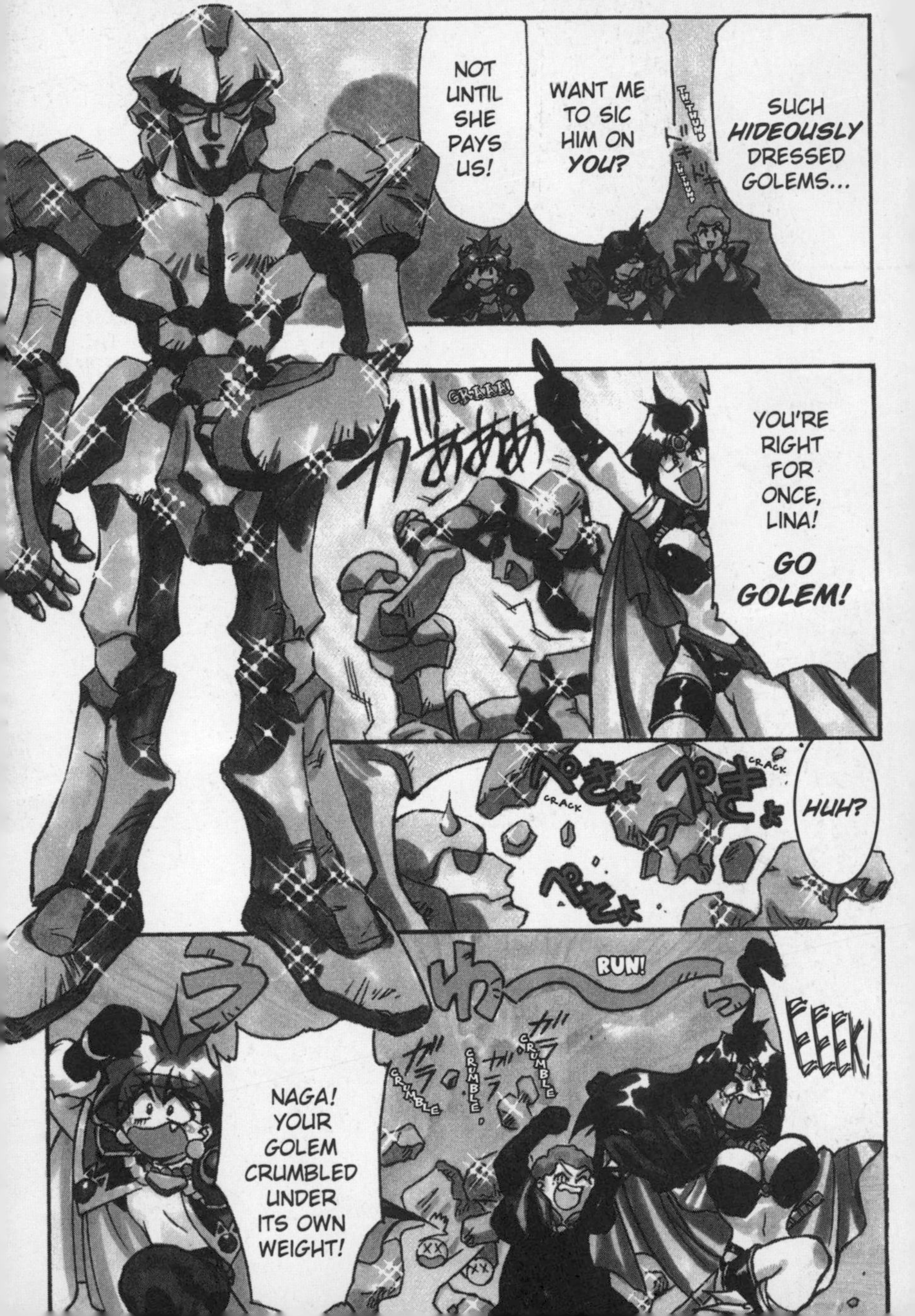
SUCH HIDEOUSLY DRESSED GOLEMS...
WANT ME TO SIC HIM ON YOU?
NOT UNTIL SHE PAYS US!
YOU'RE RIGHT FOR ONCE, LINA! GO GOLEM!
GRAAAA!
HUH?
CRACK
CRACK
EEEK!
RUN!
CRUMBLE
CRUMBLE
CRUMBLE
NAGA! YOUR GOLEM CRUMBLED UNDER ITS OWN WEIGHT!

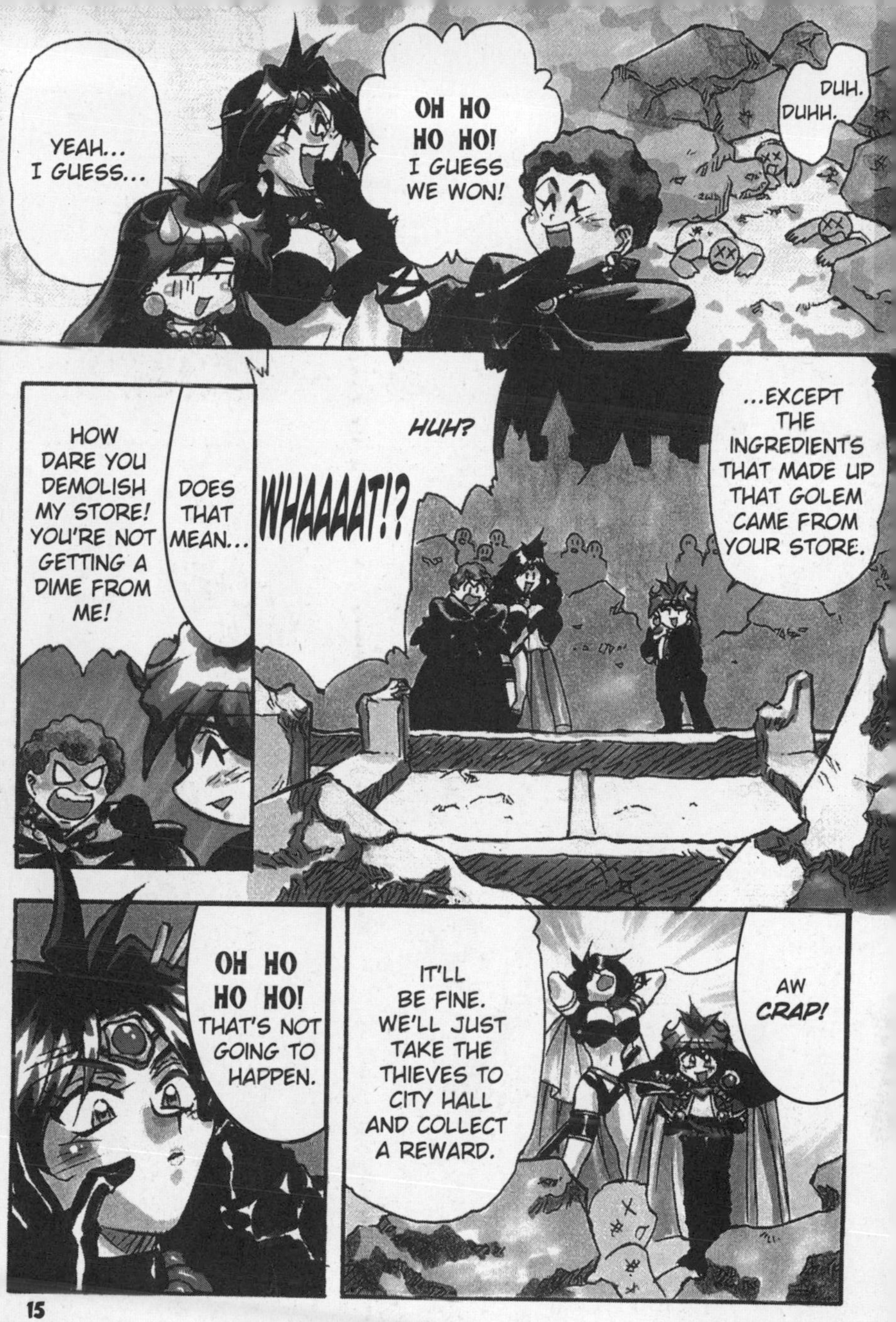
DUH. DUHH.
OH HO HO HO! I GUESS WE WON!
YEAH... I GUESS...
...EXCEPT THE INGREDIENTS THAT MADE UP THAT GOLEM CAME FROM YOUR STORE.
HUH?
WHAAAAT!?
DOES THAT MEAN...
HOW DARE YOU DEMOLISH MY STORE! YOU'RE NOT GETTING A DIME FROM ME!
AW CRAP!
IT'LL BE FINE. WE'LL JUST TAKE THE THIEVES TO CITY HALL AND COLLECT A REWARD.
OH HO HO HO! THAT'S NOT GOING TO HAPPEN.

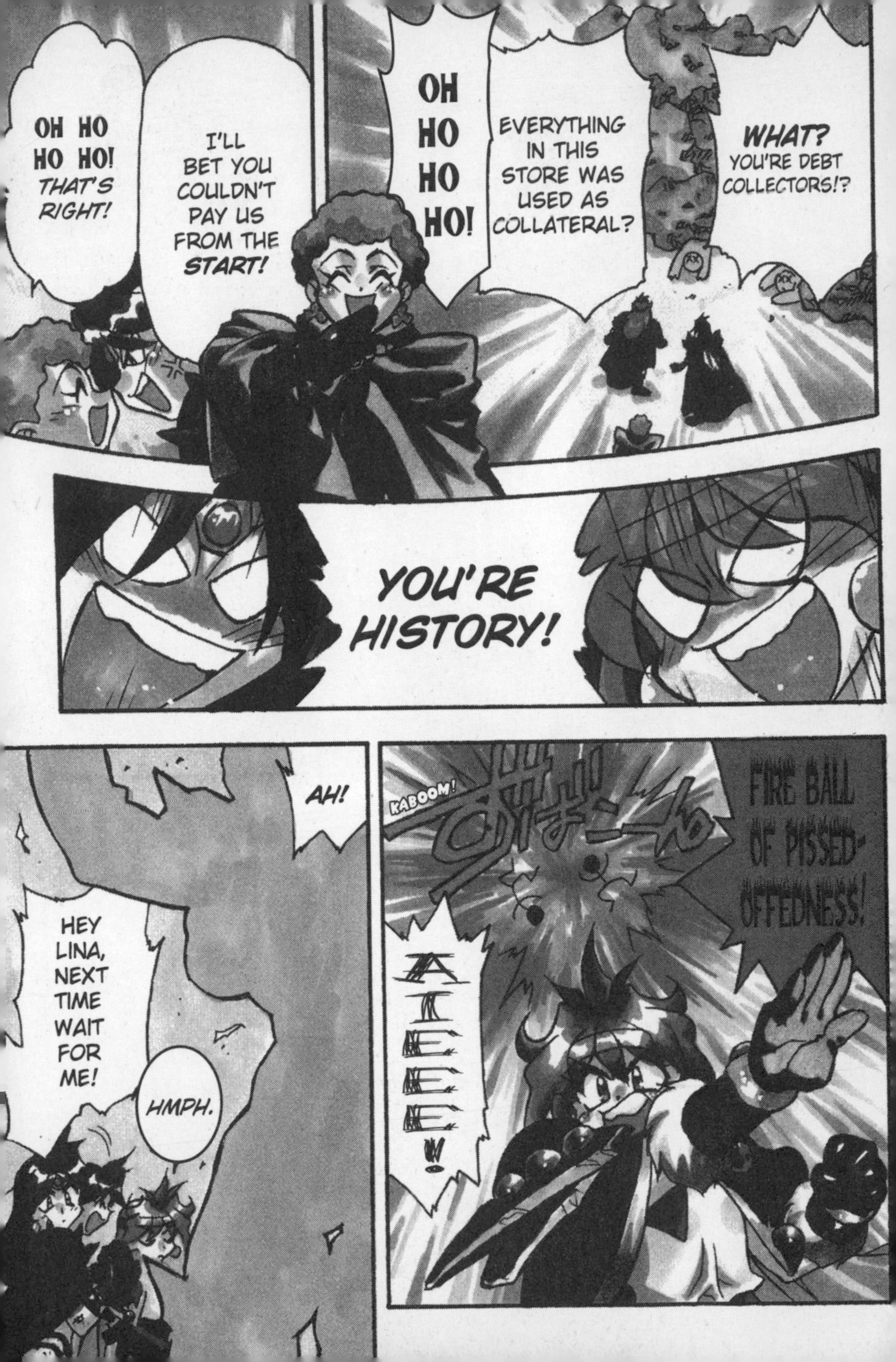
WHAT? YOU'RE DEBT COLLECTORS!?
EVERYTHING IN THIS STORE WAS USED AS COLLATERAL?
OH HO HO HO!
I'LL BET YOU COULDN'T PAY US FROM THE START!
OH HO HO HO! THAT'S RIGHT!
YOU'RE HISTORY!
FIRE BALL OF PISSED-OFFEDNESS!
KABOOM!
AIEEEE!!
AH!
HEY LINA, NEXT TIME WAIT FOR ME!
HMPH.

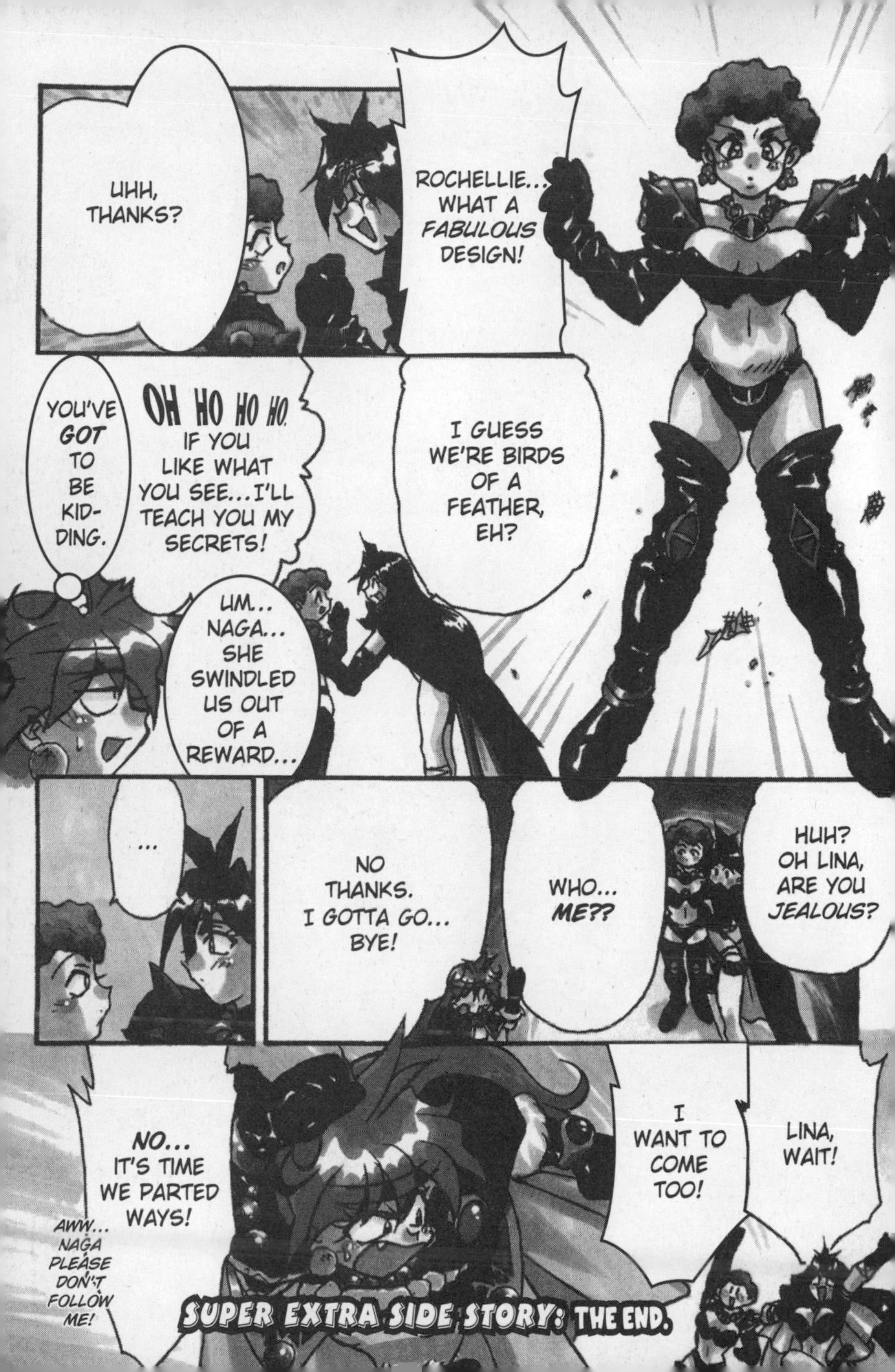
ROCHELLIE... WHAT A *FABULOUS* DESIGN!
UHH, THANKS?
I GUESS WE'RE BIRDS OF A FEATHER, EH?
OH HO HO HO. IF YOU LIKE WHAT YOU SEE...I'LL TEACH YOU MY SECRETS!
YOU'VE **GOT** TO BE KIDDING.
UM... NAGA... SHE SWINDLED US OUT OF A REWARD...
HUH? OH LINA, ARE YOU *JEALOUS?*
WHO... ***ME??***
NO THANKS. I GOTTA GO... BYE!
...
LINA, WAIT!
I WANT TO COME TOO!
NO... IT'S TIME WE PARTED WAYS!
AWW... NAGA PLEASE DON'T FOLLOW ME!
SUPER EXTRA SIDE STORY: THE END.

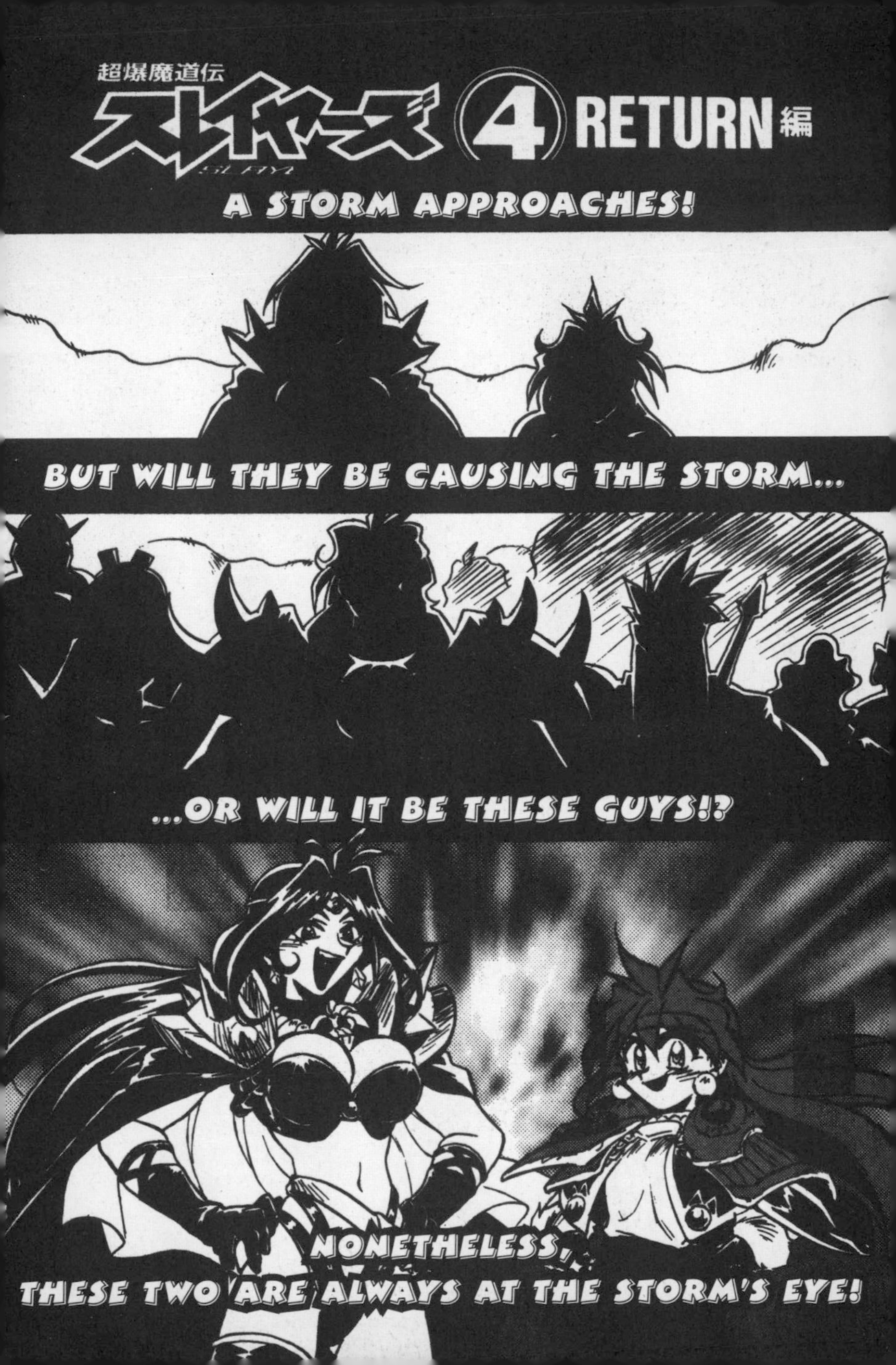
超爆魔道伝
スレイヤーズ ④ RETURN編
A STORM APPROACHES!
BUT WILL THEY BE CAUSING THE STORM...
...OR WILL IT BE THESE GUYS!?
NONETHELESS,
THESE TWO ARE ALWAYS AT THE STORM'S EYE!

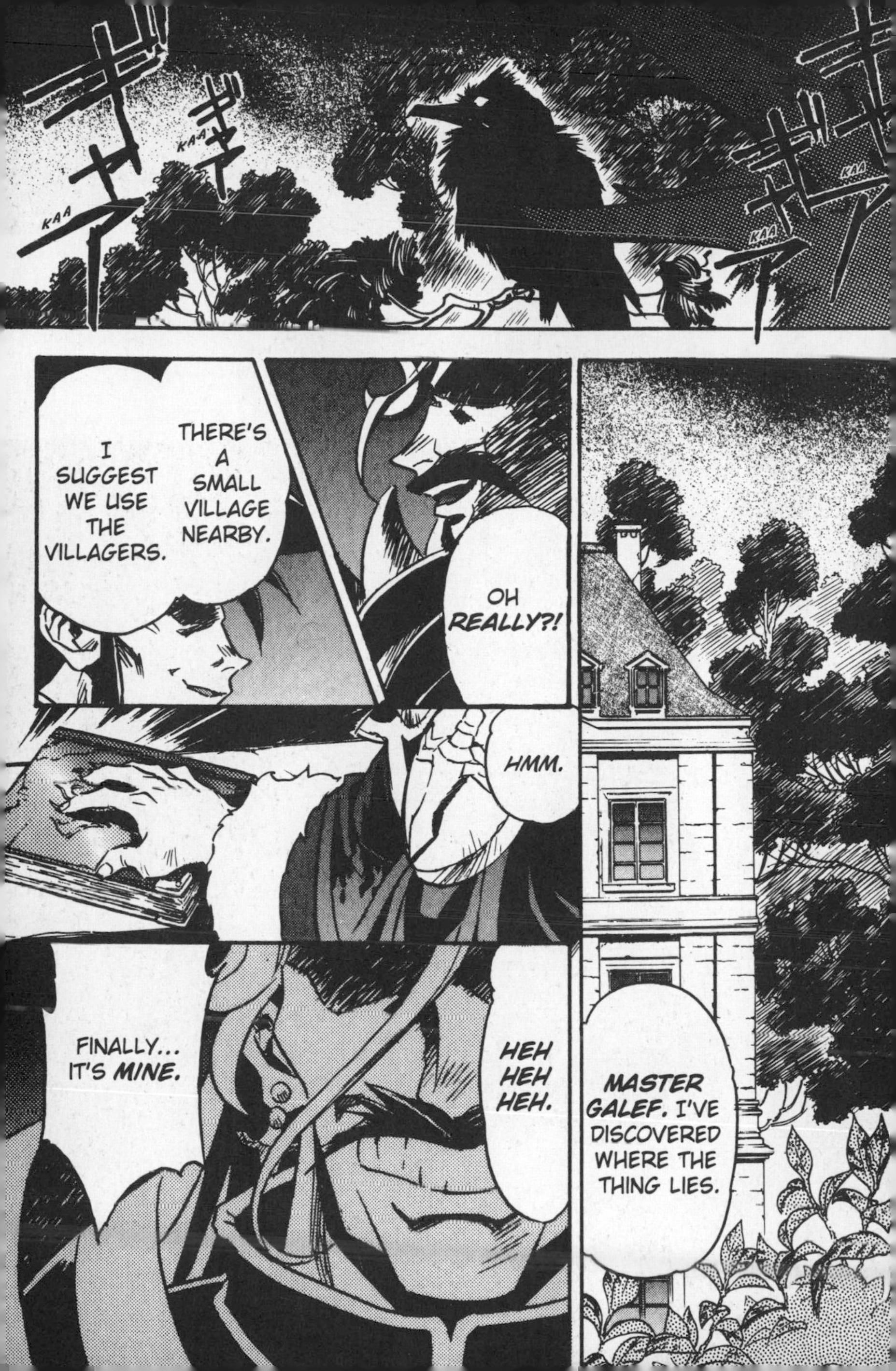
KAA
KAA
KAA
KAA
MASTER GALEF. I'VE DISCOVERED WHERE THE THING LIES.
OH REALLY?!
THERE'S A SMALL VILLAGE NEARBY.
I SUGGEST WE USE THE VILLAGERS.
HMM.
HEH HEH HEH.
FINALLY... IT'S MINE.

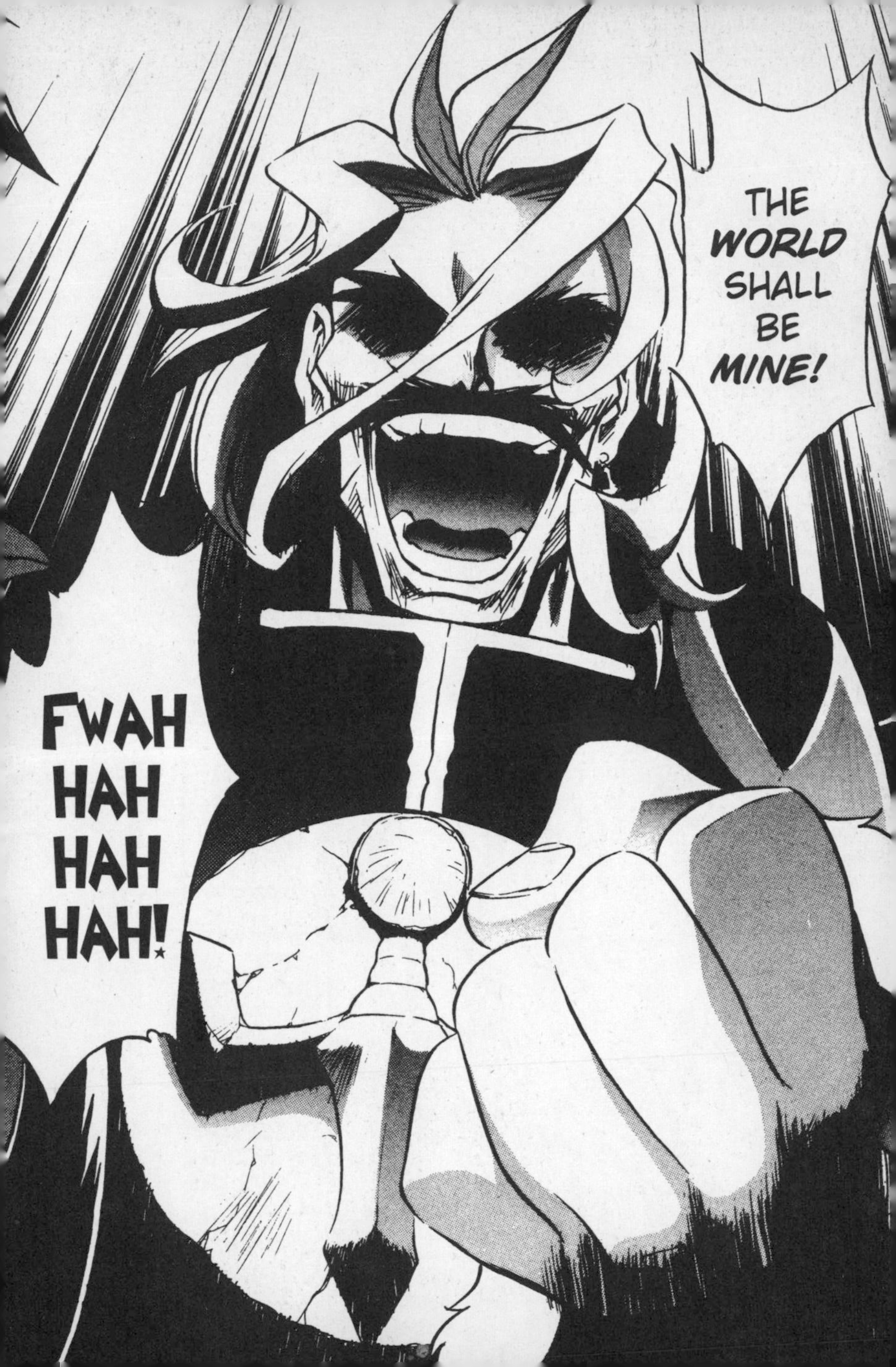
THE WORLD SHALL BE MINE!
FWAH HAH HAH HAH!

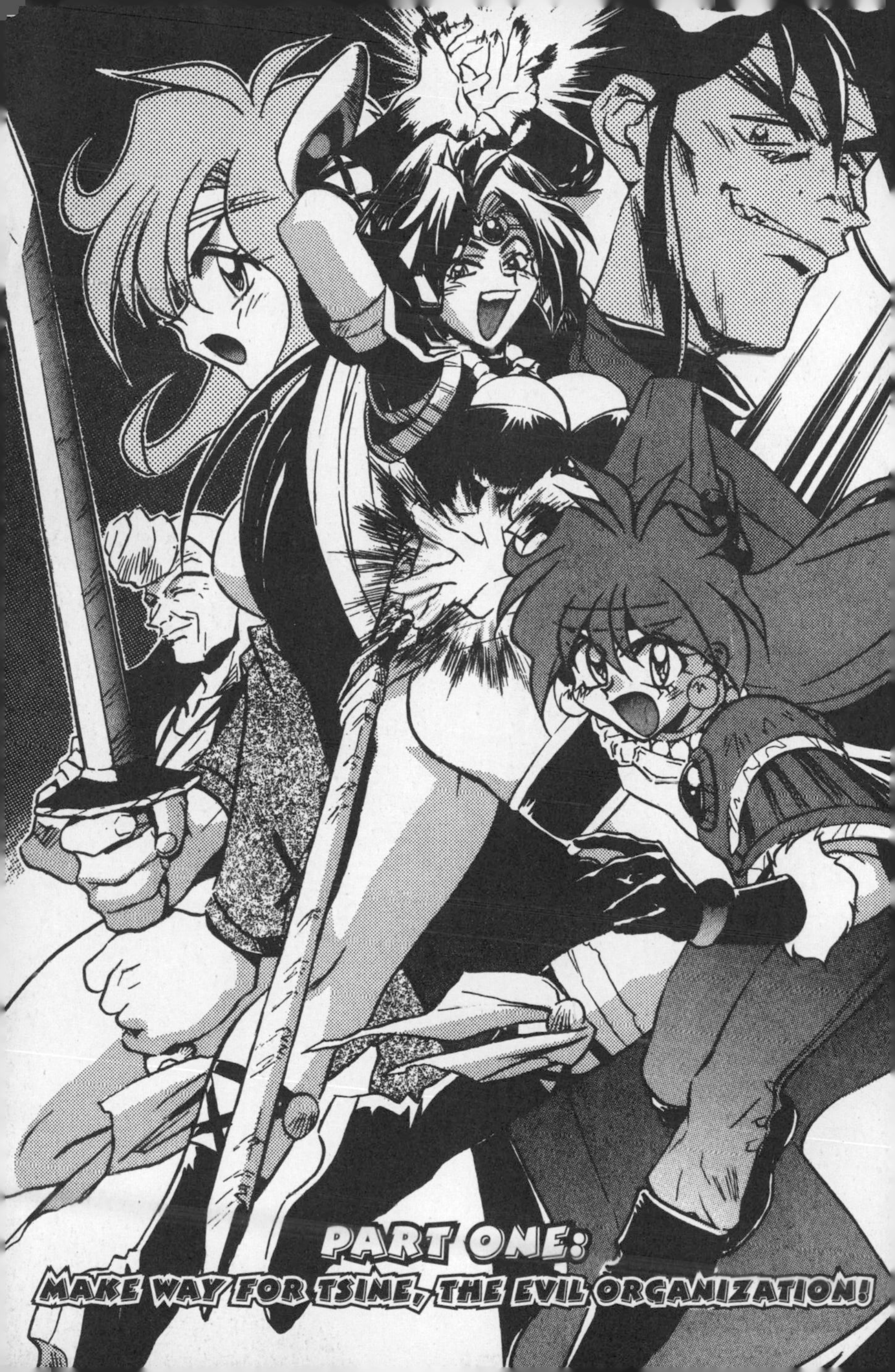
PART ONE:
MAKE WAY FOR TSINE, THE EVIL ORGANIZATION!

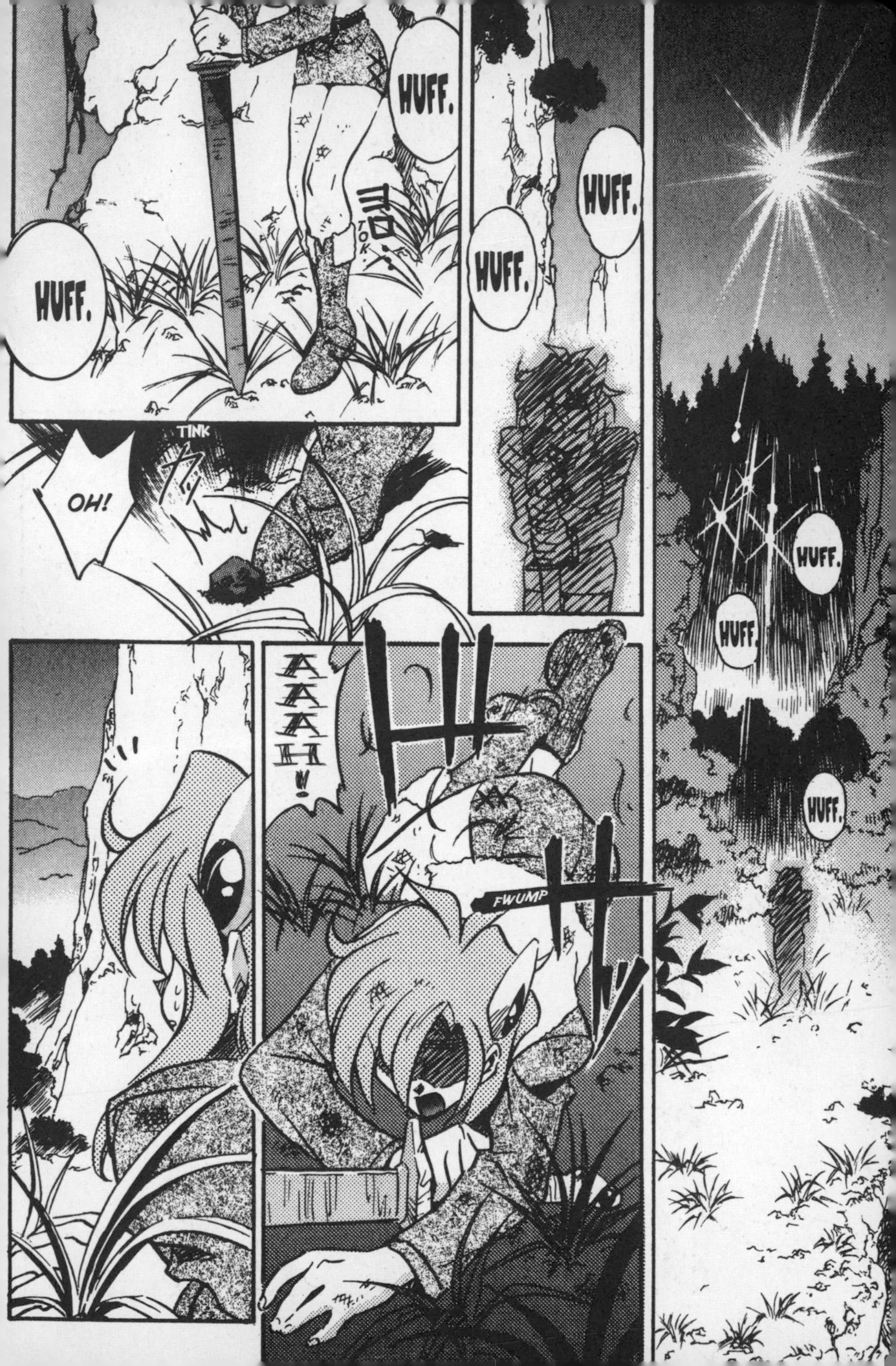
HUFF.
HUFF.
HUFF.
HUFF.
HUFF.
HUFF.
TOK
HUFF.
TINK
OH!
AAAAH!!
FWUMP

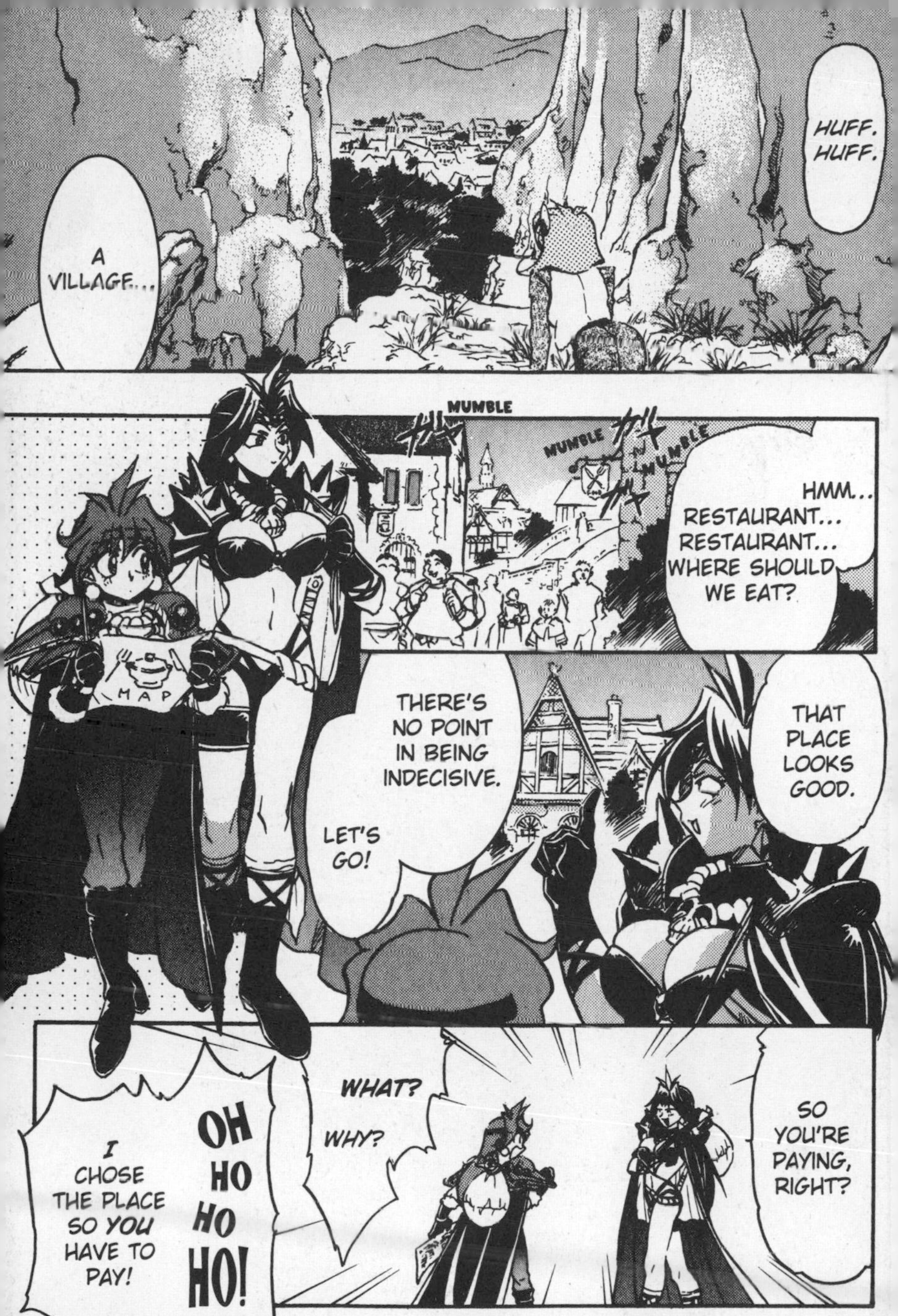
HUFF. HUFF.
A VILLAGE...
MUMBLE
MUMBLE
MUMBLE
HMM... RESTAURANT... RESTAURANT... WHERE SHOULD WE EAT?
THAT PLACE LOOKS GOOD.
THERE'S NO POINT IN BEING INDECISIVE.
LET'S GO!
MAP
SO YOU'RE PAYING, RIGHT?
WHAT?
WHY?
OH HO HO HO!
I CHOSE THE PLACE SO YOU HAVE TO PAY!

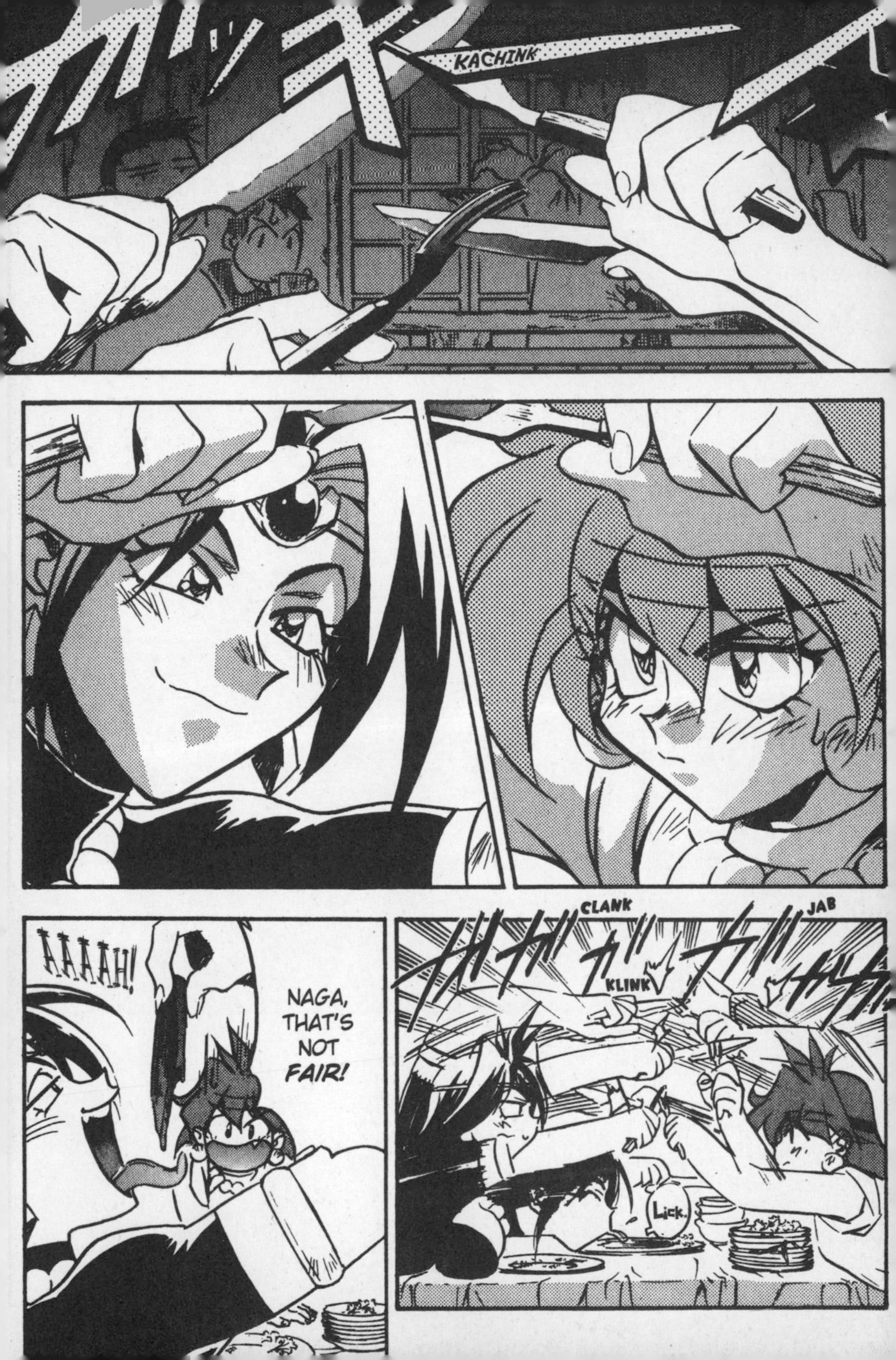
KACHINK
JAB
CLANK
KLINK
Lick
AAAAH!
NAGA, THAT'S NOT FAIR!

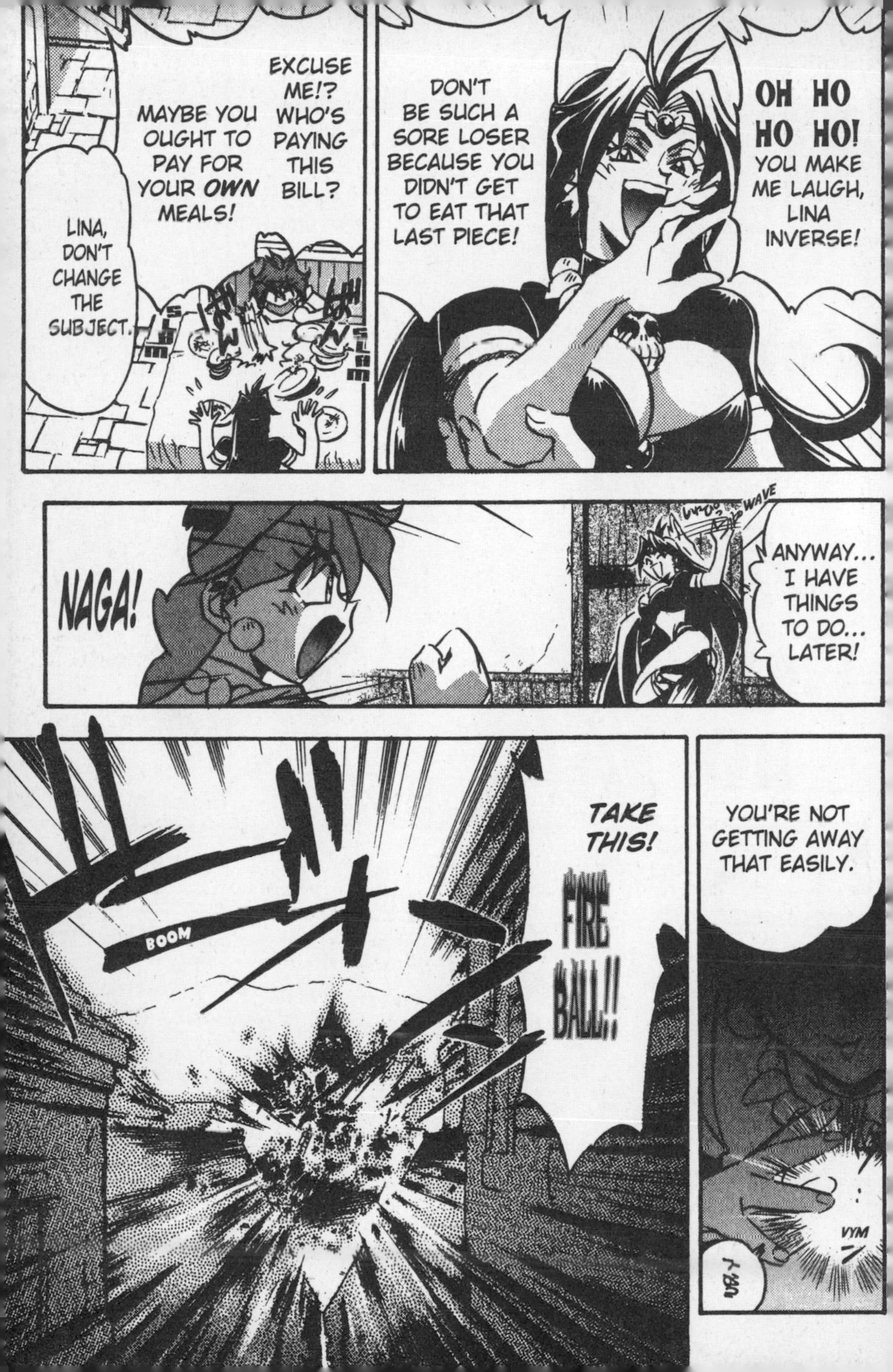
OH HO HO HO! YOU MAKE ME LAUGH, LINA INVERSE!
DON'T BE SUCH A SORE LOSER BECAUSE YOU DIDN'T GET TO EAT THAT LAST PIECE!
EXCUSE ME!? WHO'S PAYING THIS BILL?
MAYBE YOU OUGHT TO PAY FOR YOUR *OWN* MEALS!
SLAM
SLAM
LINA, DON'T CHANGE THE SUBJECT.
WAVE
ANYWAY... I HAVE THINGS TO DO... LATER!
NAGA!
YOU'RE NOT GETTING AWAY THAT EASILY.
VYM
TAKE THIS!
FIRE BALL!!
BOOM

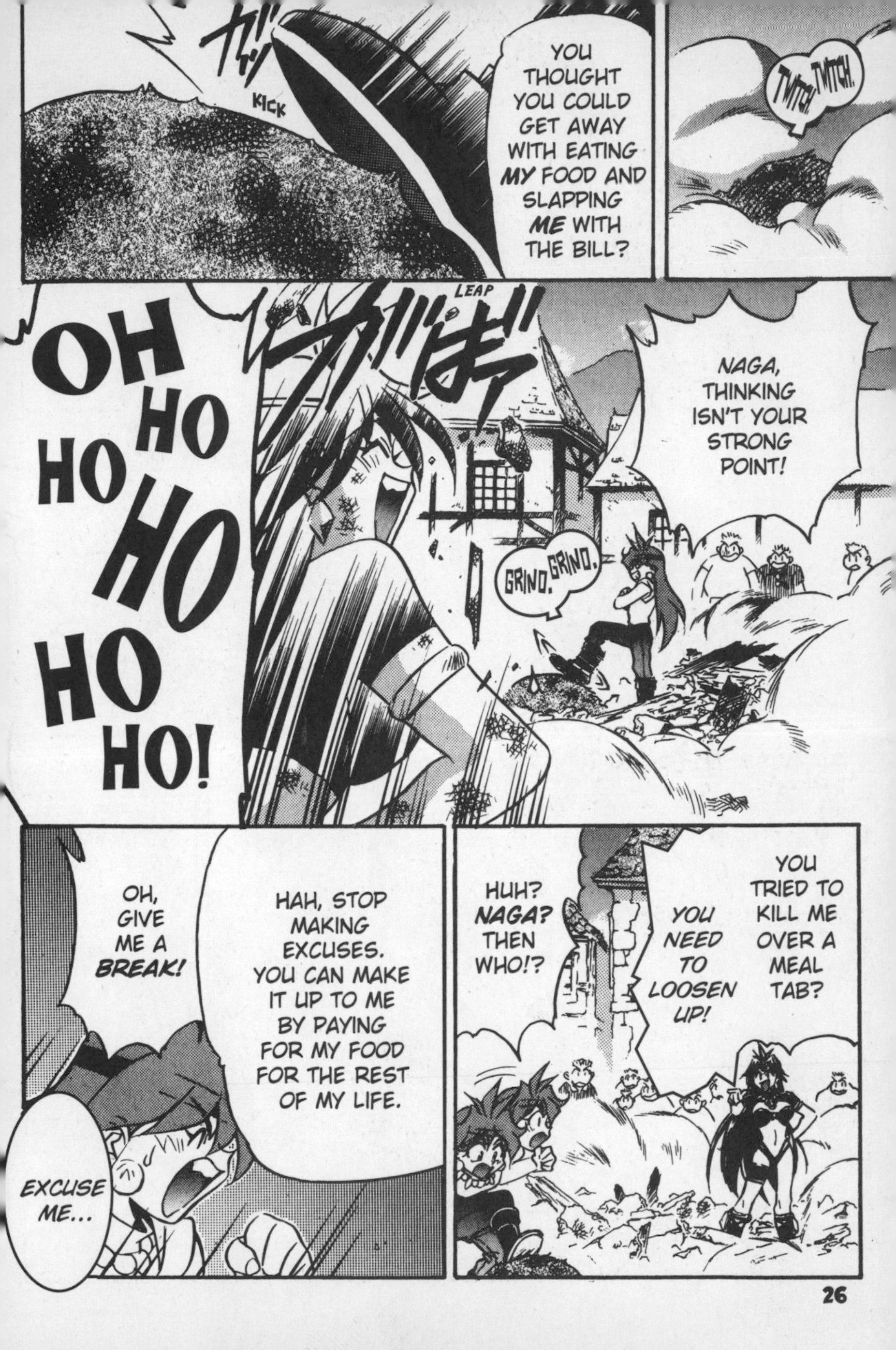
TWITCH. TWITCH.
KICK
YOU THOUGHT YOU COULD GET AWAY WITH EATING *MY* FOOD AND SLAPPING *ME* WITH THE BILL?
NAGA, THINKING ISN'T YOUR STRONG POINT!
LEAP
GRIND. GRIND.
OH HO HO HO HO HO HO!
YOU TRIED TO KILL ME OVER A MEAL TAB?
YOU NEED TO LOOSEN UP!
HUH? *NAGA?* THEN WHO!?
HAH, STOP MAKING EXCUSES. YOU CAN MAKE IT UP TO ME BY PAYING FOR MY FOOD FOR THE REST OF MY LIFE.
OH, GIVE ME A *BREAK!*
EXCUSE ME...

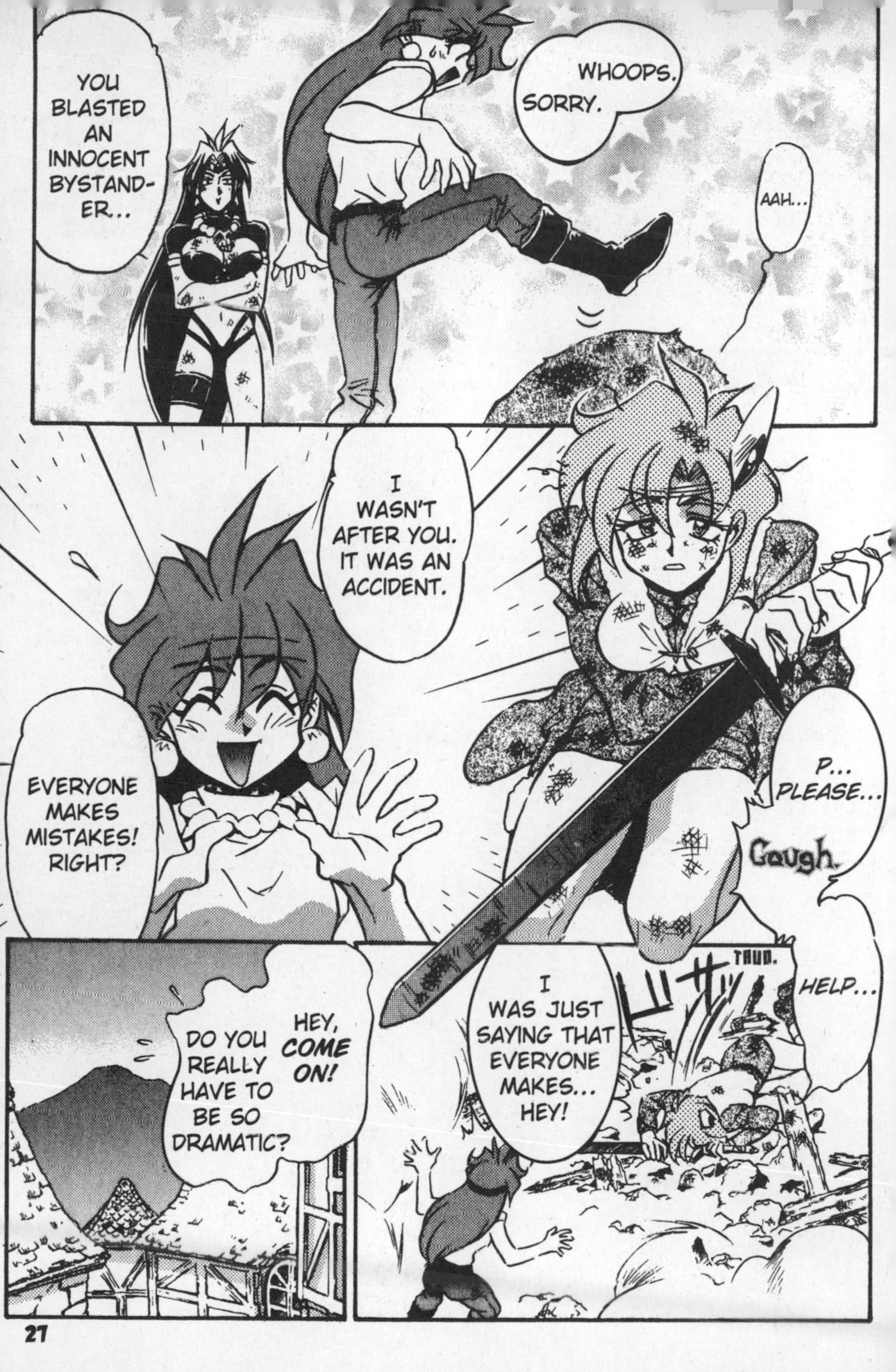
AAH...
WHOOPS. SORRY.
YOU BLASTED AN INNOCENT BYSTANDER...
P... PLEASE...
Cough.
I WASN'T AFTER YOU. IT WAS AN ACCIDENT.
EVERYONE MAKES MISTAKES! RIGHT?
HELP...
THUD.
I WAS JUST SAYING THAT EVERYONE MAKES... HEY!
HEY, **COME ON!**
DO YOU REALLY HAVE TO BE SO DRAMATIC?

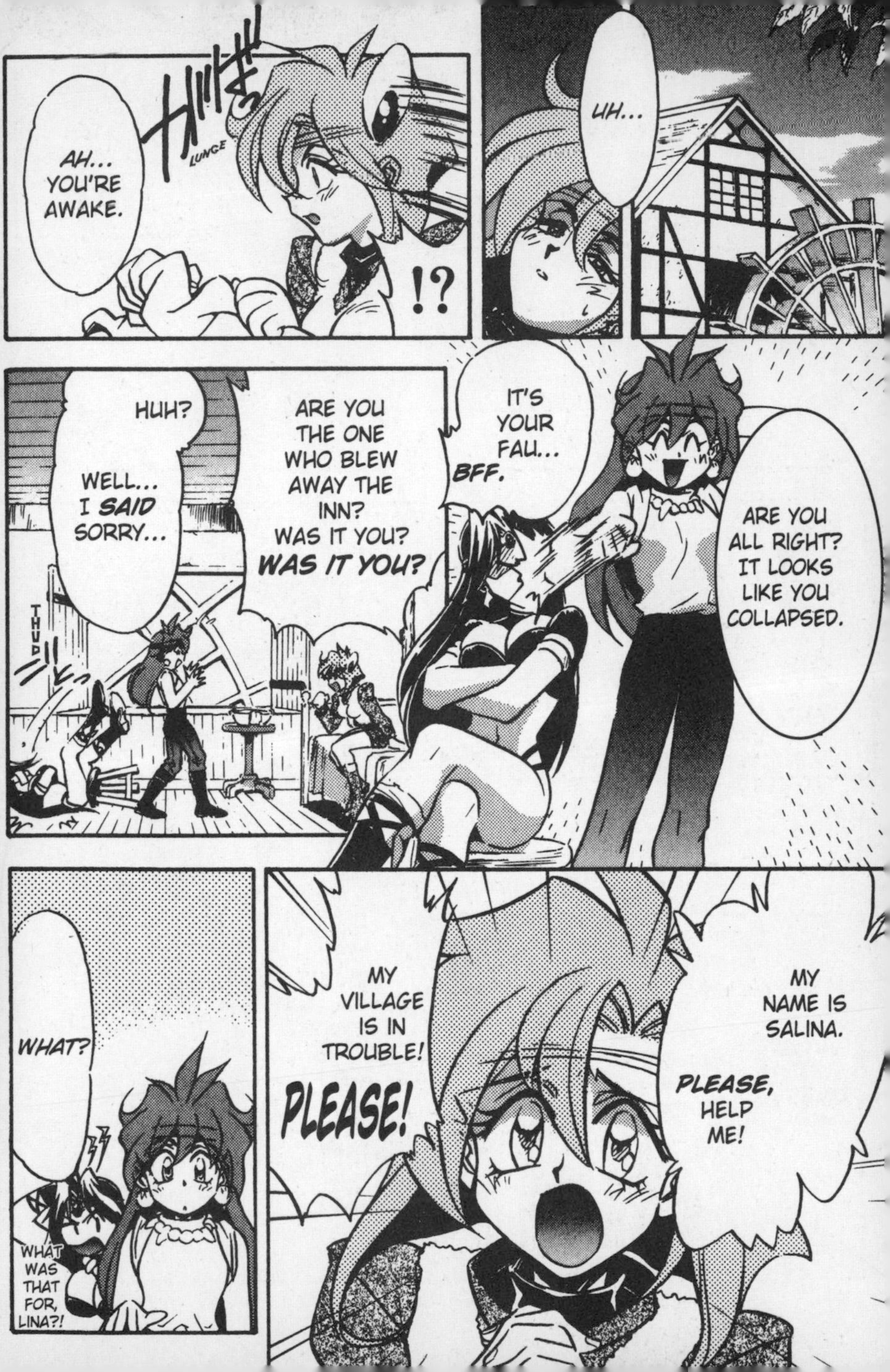
UH...
AH... YOU'RE AWAKE.
LUNGE
!?
ARE YOU ALL RIGHT? IT LOOKS LIKE YOU COLLAPSED.
IT'S YOUR FAU... BFF.
ARE YOU THE ONE WHO BLEW AWAY THE INN? WAS IT YOU? WAS IT YOU?
HUH?
WELL... I SAID SORRY...
THUD
MY NAME IS SALINA.
PLEASE, HELP ME!
MY VILLAGE IS IN TROUBLE!
PLEASE!
WHAT?
WHAT WAS THAT FOR, LINA?!

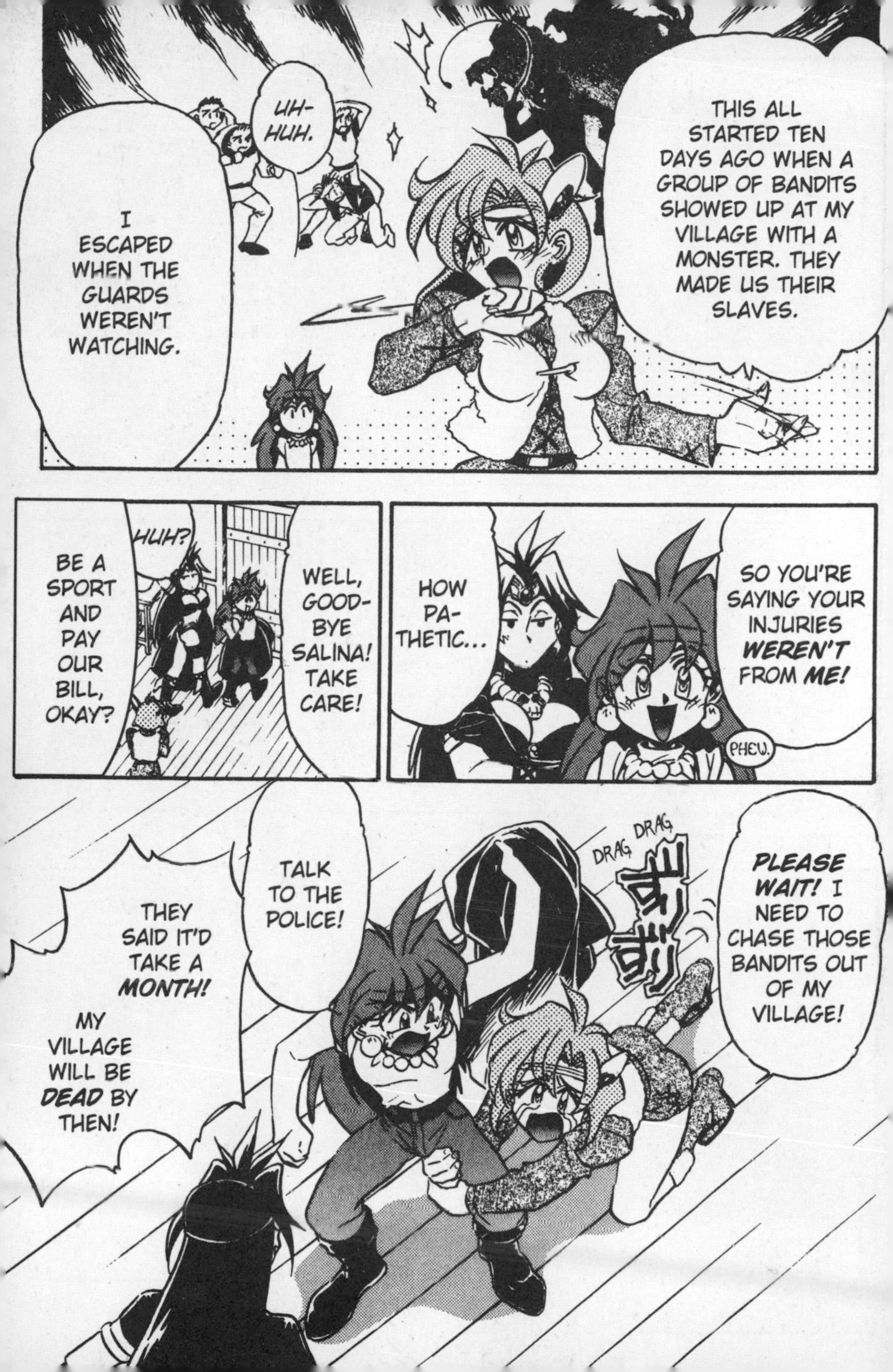
THIS ALL STARTED TEN DAYS AGO WHEN A GROUP OF BANDITS SHOWED UP AT MY VILLAGE WITH A MONSTER. THEY MADE US THEIR SLAVES.
UH-HUH.
I ESCAPED WHEN THE GUARDS WEREN'T WATCHING.
SO YOU'RE SAYING YOUR INJURIES ***WEREN'T*** FROM ***ME!***
PHEW.
HOW PA-THETIC...
WELL, GOOD-BYE SALINA! TAKE CARE!
HUH?
BE A SPORT AND PAY OUR BILL, OKAY?
PLEASE WAIT! I NEED TO CHASE THOSE BANDITS OUT OF MY VILLAGE!
DRAG DRAG
TALK TO THE POLICE!
THEY SAID IT'D TAKE A ***MONTH!***
MY VILLAGE WILL BE ***DEAD*** BY THEN!

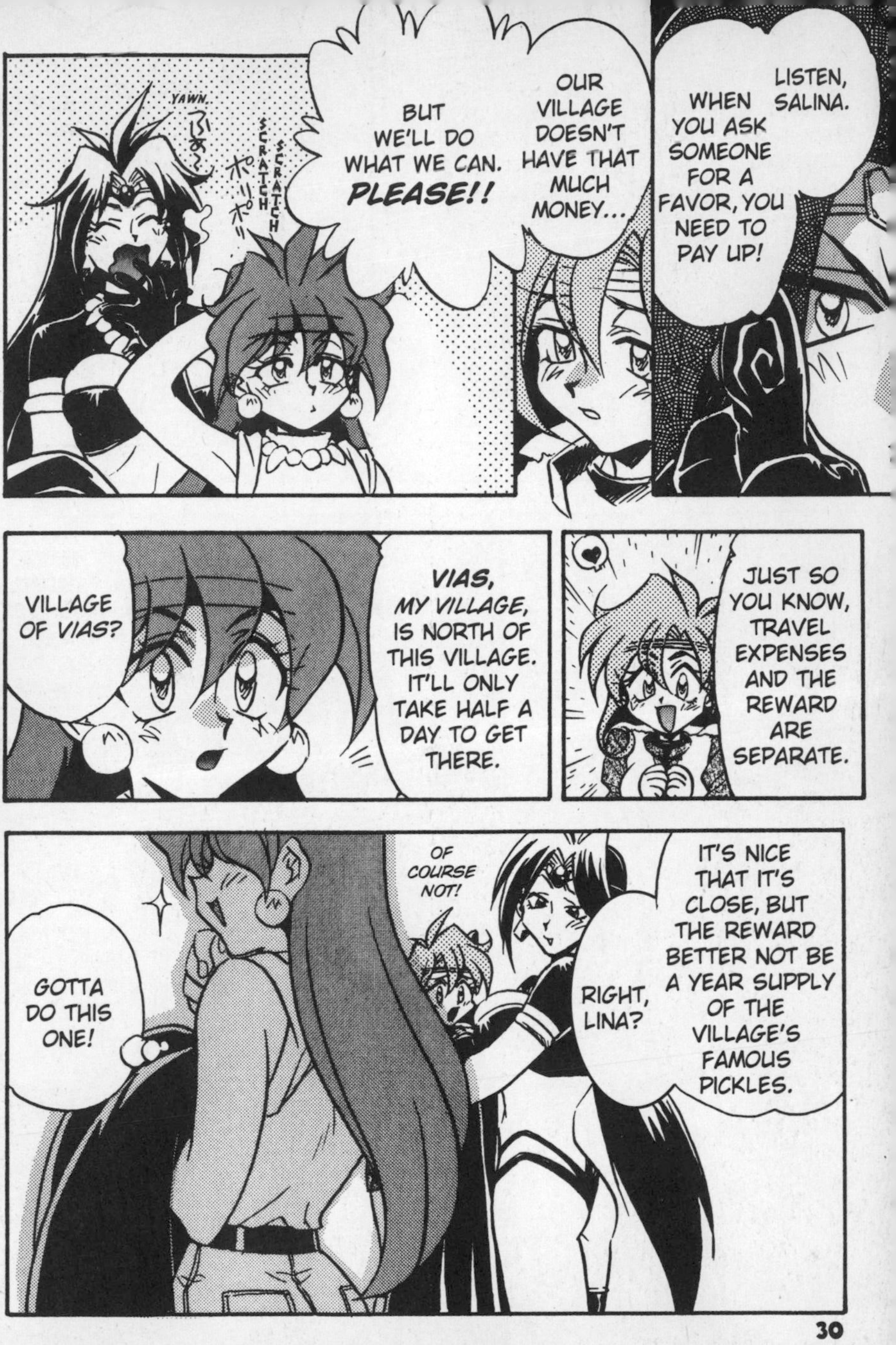
LISTEN, SALINA.
WHEN YOU ASK SOMEONE FOR A FAVOR, YOU NEED TO PAY UP!
OUR VILLAGE DOESN'T HAVE THAT MUCH MONEY...
BUT WE'LL DO WHAT WE CAN. *PLEASE!!*
YAWN.
ふあ〜
SCRATCH SCRATCH
ポリポリ
JUST SO YOU KNOW, TRAVEL EXPENSES AND THE REWARD ARE SEPARATE.
VIAS, MY VILLAGE, IS NORTH OF THIS VILLAGE. IT'LL ONLY TAKE HALF A DAY TO GET THERE.
VILLAGE OF *VIAS?*
IT'S NICE THAT IT'S CLOSE, BUT THE REWARD BETTER NOT BE A YEAR SUPPLY OF THE VILLAGE'S FAMOUS PICKLES.
RIGHT, LINA?
OF COURSE NOT!
GOTTA DO THIS ONE!

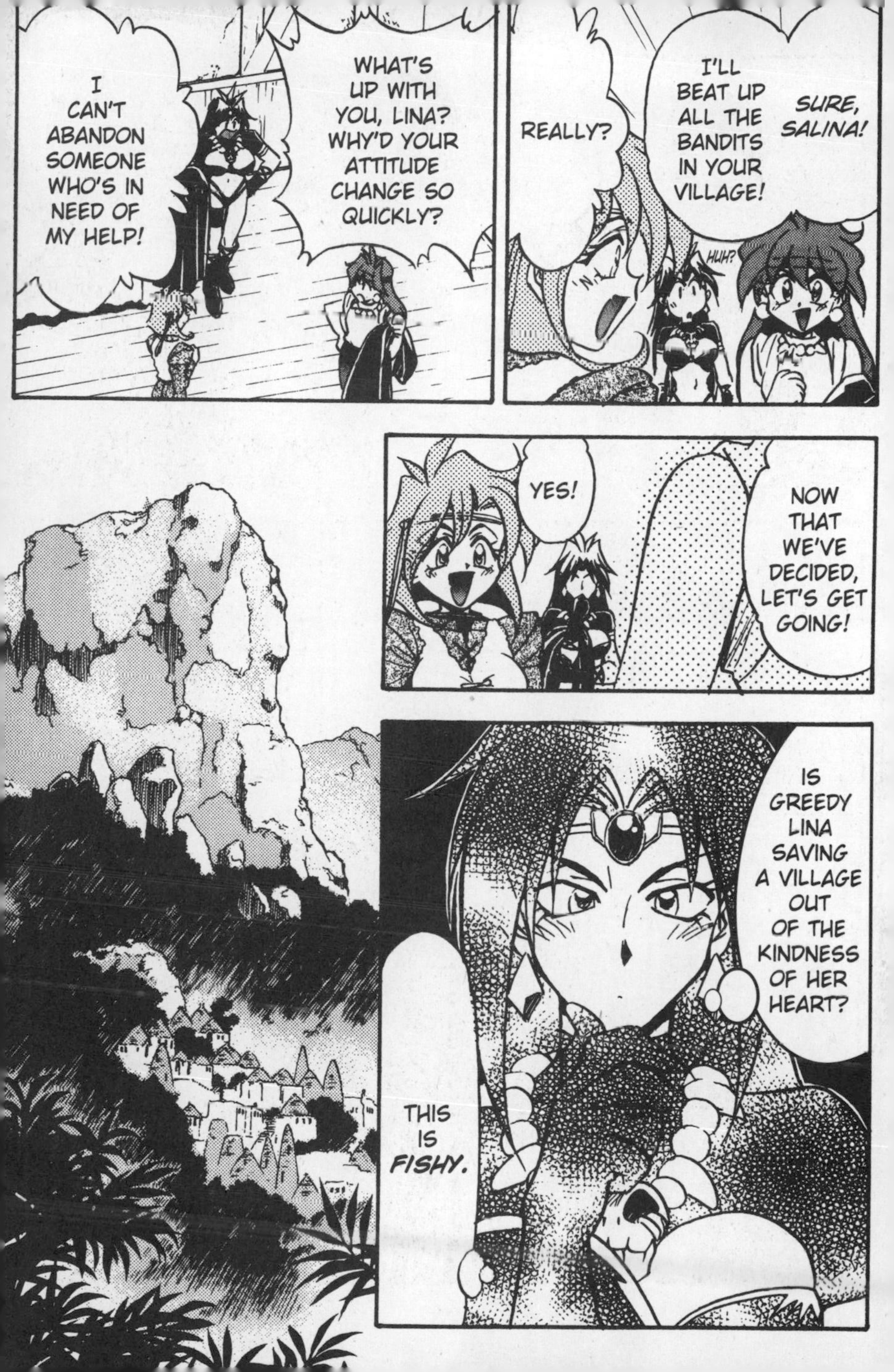
SURE, SALINA!
I'LL BEAT UP ALL THE BANDITS IN YOUR VILLAGE!
HUH?
REALLY?
WHAT'S UP WITH YOU, LINA? WHY'D YOUR ATTITUDE CHANGE SO QUICKLY?
I CAN'T ABANDON SOMEONE WHO'S IN NEED OF MY HELP!
NOW THAT WE'VE DECIDED, LET'S GET GOING!
YES!
IS GREEDY LINA SAVING A VILLAGE OUT OF THE KINDNESS OF HER HEART?
THIS IS *FISHY*.

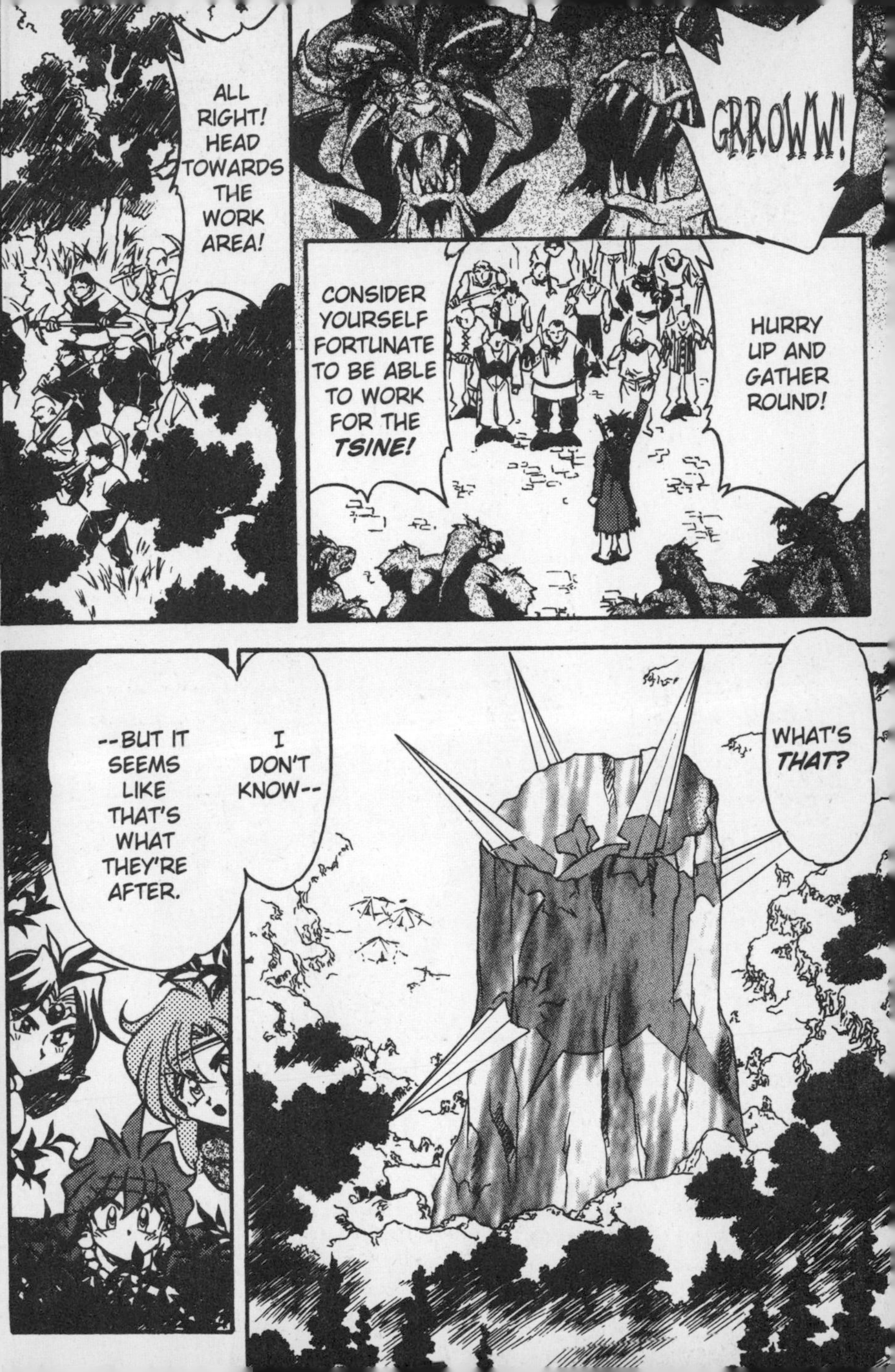
GRROWW!
HURRY UP AND GATHER ROUND!
CONSIDER YOURSELF FORTUNATE TO BE ABLE TO WORK FOR THE *TSINE!*
ALL RIGHT! HEAD TOWARDS THE WORK AREA!
WHAT'S *THAT?*
I DON'T KNOW--
--BUT IT SEEMS LIKE THAT'S WHAT THEY'RE AFTER.

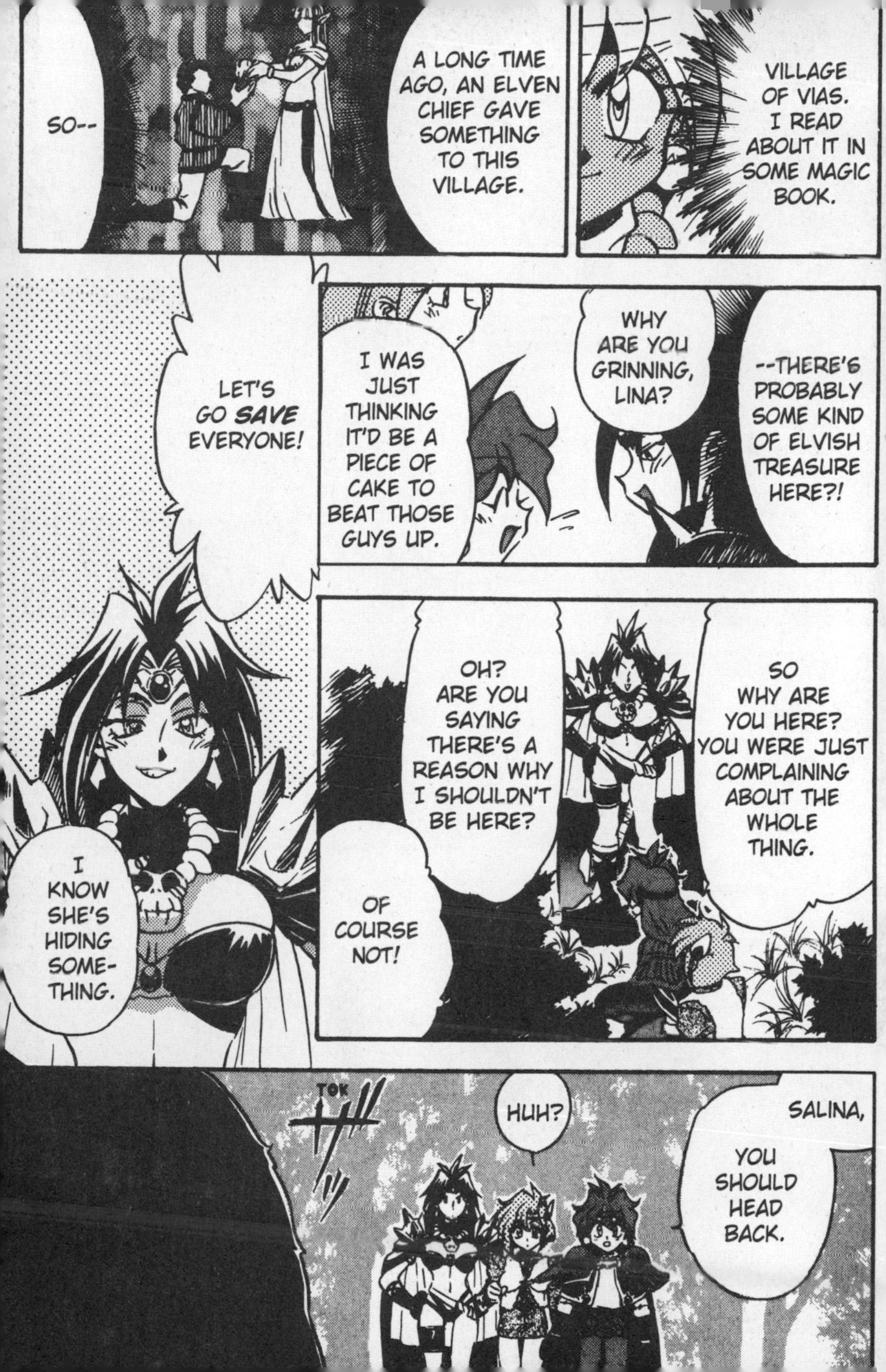
VILLAGE OF VIAS. I READ ABOUT IT IN SOME MAGIC BOOK.
A LONG TIME AGO, AN ELVEN CHIEF GAVE SOMETHING TO THIS VILLAGE.
SO--
--THERE'S PROBABLY SOME KIND OF ELVISH TREASURE HERE?!
WHY ARE YOU GRINNING, LINA?
I WAS JUST THINKING IT'D BE A PIECE OF CAKE TO BEAT THOSE GUYS UP.
SO WHY ARE YOU HERE? YOU WERE JUST COMPLAINING ABOUT THE WHOLE THING.
OH? ARE YOU SAYING THERE'S A REASON WHY I SHOULDN'T BE HERE?
OF COURSE NOT!
LET'S GO **SAVE** EVERYONE!
I KNOW SHE'S HIDING SOME-THING.
SALINA,
YOU SHOULD HEAD BACK.
HUH?
TOK

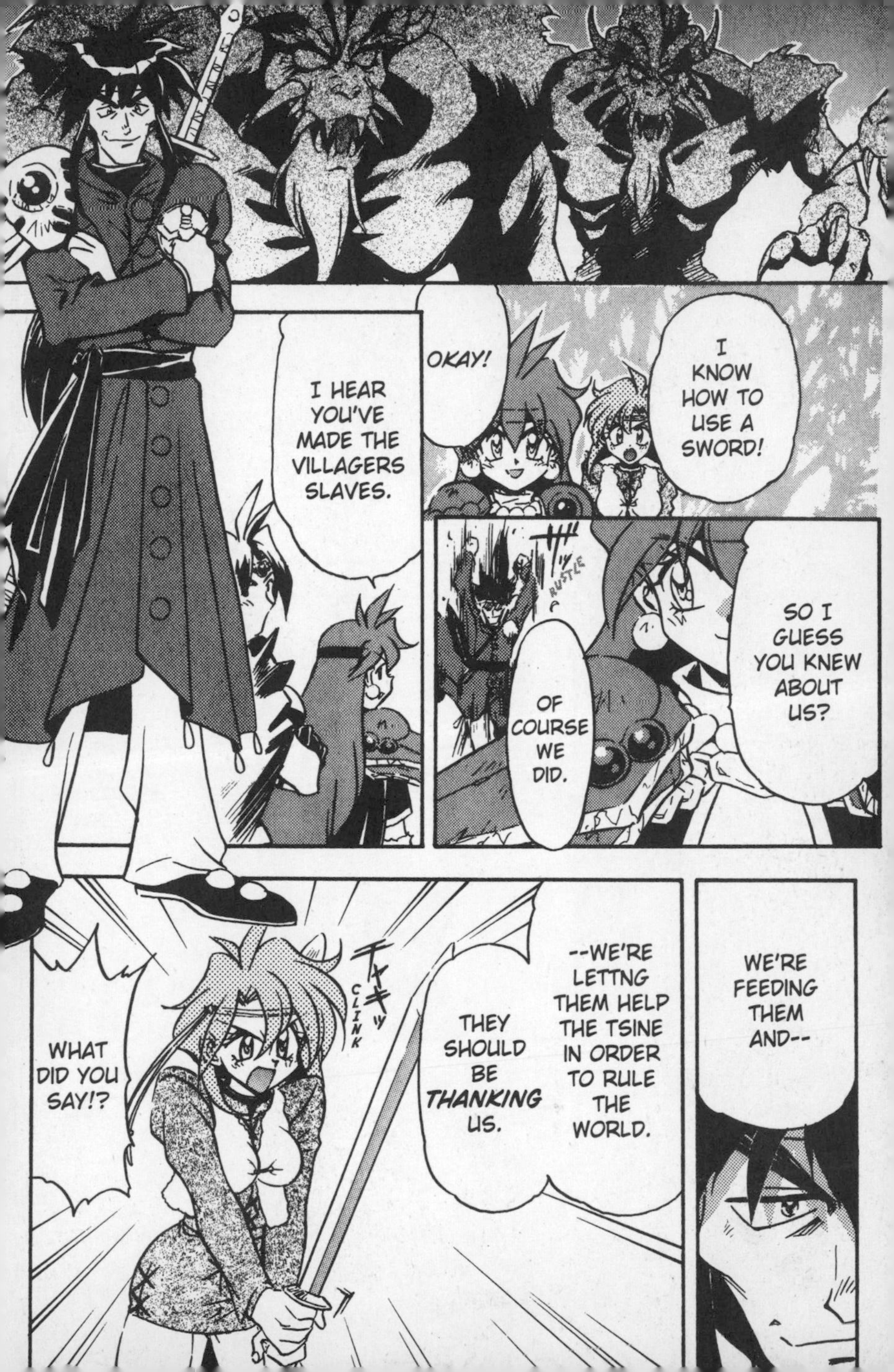

I KNOW HOW TO USE A SWORD!
OKAY!
SO I GUESS YOU KNEW ABOUT US?
RUSTLE
OF COURSE WE DID.
I HEAR YOU'VE MADE THE VILLAGERS SLAVES.
WE'RE FEEDING THEM AND--
--WE'RE LETTNG THEM HELP THE TSINE IN ORDER TO RULE THE WORLD.
THEY SHOULD BE *THANKING* US.
CLINK
WHAT DID YOU SAY!?

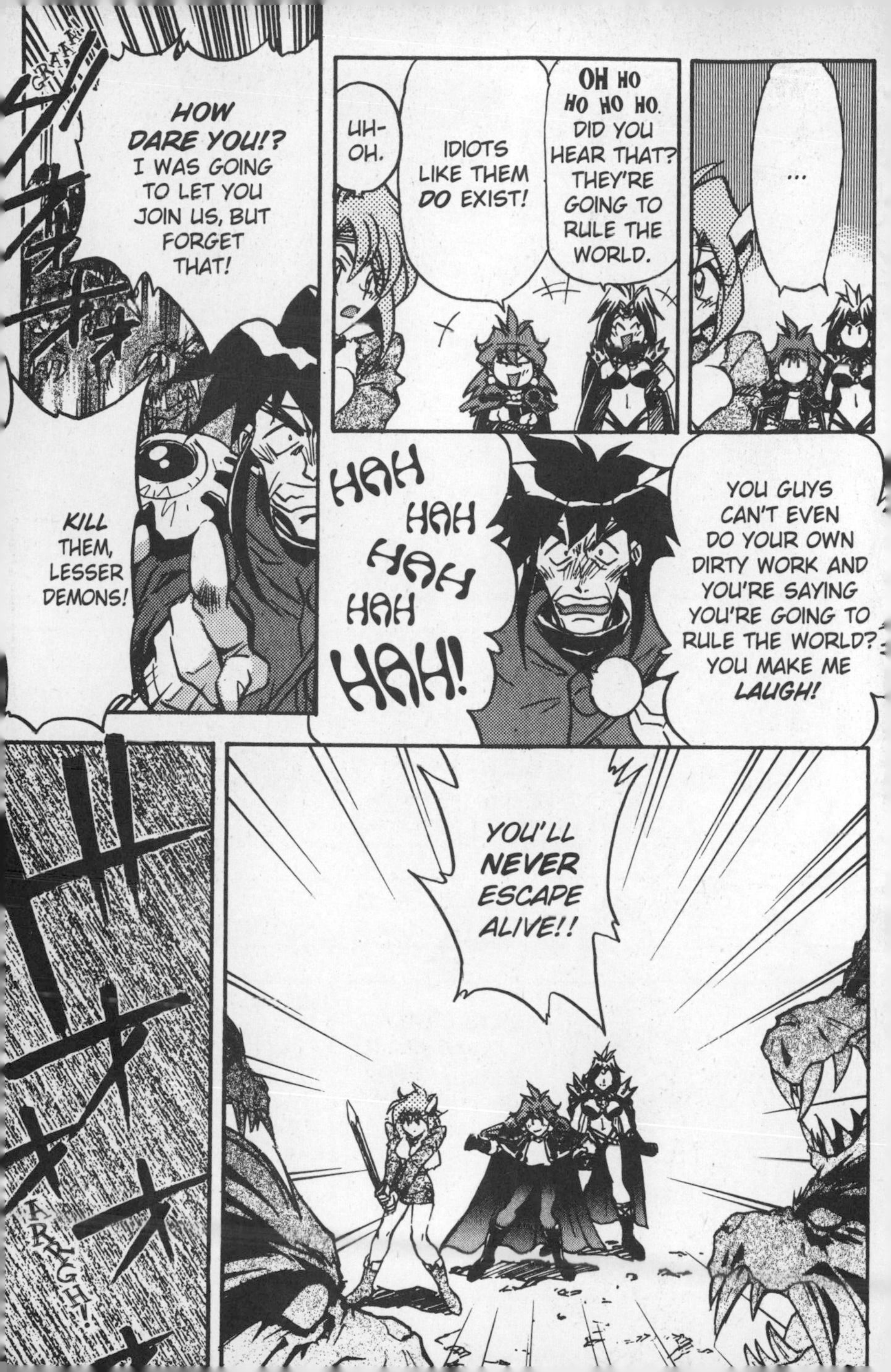
...
OH HO HO HO HO. DID YOU HEAR THAT? THEY'RE GOING TO RULE THE WORLD.
IDIOTS LIKE THEM DO EXIST!
UH-OH.
YOU GUYS CAN'T EVEN DO YOUR OWN DIRTY WORK AND YOU'RE SAYING YOU'RE GOING TO RULE THE WORLD? YOU MAKE ME LAUGH!
HAH HAH HAH HAH HAH!
GRAAA!!
HOW DARE YOU!? I WAS GOING TO LET YOU JOIN US, BUT FORGET THAT!
KILL THEM, LESSER DEMONS!
YOU'LL NEVER ESCAPE ALIVE!!
ARRGH!

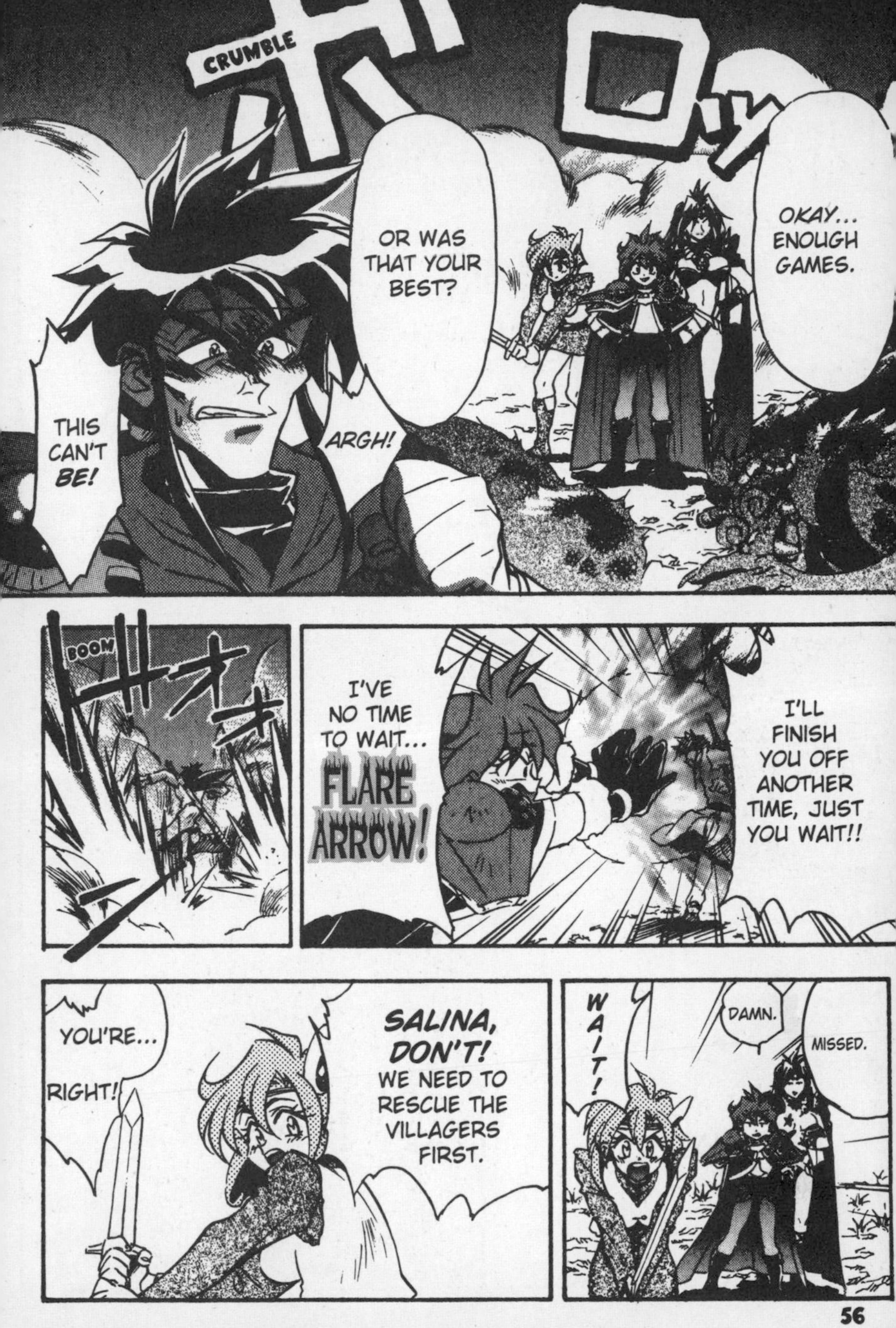
CRUMBLE
OKAY... ENOUGH GAMES.
OR WAS THAT YOUR BEST?
ARGH!
THIS CAN'T BE!
I'LL FINISH YOU OFF ANOTHER TIME, JUST YOU WAIT!!
I'VE NO TIME TO WAIT... FLARE ARROW!
BOOM
DAMN.
MISSED.
WAIT!
SALINA, DON'T! WE NEED TO RESCUE THE VILLAGERS FIRST.
YOU'RE...
RIGHT!

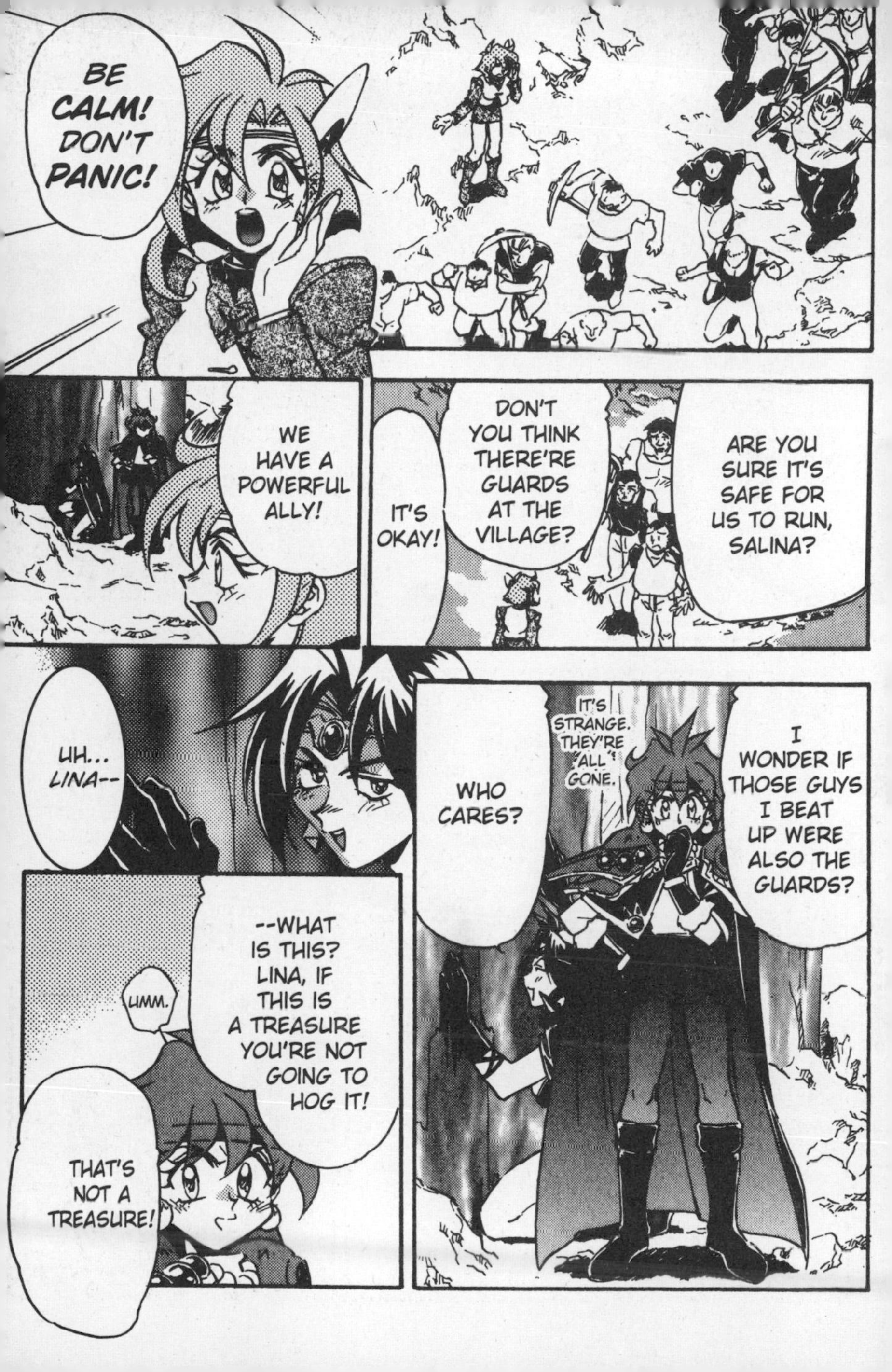
BE CALM! DON'T PANIC!
ARE YOU SURE IT'S SAFE FOR US TO RUN, SALINA?
DON'T YOU THINK THERE'RE GUARDS AT THE VILLAGE?
IT'S OKAY!
WE HAVE A POWERFUL ALLY!
I WONDER IF THOSE GUYS I BEAT UP WERE ALSO THE GUARDS?
IT'S STRANGE. THEY'RE ALL GONE.
WHO CARES?
UH... LINA--
--WHAT IS THIS? LINA, IF THIS IS A TREASURE YOU'RE NOT GOING TO HOG IT!
UMM.
THAT'S NOT A TREASURE!

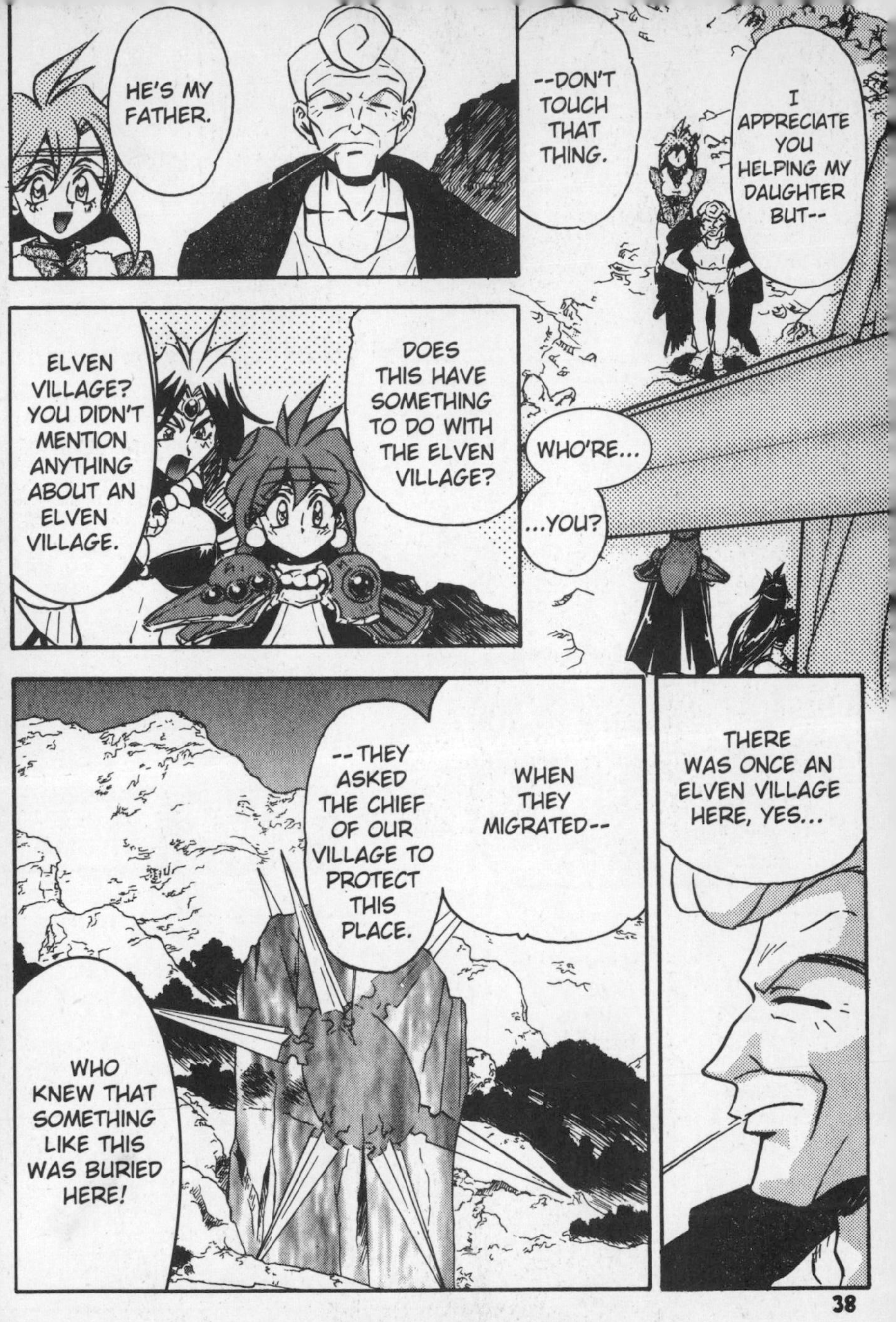
I APPRECIATE YOU HELPING MY DAUGHTER BUT--
WHO'RE...
...YOU?
--DON'T TOUCH THAT THING.
HE'S MY FATHER.
DOES THIS HAVE SOMETHING TO DO WITH THE ELVEN VILLAGE?
ELVEN VILLAGE? YOU DIDN'T MENTION ANYTHING ABOUT AN ELVEN VILLAGE.
THERE WAS ONCE AN ELVEN VILLAGE HERE, YES...
WHEN THEY MIGRATED--
--THEY ASKED THE CHIEF OF OUR VILLAGE TO PROTECT THIS PLACE.
WHO KNEW THAT SOMETHING LIKE THIS WAS BURIED HERE!

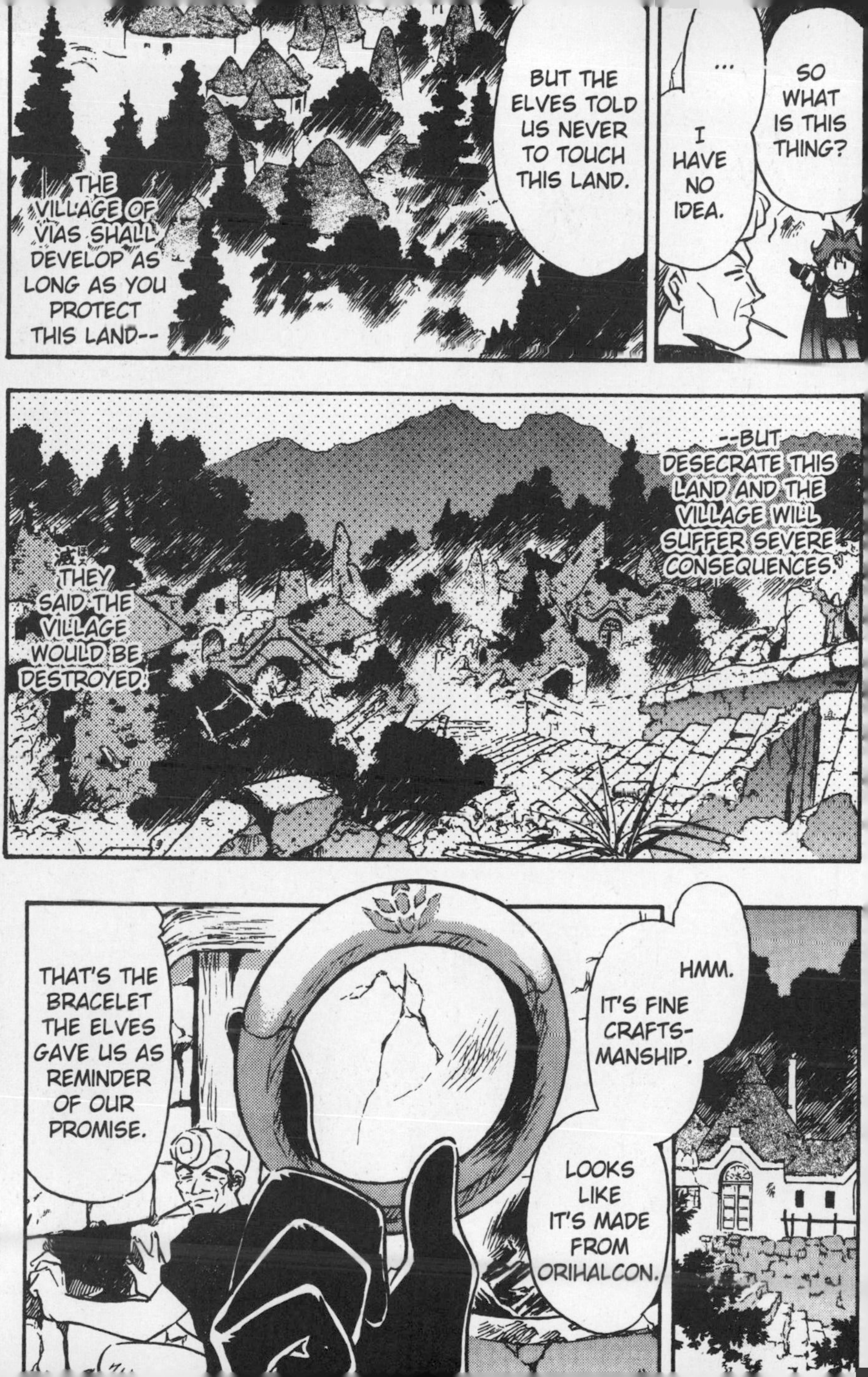
SO WHAT IS THIS THING?
... I HAVE NO IDEA.
BUT THE ELVES TOLD US NEVER TO TOUCH THIS LAND.
THE VILLAGE OF VIAS SHALL DEVELOP AS LONG AS YOU PROTECT THIS LAND--
--BUT DESECRATE THIS LAND AND THE VILLAGE WILL SUFFER SEVERE CONSEQUENCES.
THEY SAID THE VILLAGE WOULD BE DESTROYED.
HMM.
IT'S FINE CRAFTS-MANSHIP.
LOOKS LIKE IT'S MADE FROM ORIHALCON.
THAT'S THE BRACELET THE ELVES GAVE US AS REMINDER OF OUR PROMISE.

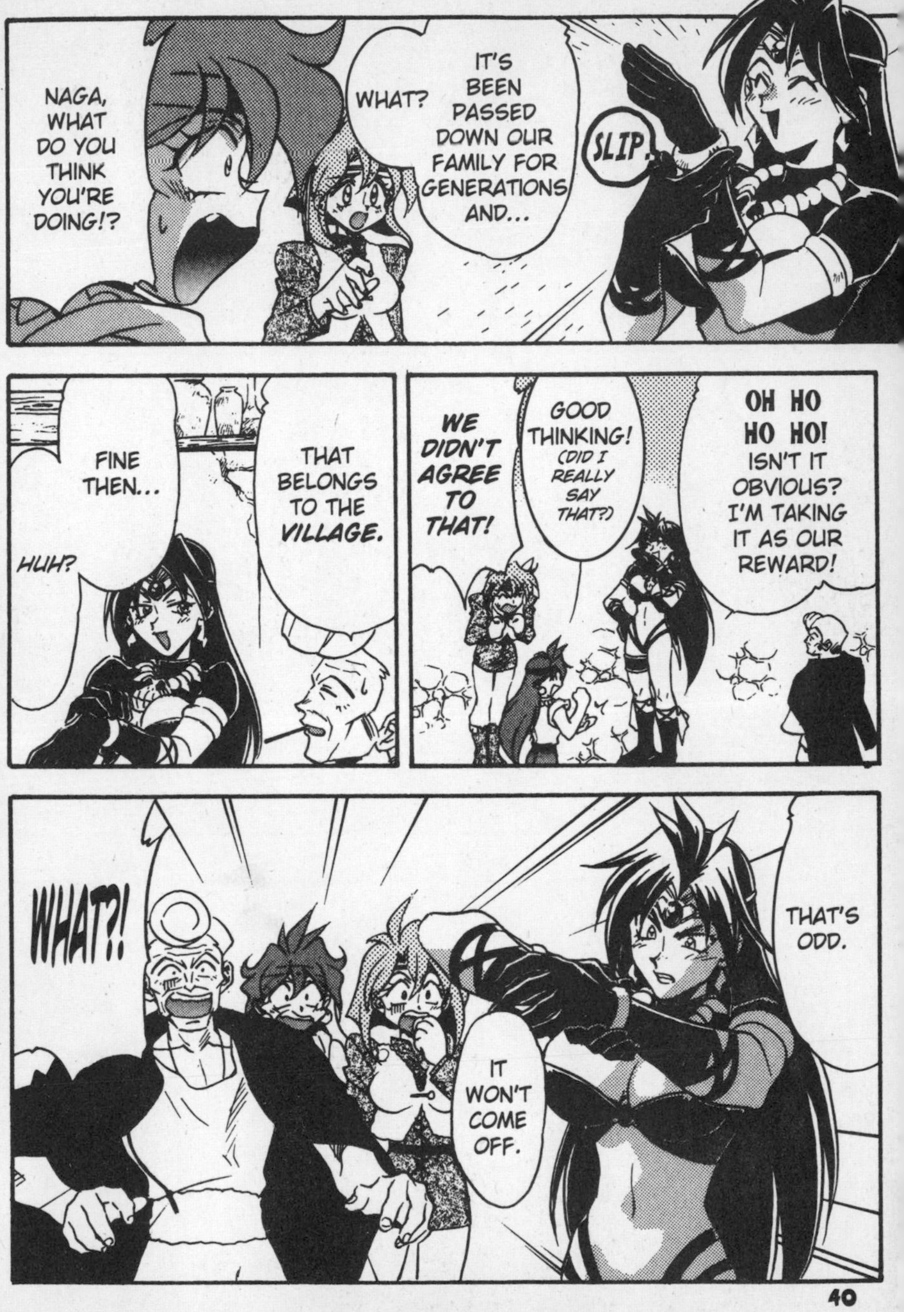
IT'S BEEN PASSED DOWN OUR FAMILY FOR GENERATIONS AND...
SLIP.
WHAT?
NAGA, WHAT DO YOU THINK YOU'RE DOING!?
OH HO HO HO! ISN'T IT OBVIOUS? I'M TAKING IT AS OUR REWARD!
GOOD THINKING! (DID I REALLY SAY THAT?)
WE DIDN'T AGREE TO THAT!
THAT BELONGS TO THE VILLAGE.
FINE THEN...
HUH?
THAT'S ODD.
IT WON'T COME OFF.
WHAT?!

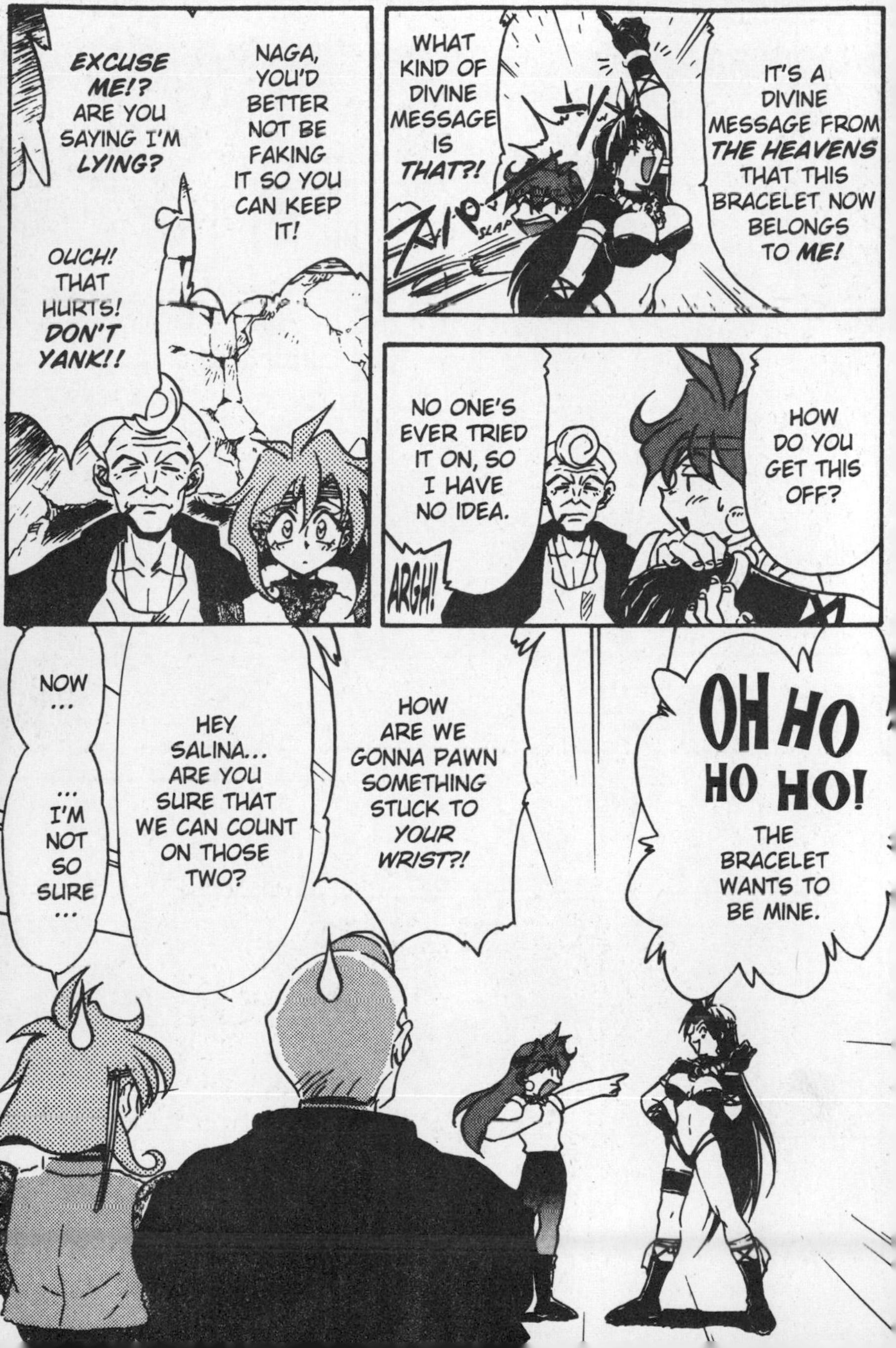
IT'S A DIVINE MESSAGE FROM THE HEAVENS THAT THIS BRACELET NOW BELONGS TO ME!
WHAT KIND OF DIVINE MESSAGE IS THAT?!
ZIP
SLAP
HOW DO YOU GET THIS OFF?
NO ONE'S EVER TRIED IT ON, SO I HAVE NO IDEA.
ARGH!
NAGA, YOU'D BETTER NOT BE FAKING IT SO YOU CAN KEEP IT!
EXCUSE ME!? ARE YOU SAYING I'M LYING?
OUCH! THAT HURTS! DON'T YANK!!
OH HO HO HO! THE BRACELET WANTS TO BE MINE.
HOW ARE WE GONNA PAWN SOMETHING STUCK TO YOUR WRIST?!
HEY SALINA... ARE YOU SURE THAT WE CAN COUNT ON THOSE TWO?
NOW... ...I'M NOT SO SURE...

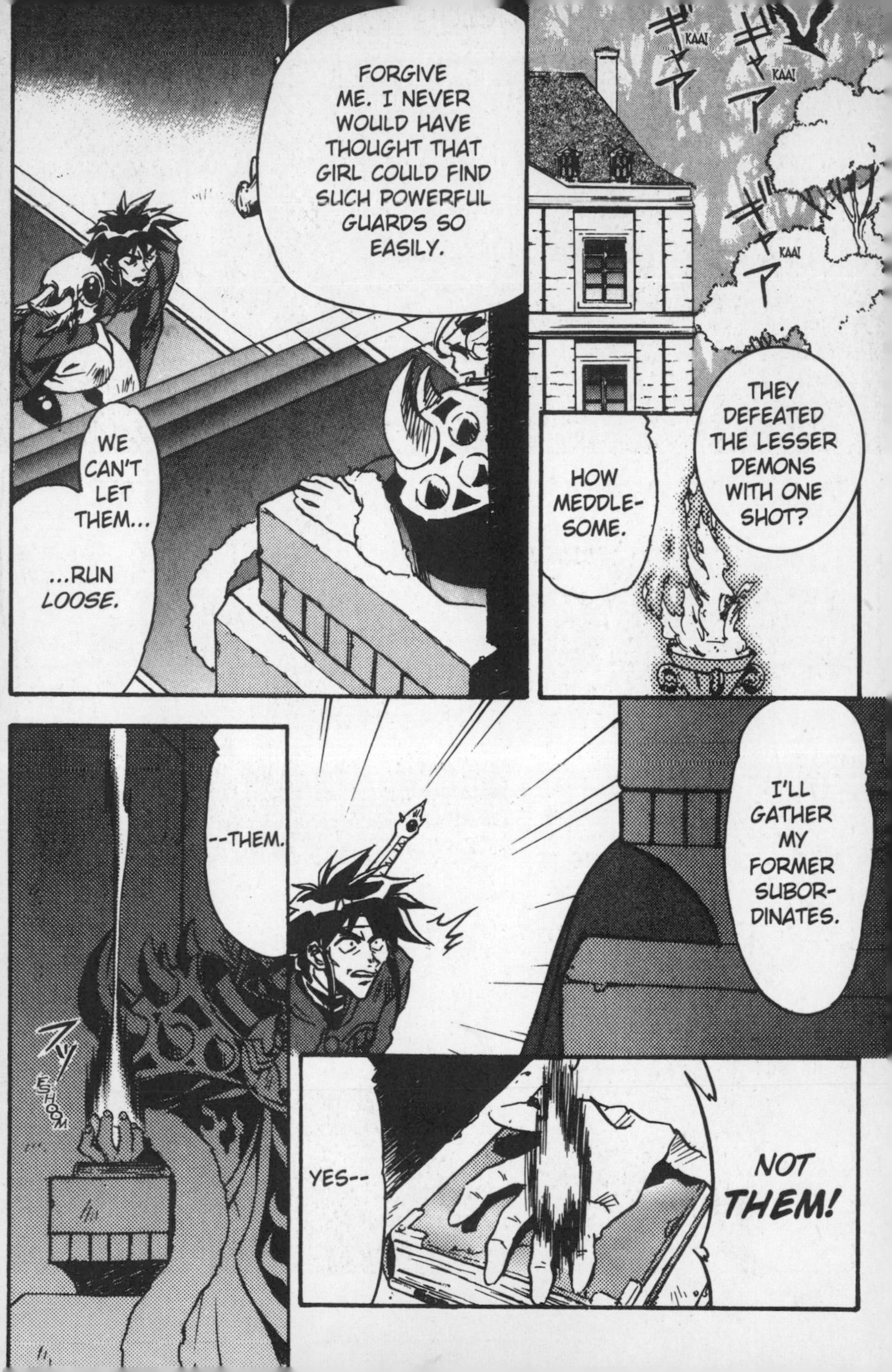
KAAI
KAAI
KAAI
THEY DEFEATED THE LESSER DEMONS WITH ONE SHOT?
HOW MEDDLE-SOME.
FORGIVE ME. I NEVER WOULD HAVE THOUGHT THAT GIRL COULD FIND SUCH POWERFUL GUARDS SO EASILY.
WE CAN'T LET THEM...
...RUN LOOSE.
I'LL GATHER MY FORMER SUBOR-DINATES.
NOT THEM!
YES--
--THEM.
ESHOOM

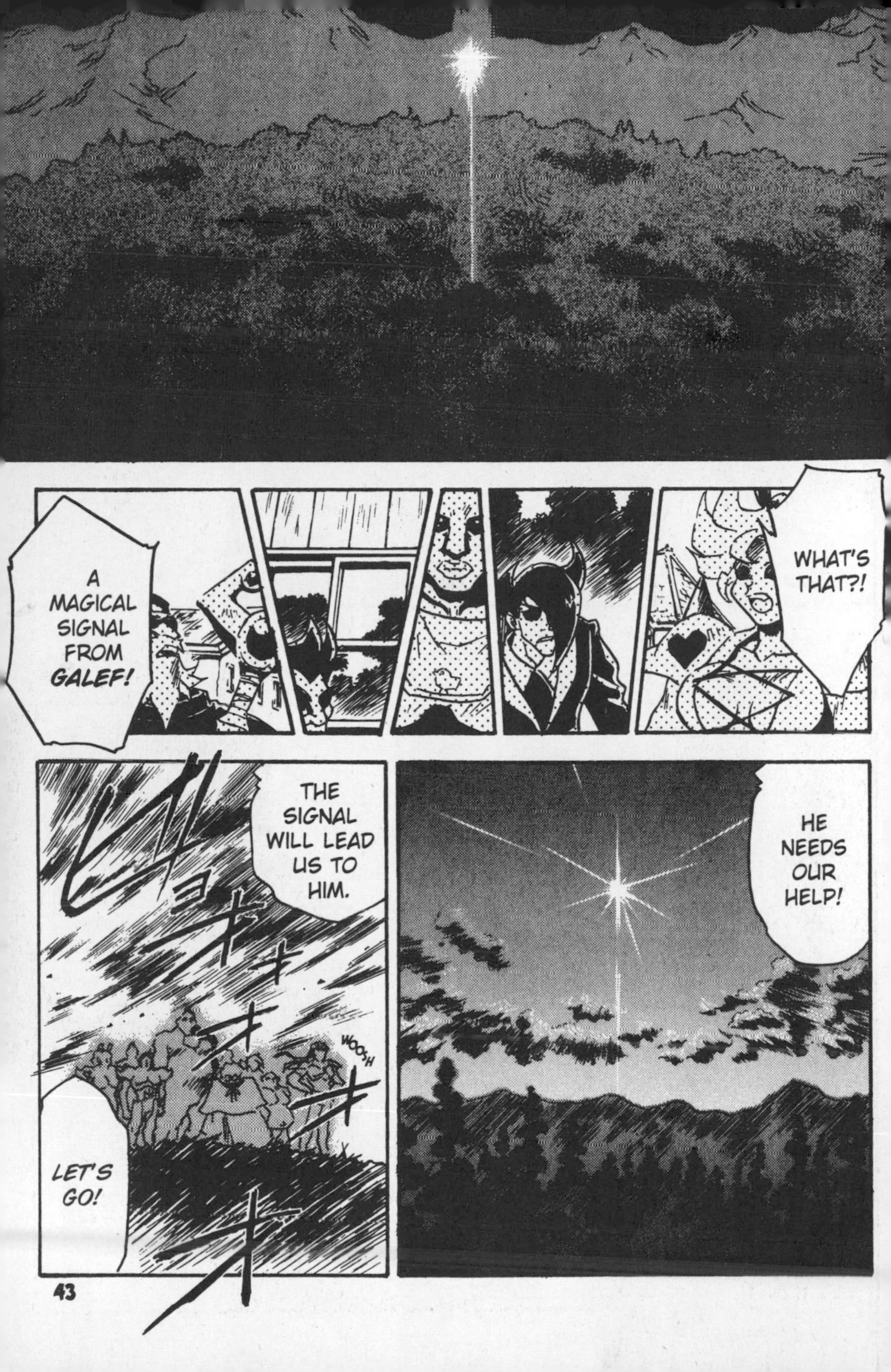
WHAT'S THAT?!
A MAGICAL SIGNAL FROM *GALEF!*
HE NEEDS OUR HELP!
THE SIGNAL WILL LEAD US TO HIM.
WOOSH
LET'S GO!

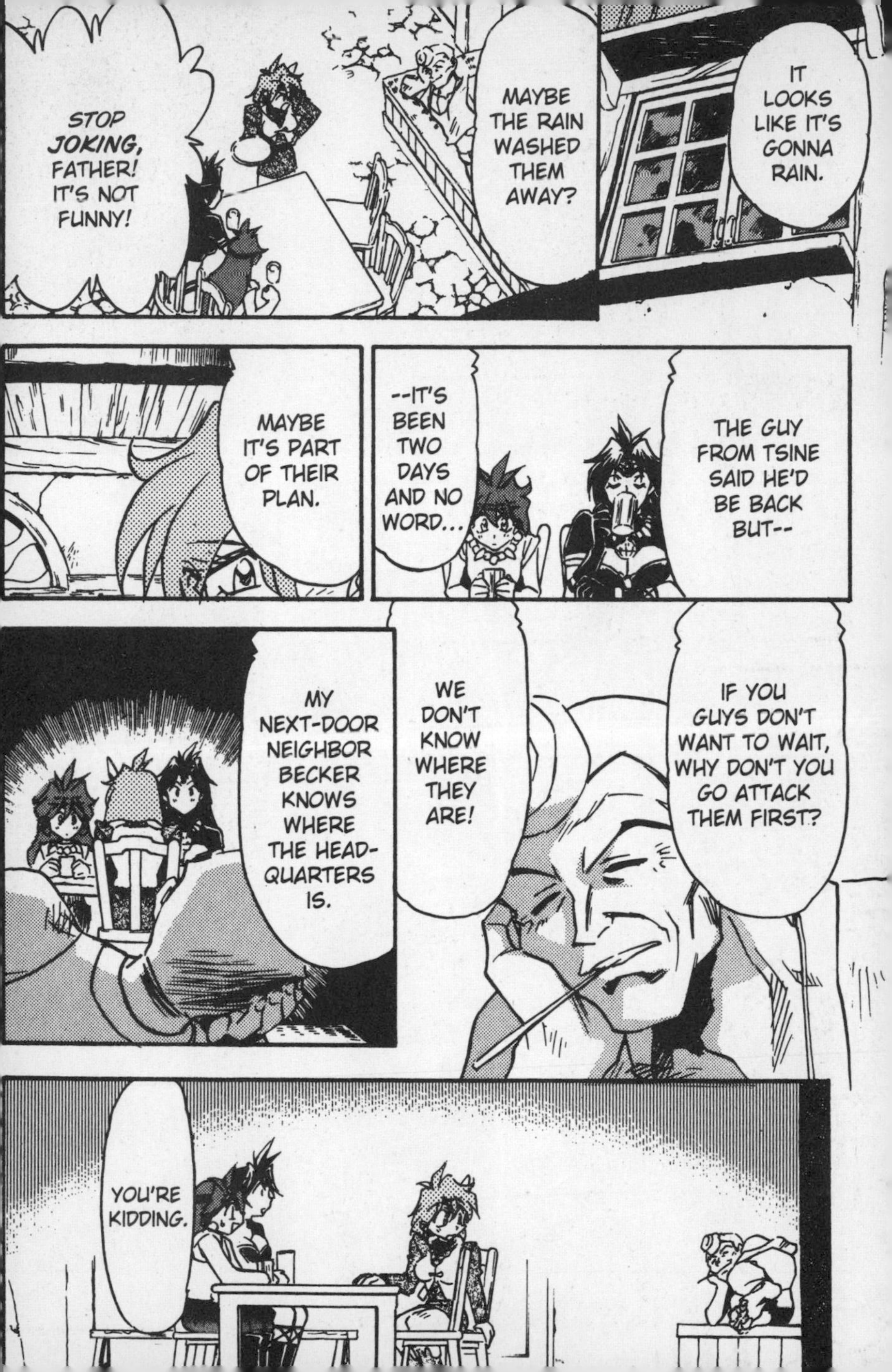
IT LOOKS LIKE IT'S GONNA RAIN.
MAYBE THE RAIN WASHED THEM AWAY?
STOP *JOKING*, FATHER! IT'S NOT FUNNY!
THE GUY FROM TSINE SAID HE'D BE BACK BUT--
--IT'S BEEN TWO DAYS AND NO WORD...
MAYBE IT'S PART OF THEIR PLAN.
IF YOU GUYS DON'T WANT TO WAIT, WHY DON'T YOU GO ATTACK THEM FIRST?
WE DON'T KNOW WHERE THEY ARE!
MY NEXT-DOOR NEIGHBOR BECKER KNOWS WHERE THE HEAD-QUARTERS IS.
YOU'RE KIDDING.

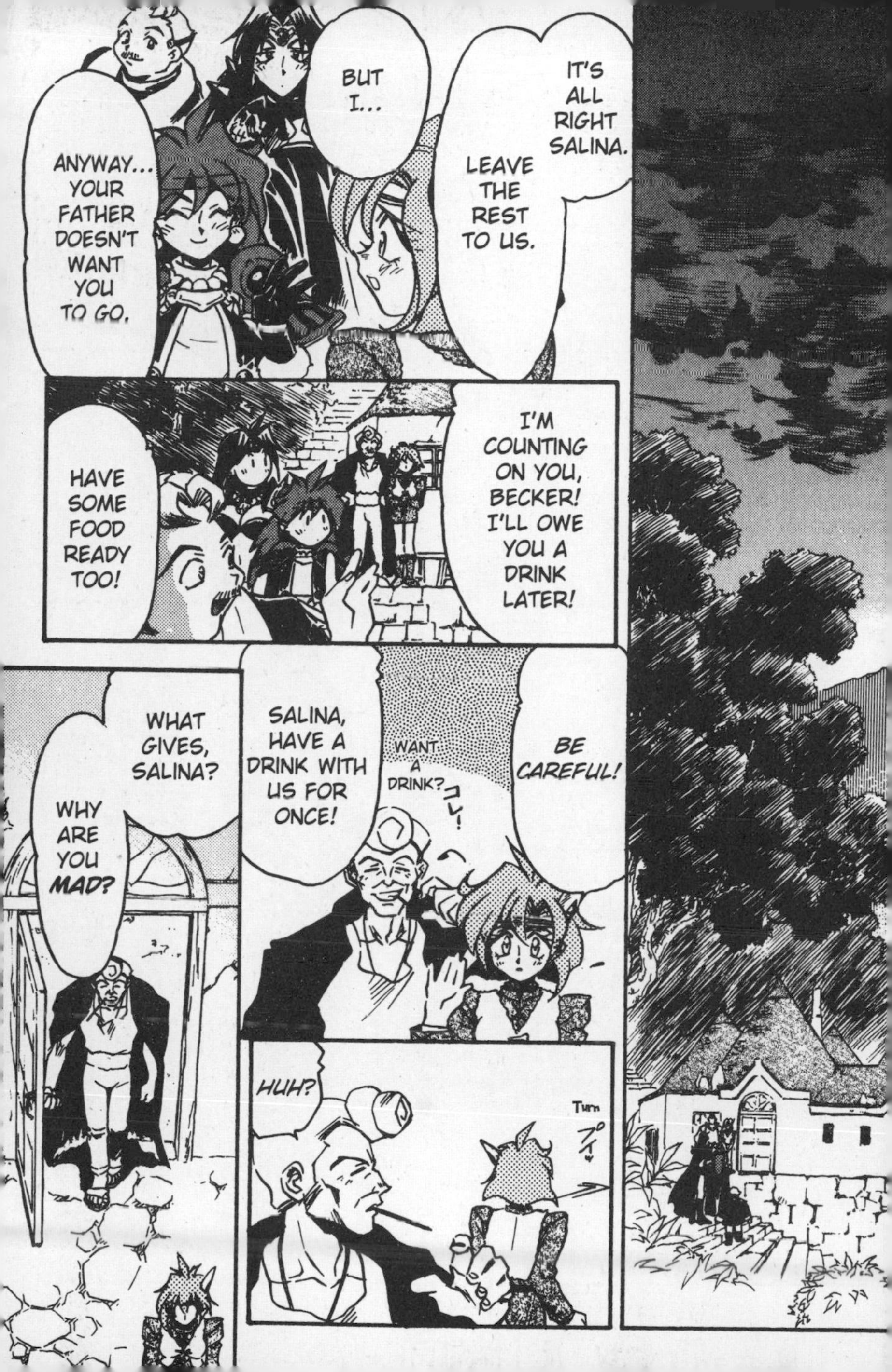
IT'S ALL RIGHT SALINA.
LEAVE THE REST TO US.
BUT I...
ANYWAY... YOUR FATHER DOESN'T WANT YOU TO GO.
I'M COUNTING ON YOU, BECKER! I'LL OWE YOU A DRINK LATER!
HAVE SOME FOOD READY TOO!
BE CAREFUL!
WANT A DRINK?
SALINA, HAVE A DRINK WITH US FOR ONCE!
HUH?
Turn
WHAT GIVES, SALINA?
WHY ARE YOU *MAD?*

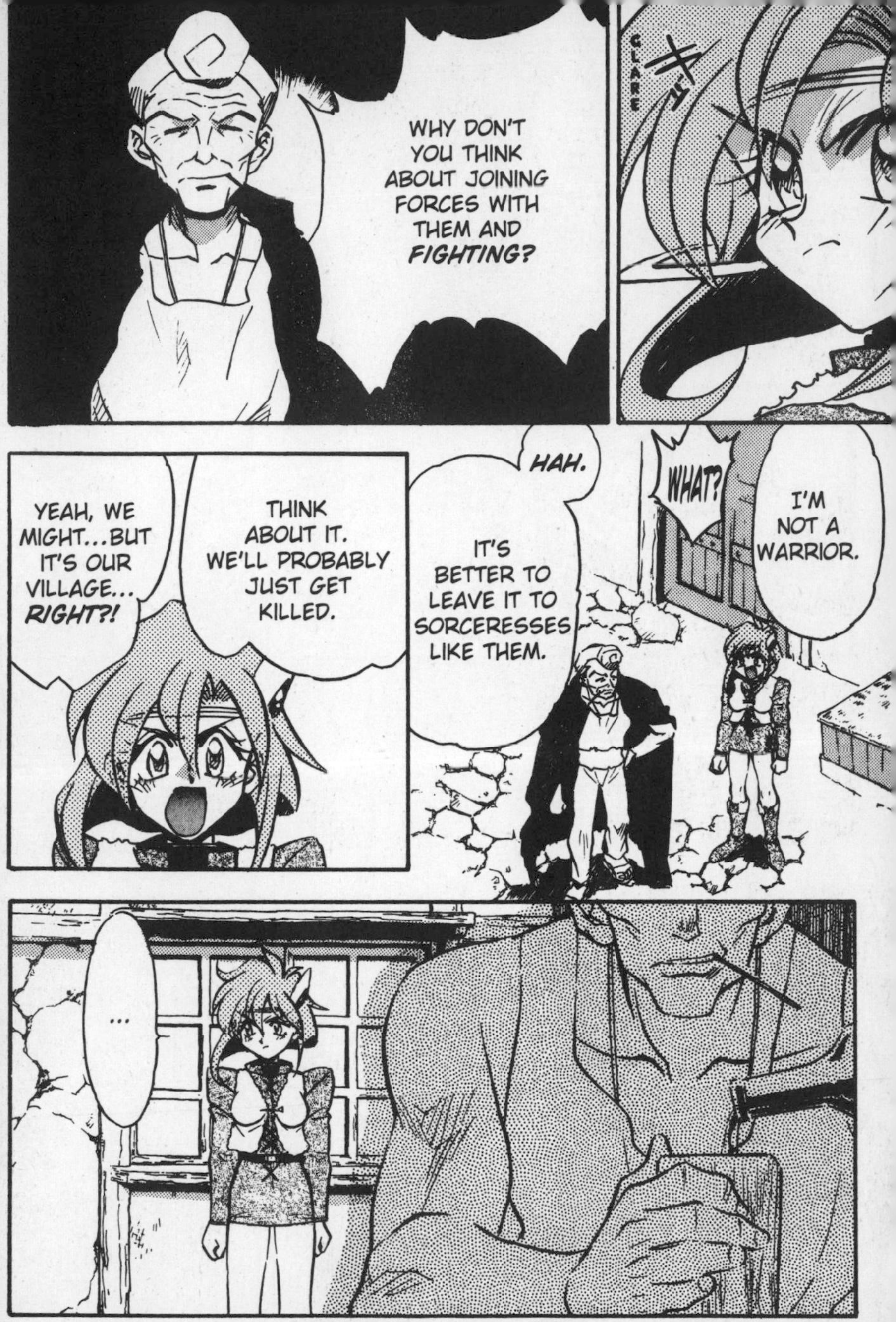
GLARE
WHY DON'T YOU THINK ABOUT JOINING FORCES WITH THEM AND *FIGHTING?*
I'M NOT A WARRIOR.
WHAT?
HAH.
IT'S BETTER TO LEAVE IT TO SORCERESSES LIKE THEM.
THINK ABOUT IT. WE'LL PROBABLY JUST GET KILLED.
YEAH, WE MIGHT...BUT IT'S OUR VILLAGE... *RIGHT?!*
...

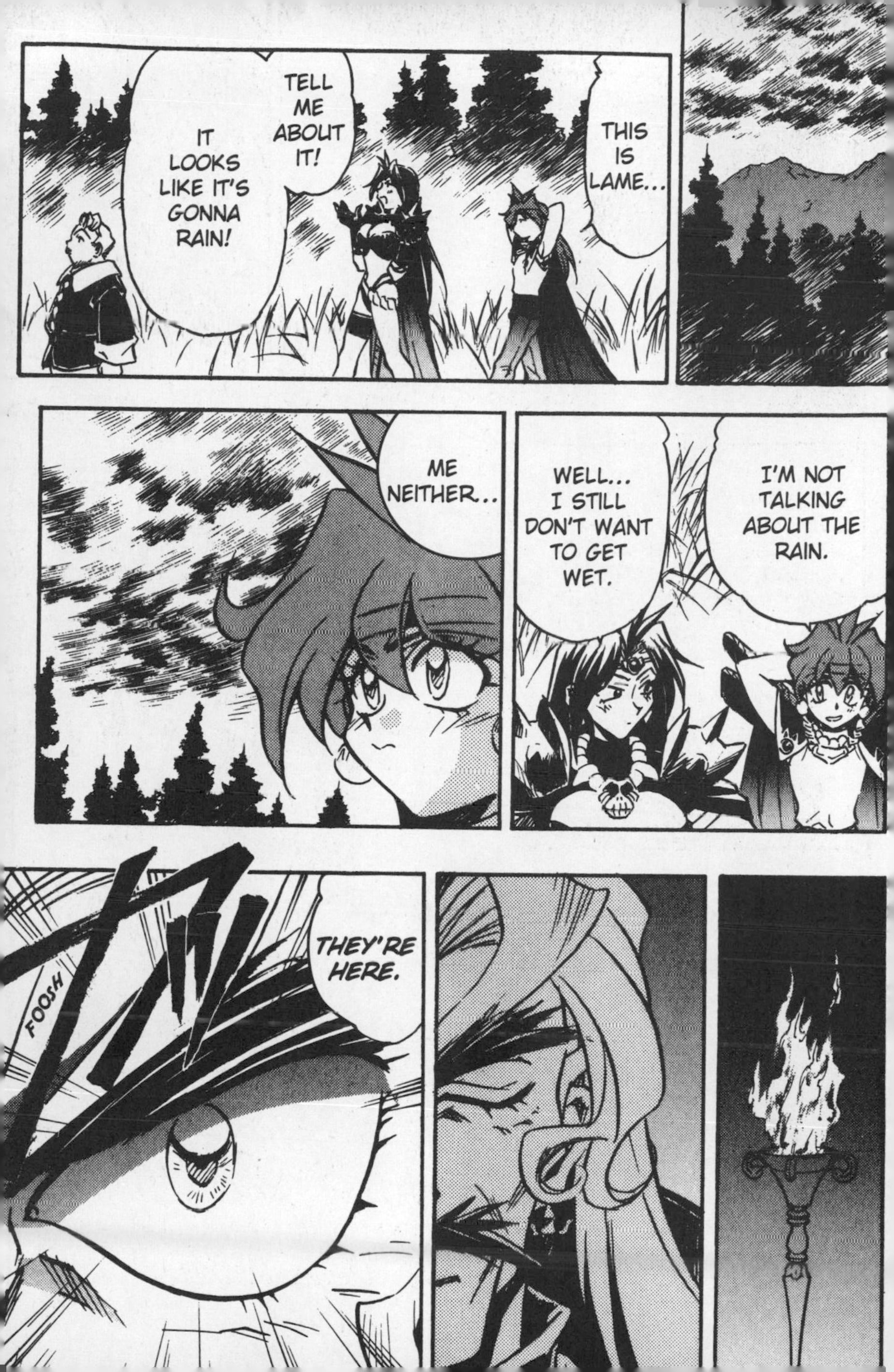
THIS IS LAME...
TELL ME ABOUT IT!
IT LOOKS LIKE IT'S GONNA RAIN!
I'M NOT TALKING ABOUT THE RAIN.
WELL... I STILL DON'T WANT TO GET WET.
ME NEITHER...
THEY'RE HERE.
FOOSH

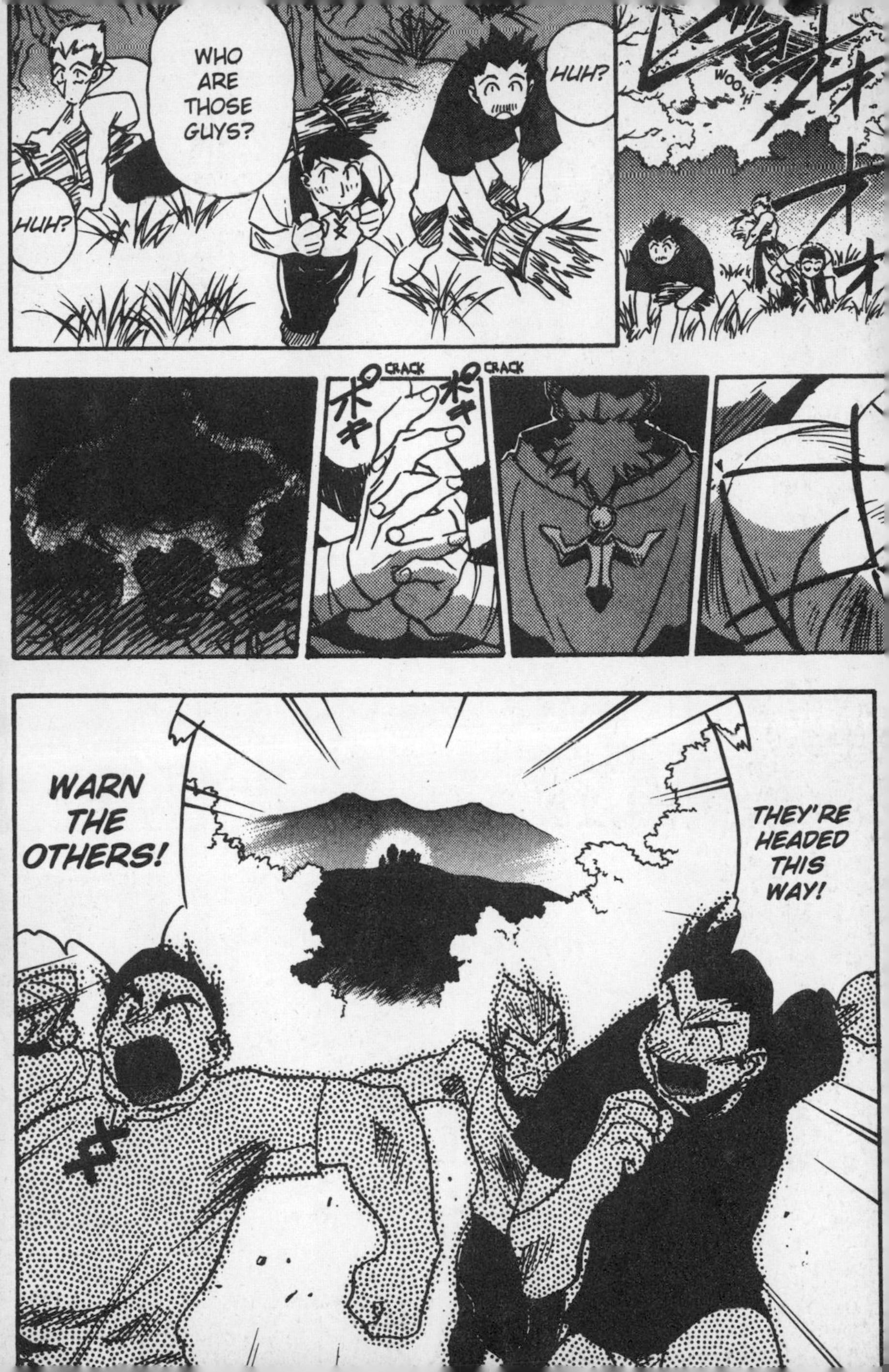
WOOSH
HUH?
WHO ARE THOSE GUYS?
HUH?
ポキ
CRACK
ポキ
CRACK
THEY'RE HEADED THIS WAY!
WARN THE OTHERS!

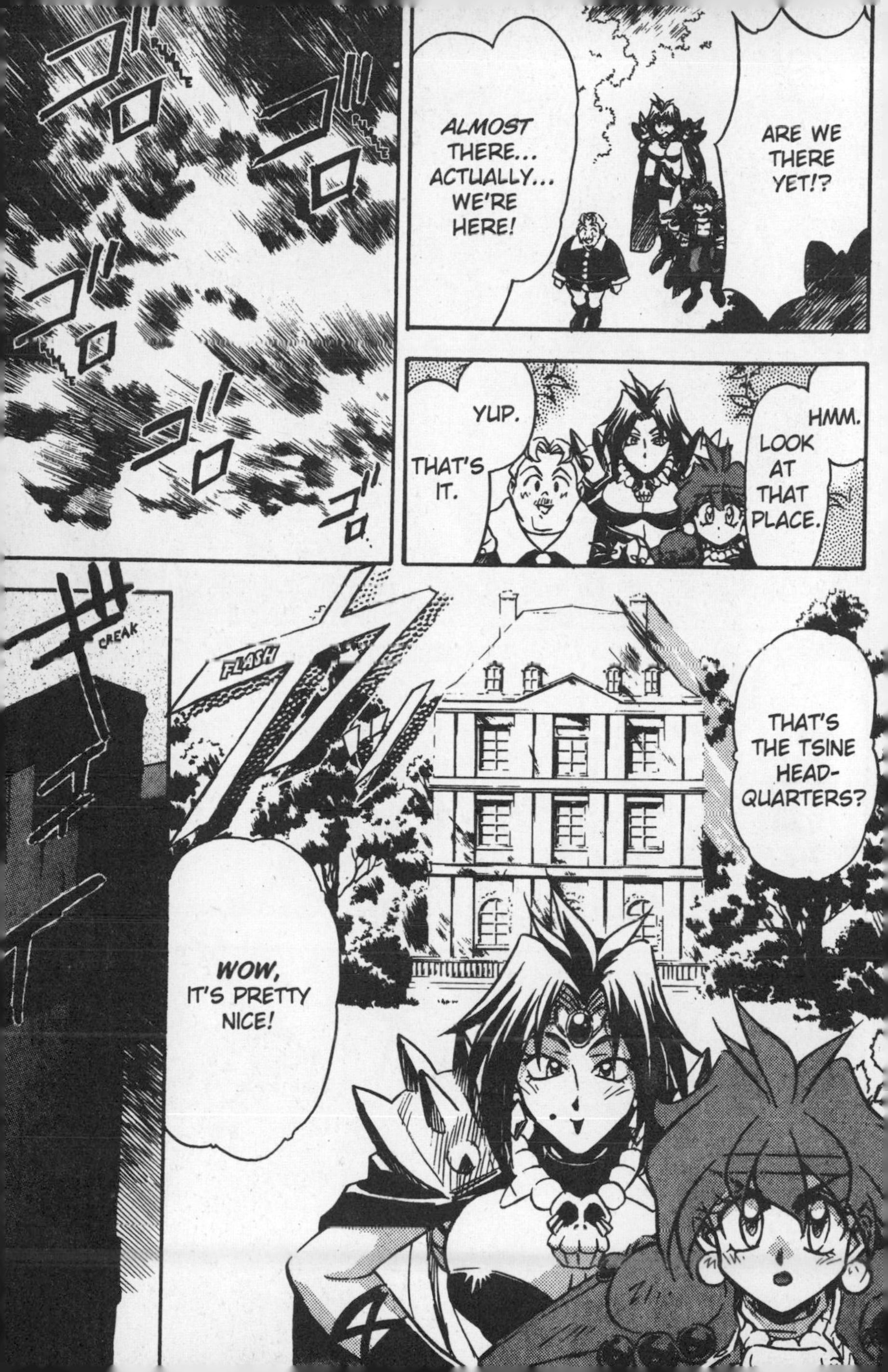
ARE WE THERE YET!?
ALMOST THERE... ACTUALLY... WE'RE HERE!
HMM. LOOK AT THAT PLACE.
YUP.
THAT'S IT.
ゴロゴロ
RUMBLE
ゴロゴロ
RUMBLE
ゴロゴロ
RUMBLE
ゴロゴロ
THAT'S THE TSINE HEAD-QUARTERS?
FLASH
CREAK
WOW, IT'S PRETTY NICE!

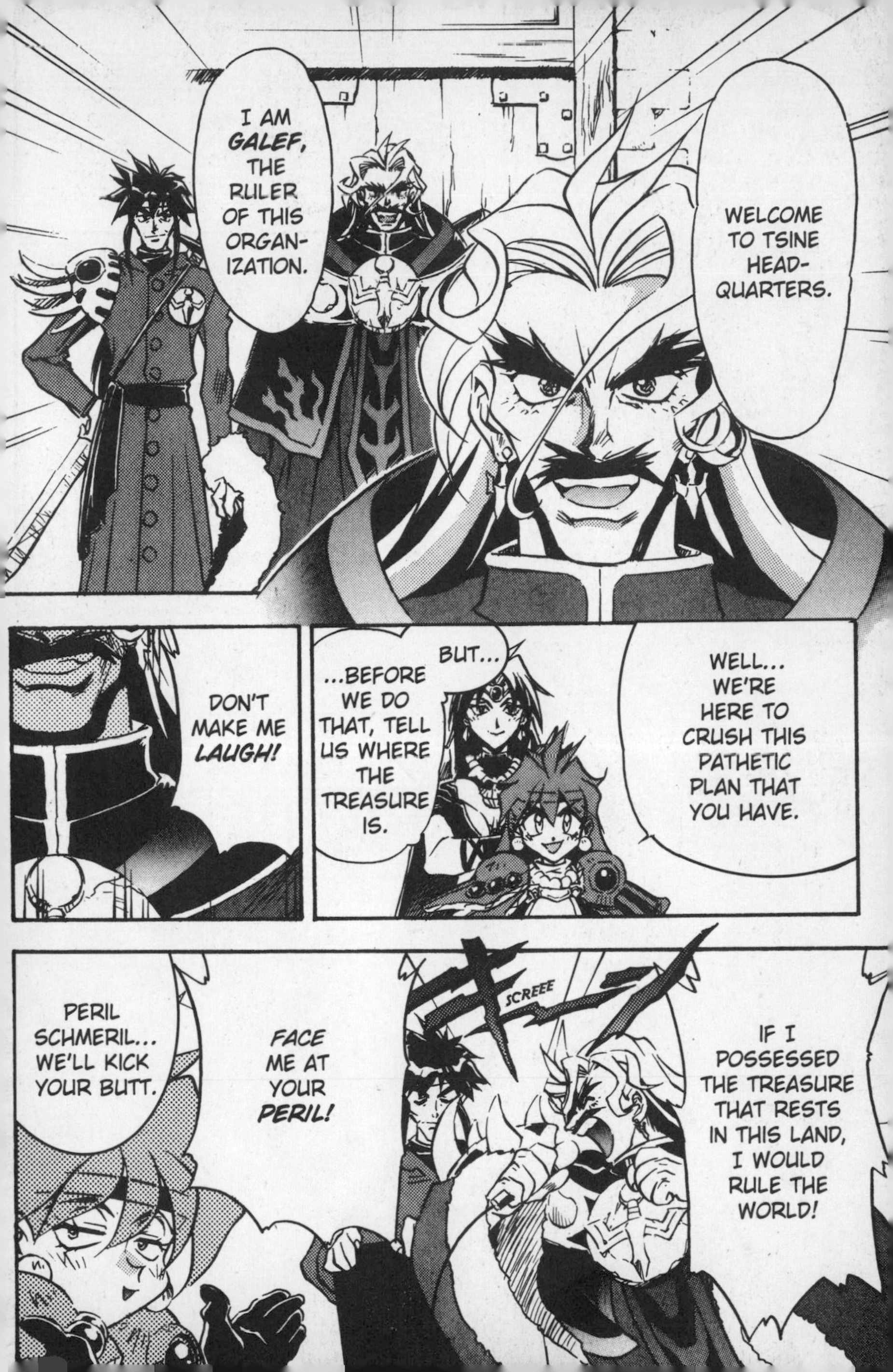
WELCOME TO TSINE HEAD-QUARTERS.
I AM *GALEF*, THE RULER OF THIS ORGAN-IZATION.
WELL... WE'RE HERE TO CRUSH THIS PATHETIC PLAN THAT YOU HAVE.
BUT...
...BEFORE WE DO THAT, TELL US WHERE THE TREASURE IS.
DON'T MAKE ME *LAUGH!*
IF I POSSESSED THE TREASURE THAT RESTS IN THIS LAND, I WOULD RULE THE WORLD!
SCREEE
FACE ME AT YOUR *PERIL!*
PERIL SCHMERIL... WE'LL KICK YOUR BUTT.

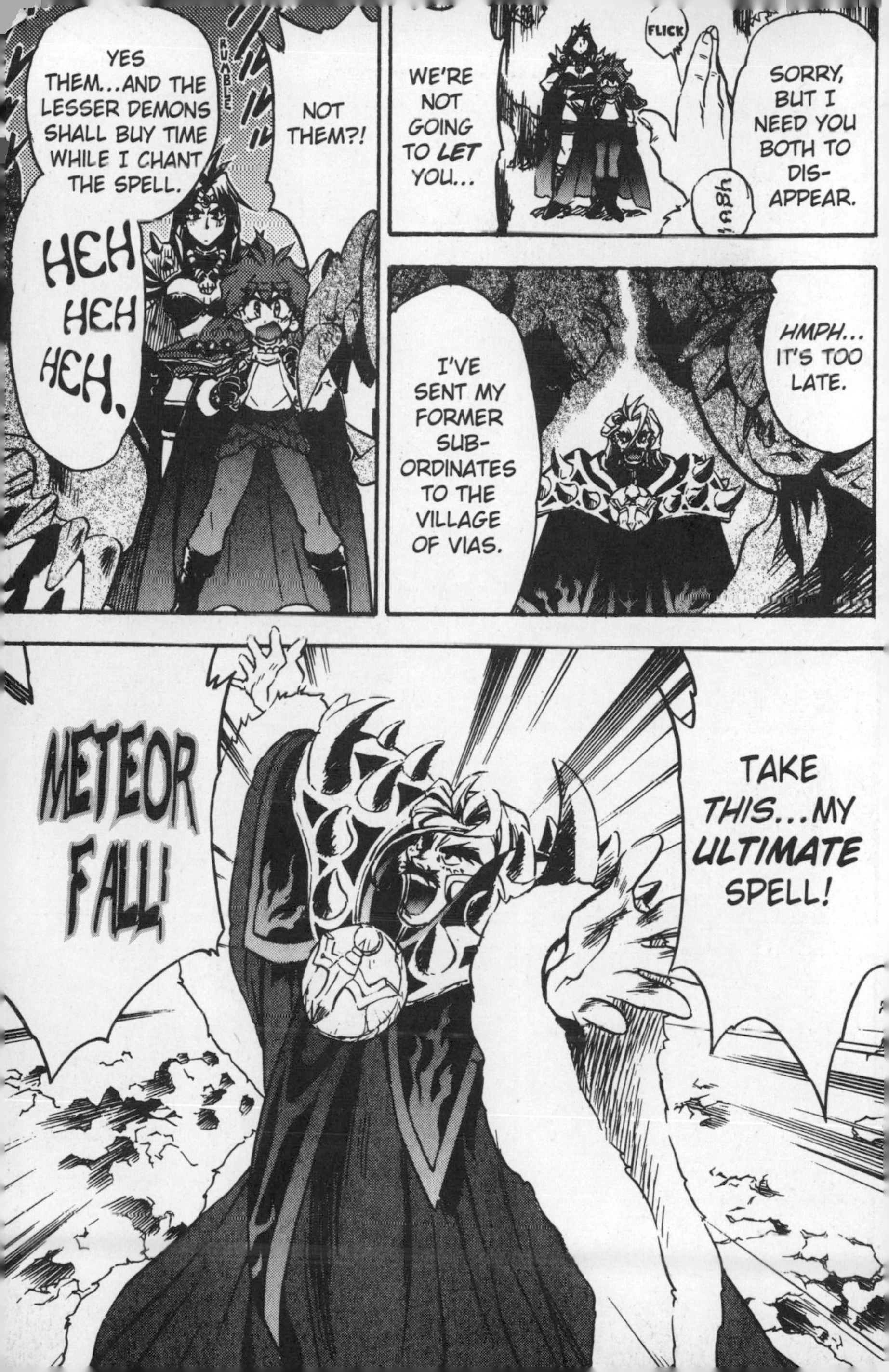
FLICK
SORRY, BUT I NEED YOU BOTH TO DIS-APPEAR.
UGH!
WE'RE NOT GOING TO LET YOU...
HMPH... IT'S TOO LATE.
I'VE SENT MY FORMER SUB-ORDINATES TO THE VILLAGE OF VIAS.
NOT THEM?!
YES THEM...AND THE LESSER DEMONS SHALL BUY TIME WHILE I CHANT THE SPELL.
RUMBLE
HEH HEH HEH.
TAKE THIS...MY ULTIMATE SPELL!
METEOR FALL!

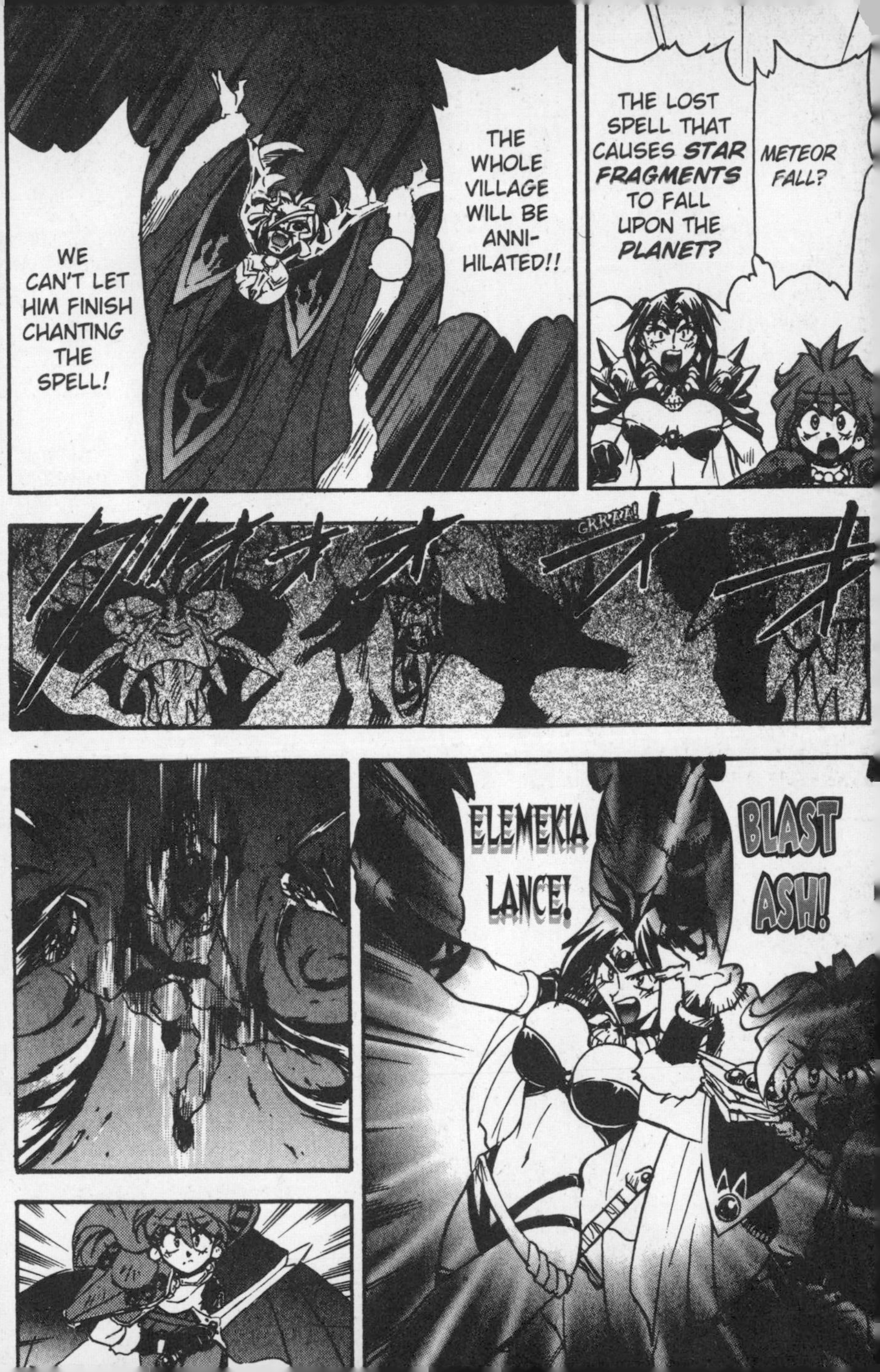
METEOR FALL?
THE LOST SPELL THAT CAUSES STAR FRAGMENTS TO FALL UPON THE PLANET?
THE WHOLE VILLAGE WILL BE ANNI-HILATED!!
WE CAN'T LET HIM FINISH CHANTING THE SPELL!
GRRAAA!
BLAST ASH!
ELEMEKIA LANCE!

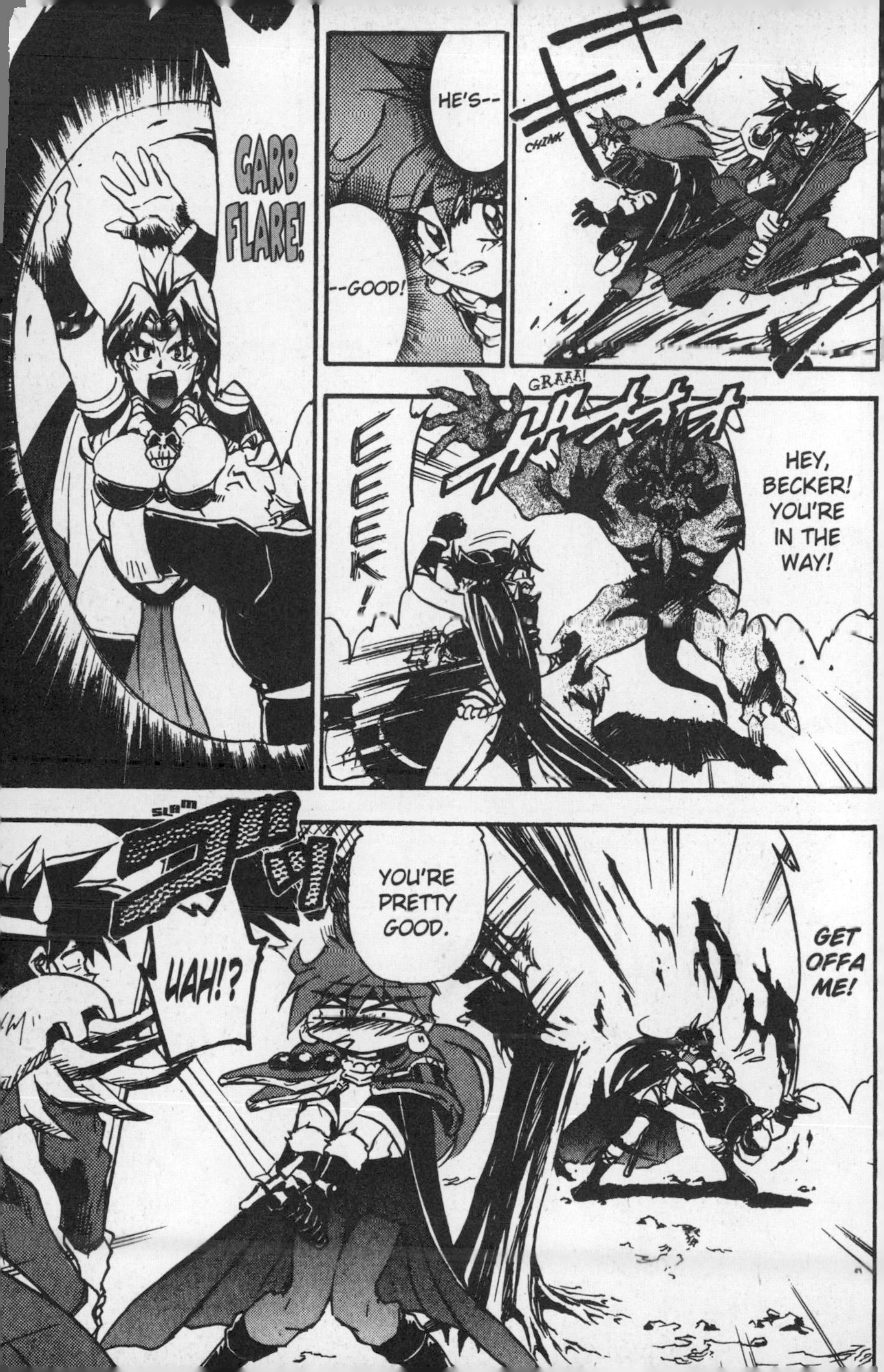
CHINK
HE'S--
--GOOD!
GRAAA!
HEY, BECKER! YOU'RE IN THE WAY!
EEEEK!
GARB FLARE!
GET OFFA ME!
YOU'RE PRETTY GOOD.
UAH!?
SLAM

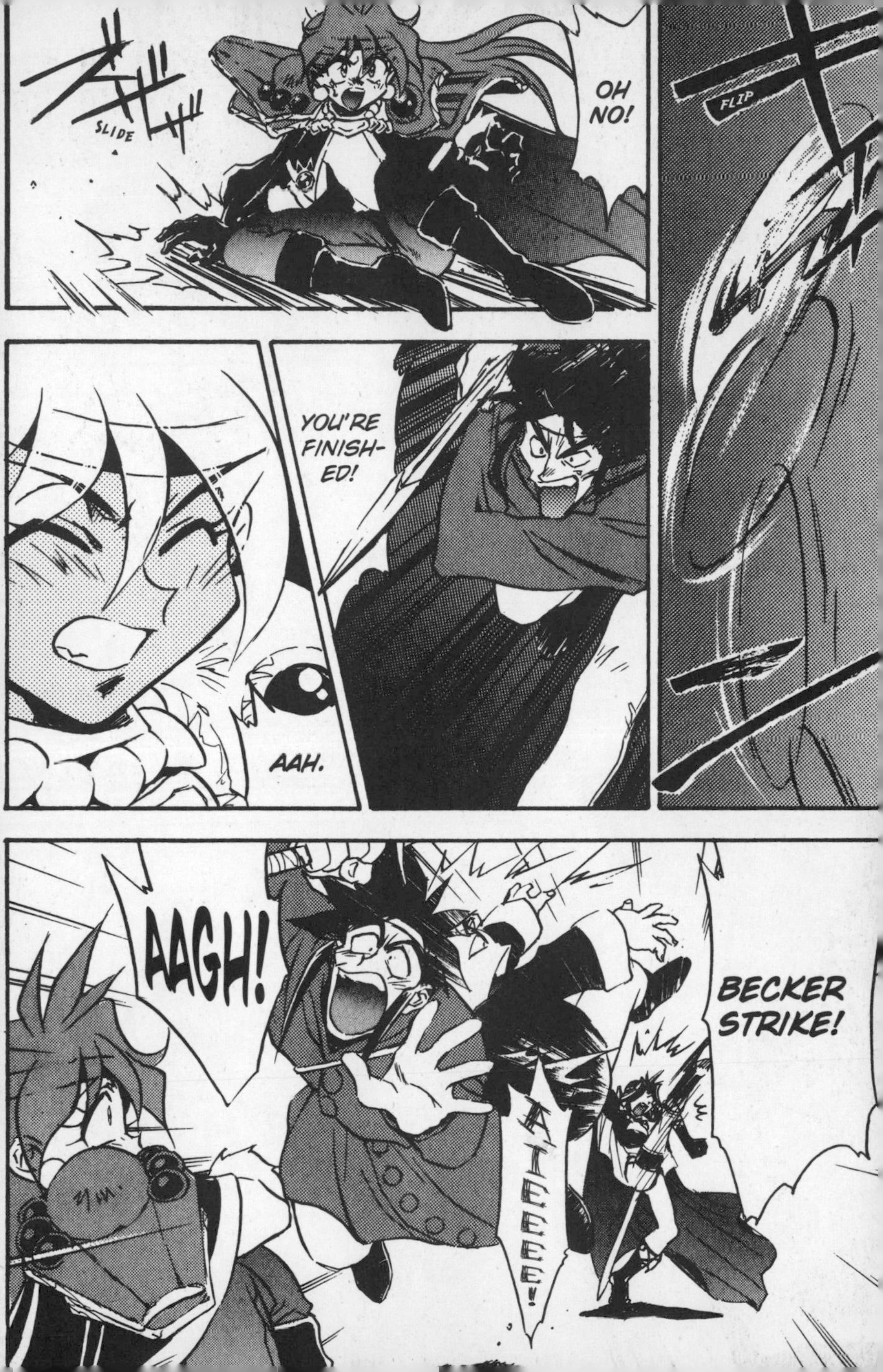
FLIP
OH NO!
SLIDE
YOU'RE FINISH-ED!
AAH.
BECKER STRIKE!
AAGH!
AIEEEE!

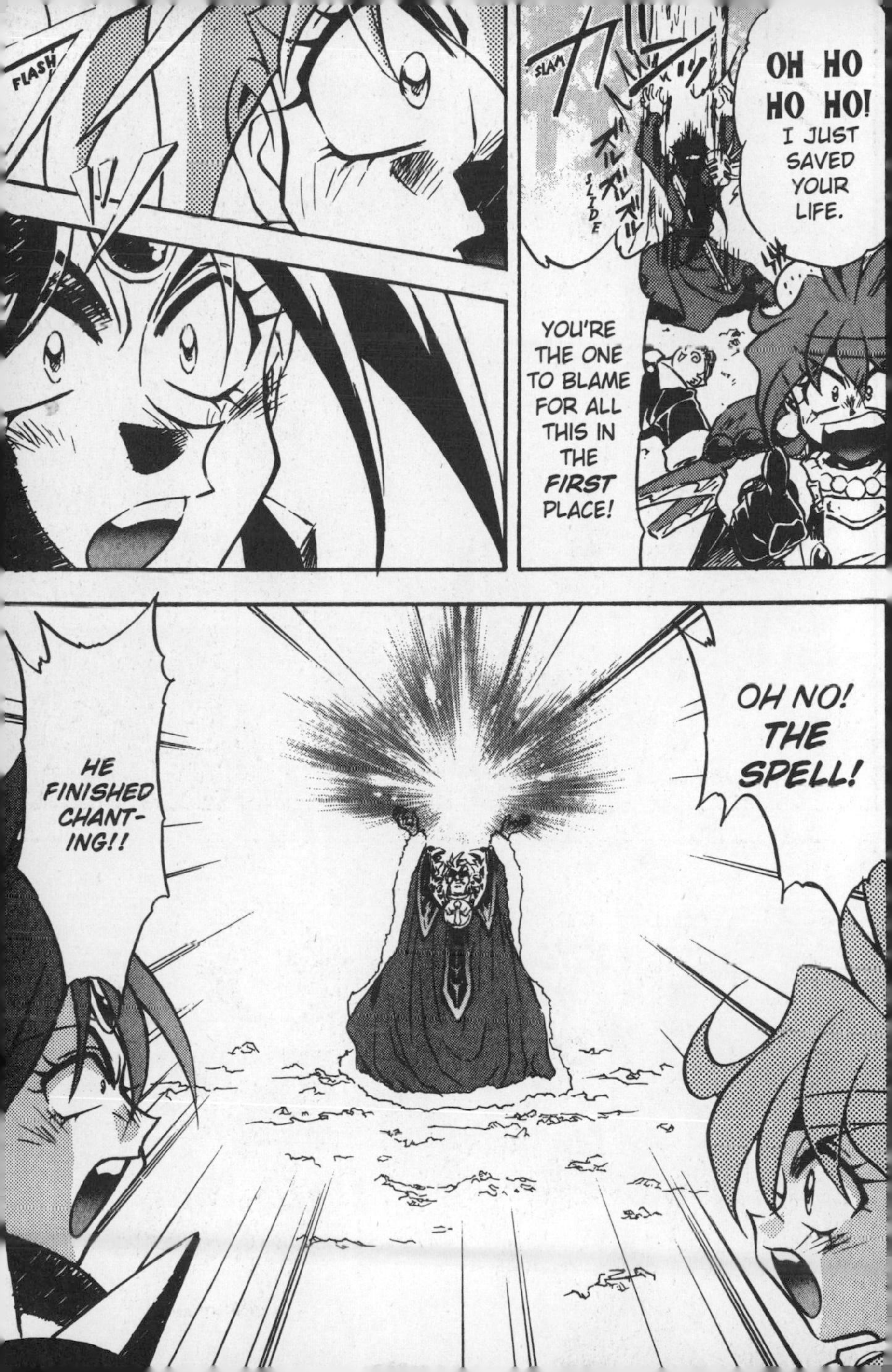
OH HO HO HO! I JUST SAVED YOUR LIFE.
SLAM
SLIDE
YOU'RE THE ONE TO BLAME FOR ALL THIS IN THE *FIRST* PLACE!
FLASH
OH NO! *THE SPELL!*
HE FINISHED CHANTING!!

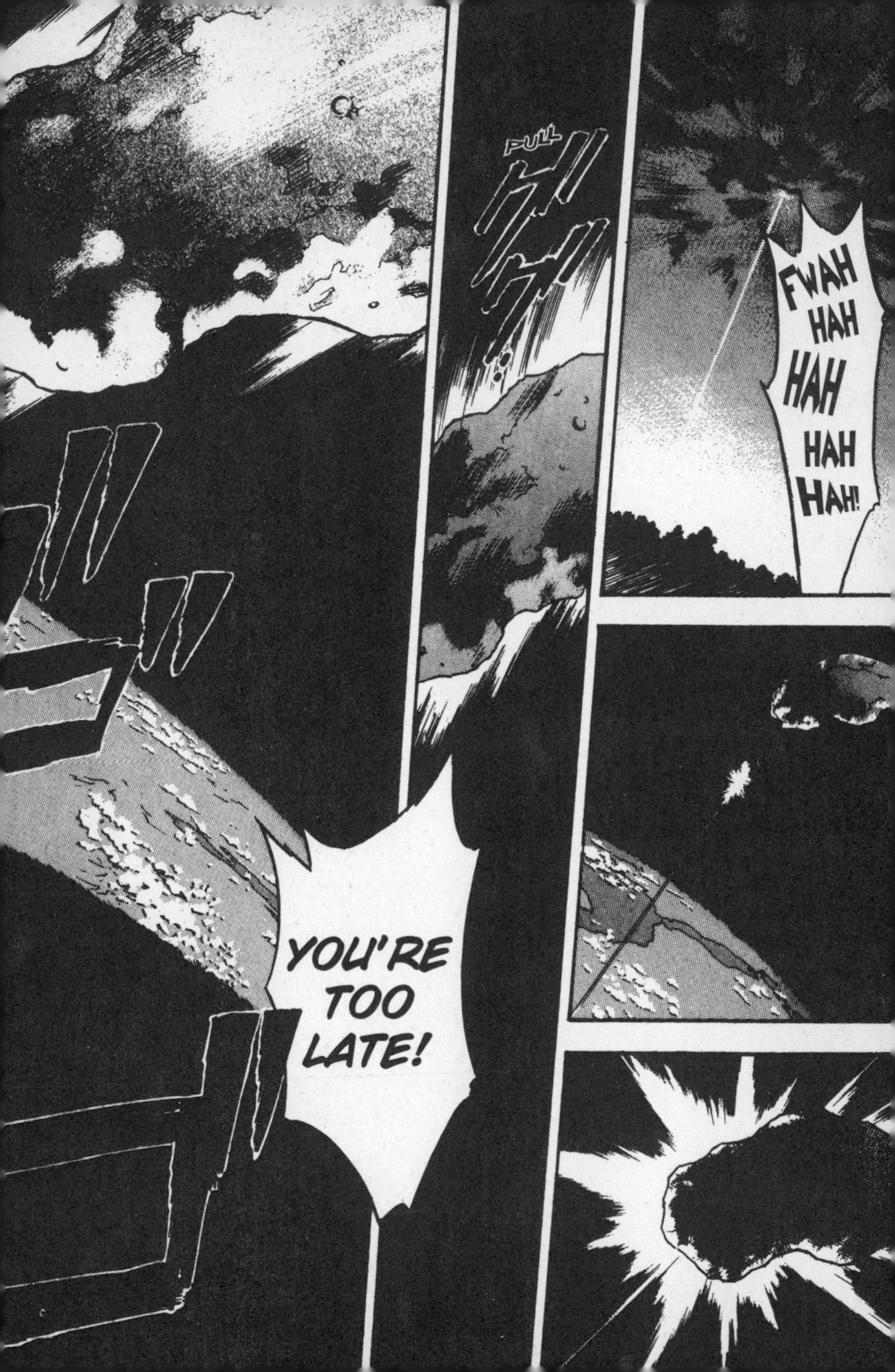
FWAH HAH HAH HAH HAH!
PULL
YOU'RE TOO LATE!

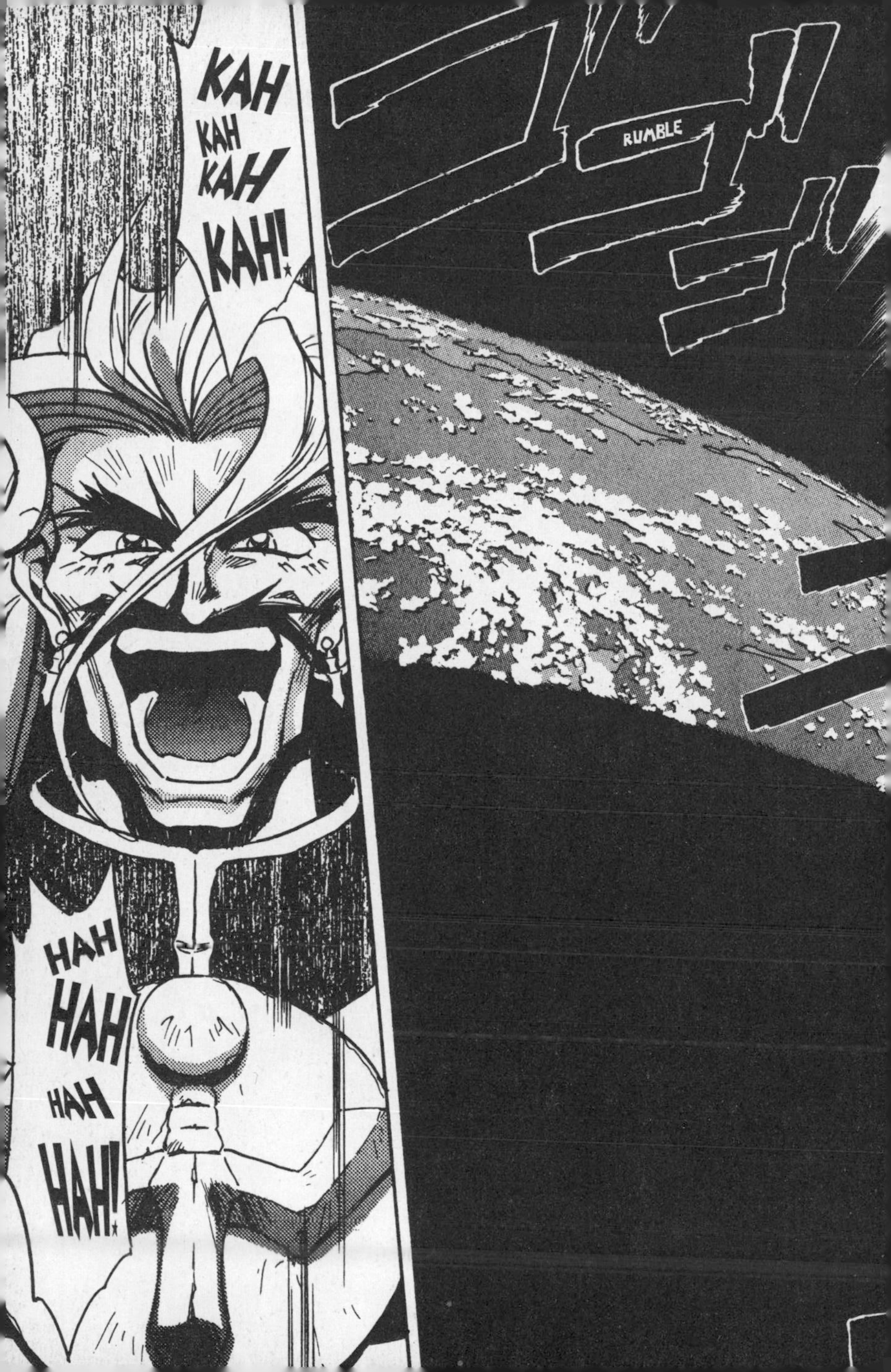
RUMBLE
KAH KAH KAH KAH!
HAH HAH HAH HAH!

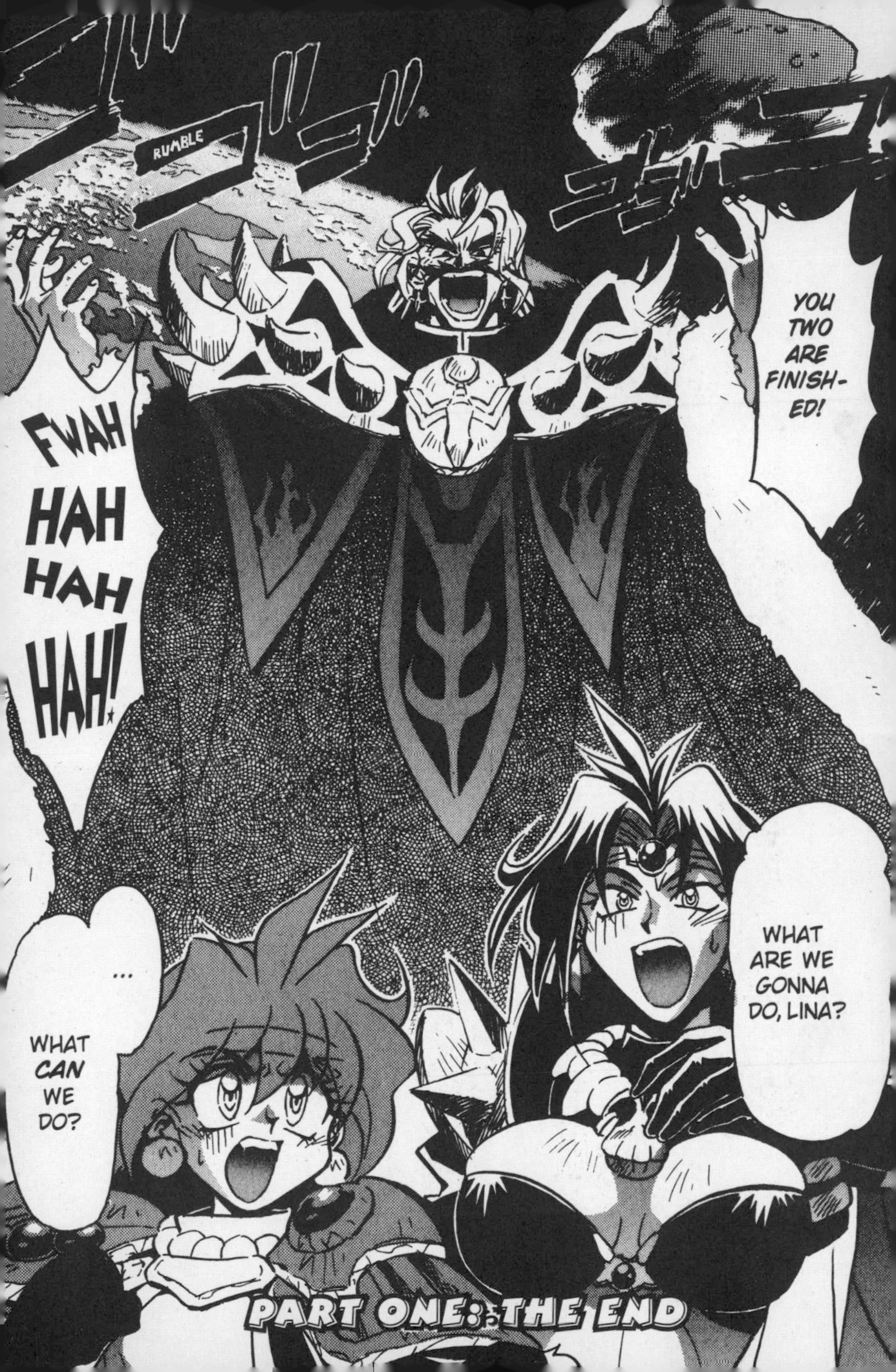
RUMBLE
YOU TWO ARE FINISHED!
FWAH HAH HAH HAH!
WHAT ARE WE GONNA DO, LINA?
...
WHAT CAN WE DO?
PART ONE: THE END

LINA & NAGA.

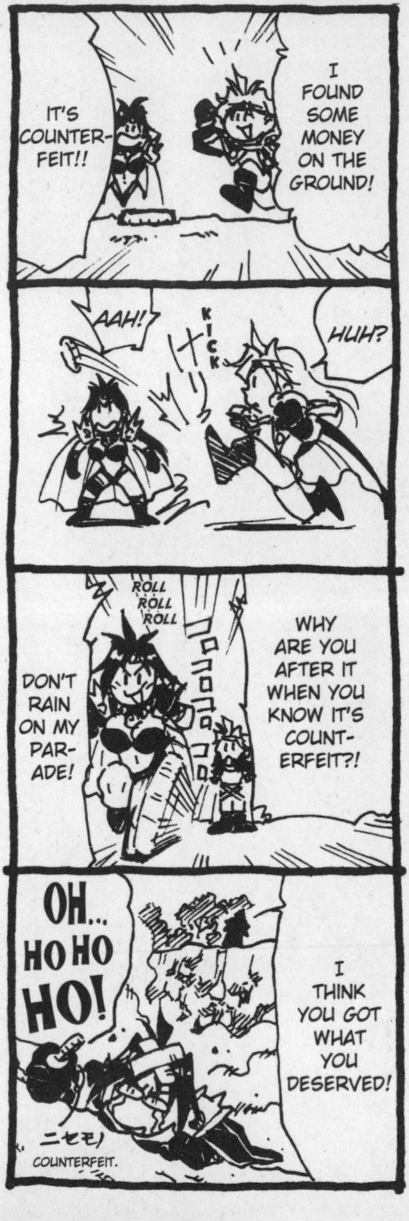
I FOUND SOME MONEY ON THE GROUND!
IT'S COUNTER-FEIT!!
HUH?
KICK
AAH!
WHY ARE YOU AFTER IT WHEN YOU KNOW IT'S COUNT-ERFEIT?!
ROLL ROLL ROLL
DON'T RAIN ON MY PAR-ADE!
I THINK YOU GOT WHAT YOU DESERVED!
OH... HO HO HO!
ニセモノ
COUNTERFEIT.

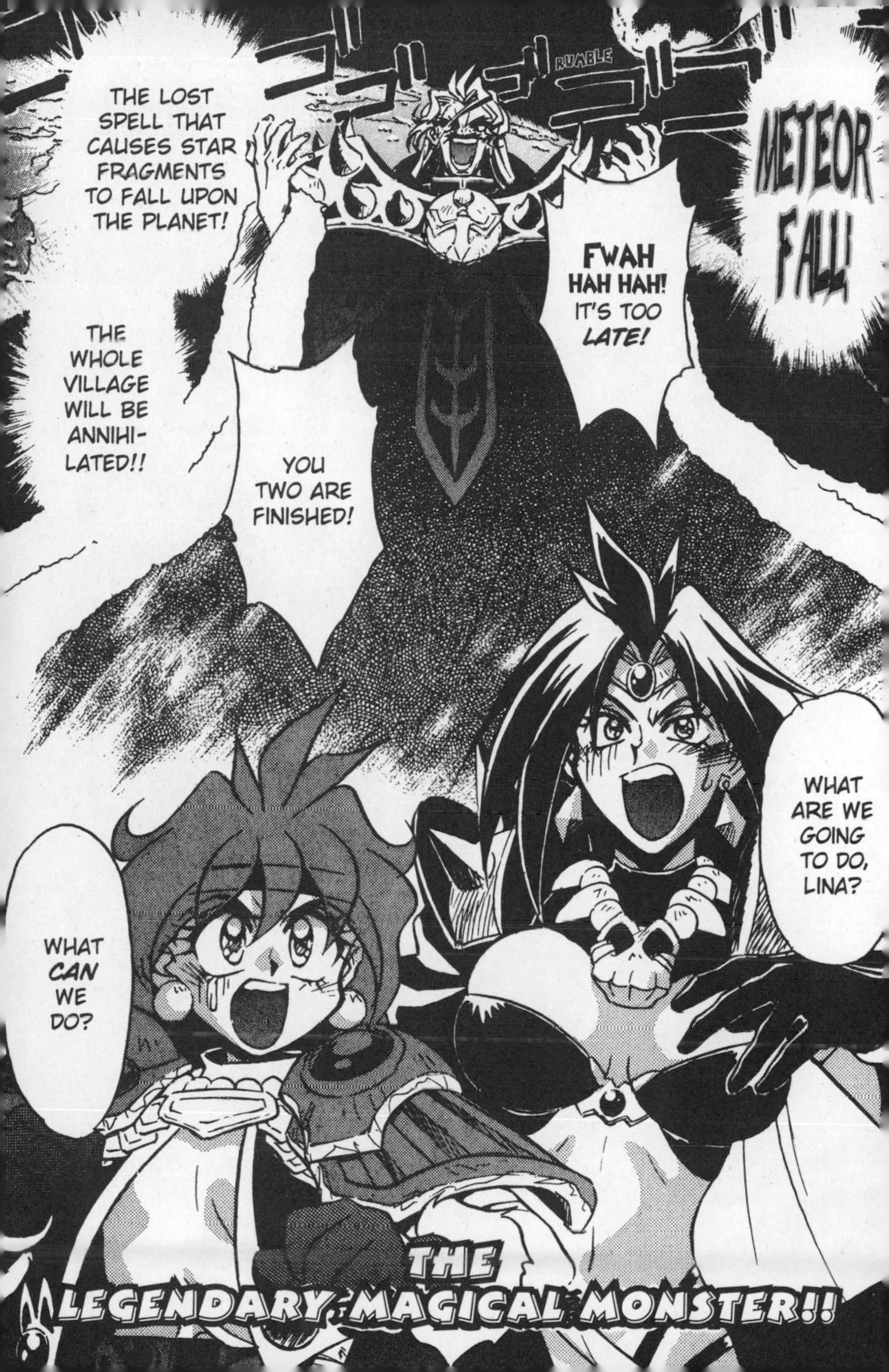
RUMBLE
METEOR FALL!!
FWAH HAH HAH! IT'S TOO LATE!
THE LOST SPELL THAT CAUSES STAR FRAGMENTS TO FALL UPON THE PLANET!
THE WHOLE VILLAGE WILL BE ANNIHI-LATED!!
YOU TWO ARE FINISHED!
WHAT ARE WE GOING TO DO, LINA?
WHAT CAN WE DO?
THE LEGENDARY MAGICAL MONSTER!!

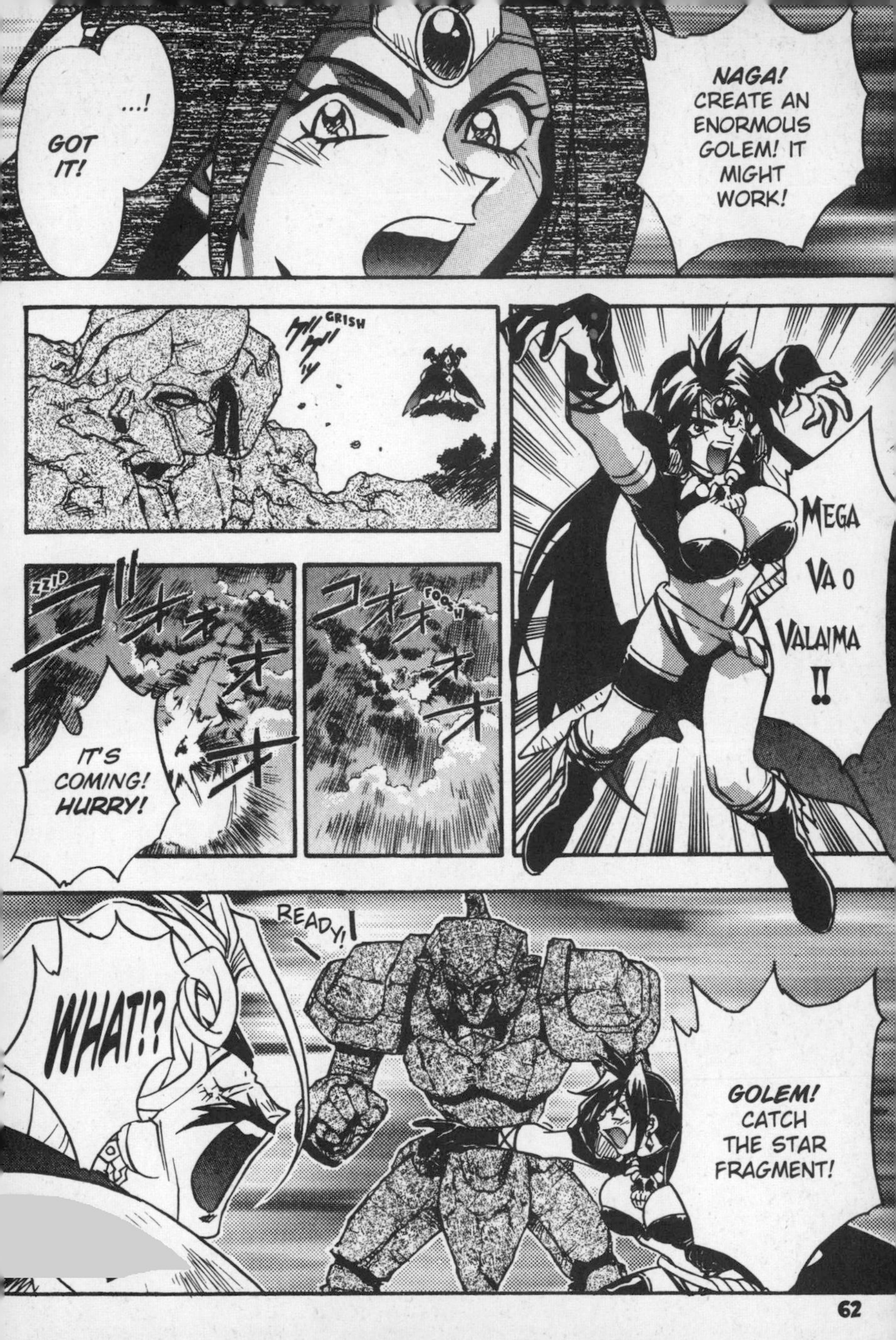
NAGA! CREATE AN ENORMOUS GOLEM! IT MIGHT WORK!
...!
GOT IT!
MEGA VA O VALAIMA !!
GRISH
FOOSH
ZZIP
IT'S COMING! HURRY!
GOLEM! CATCH THE STAR FRAGMENT!
READY!
WHAT!?

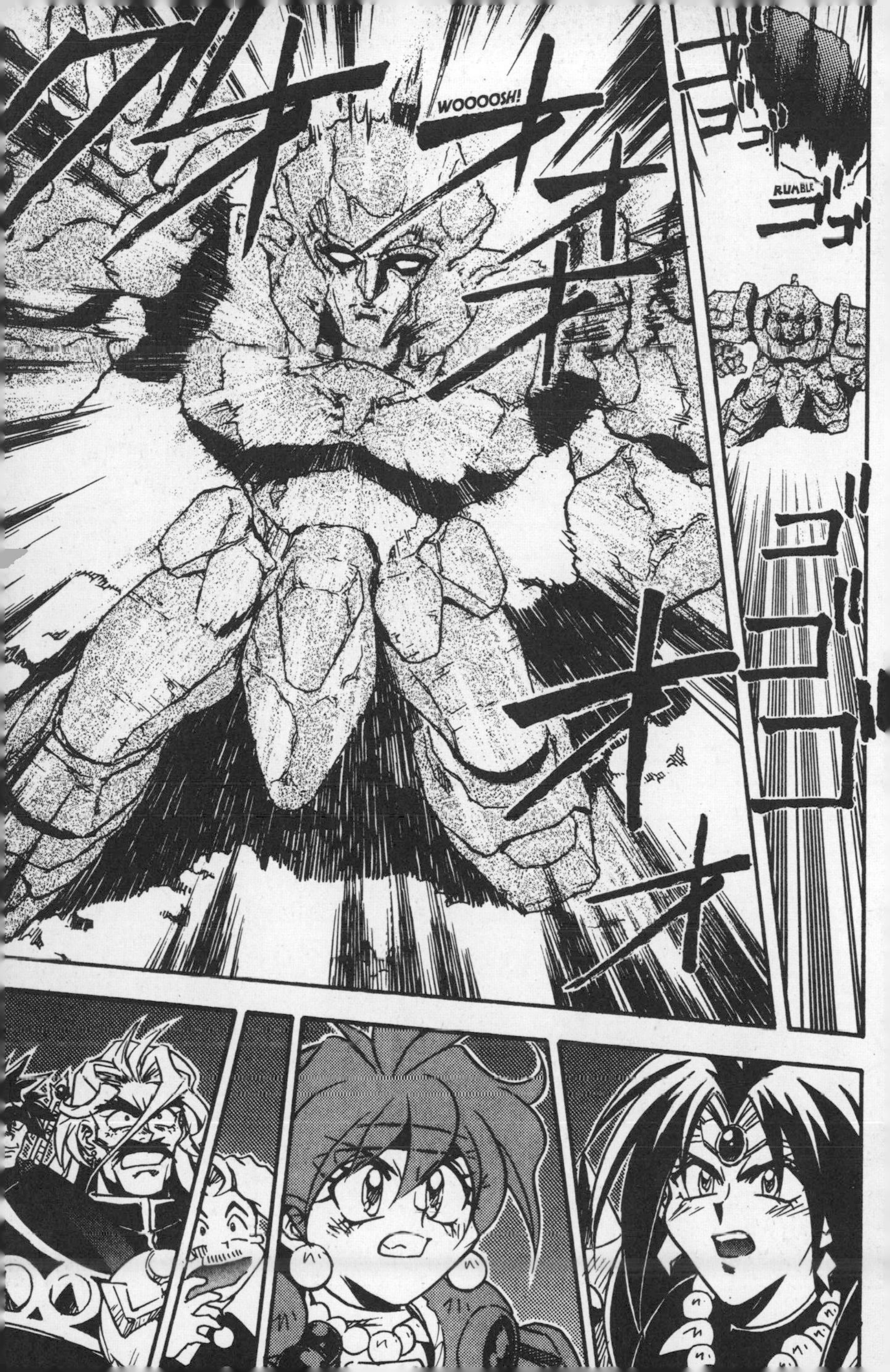
RUMBLE
WOOOOSH!

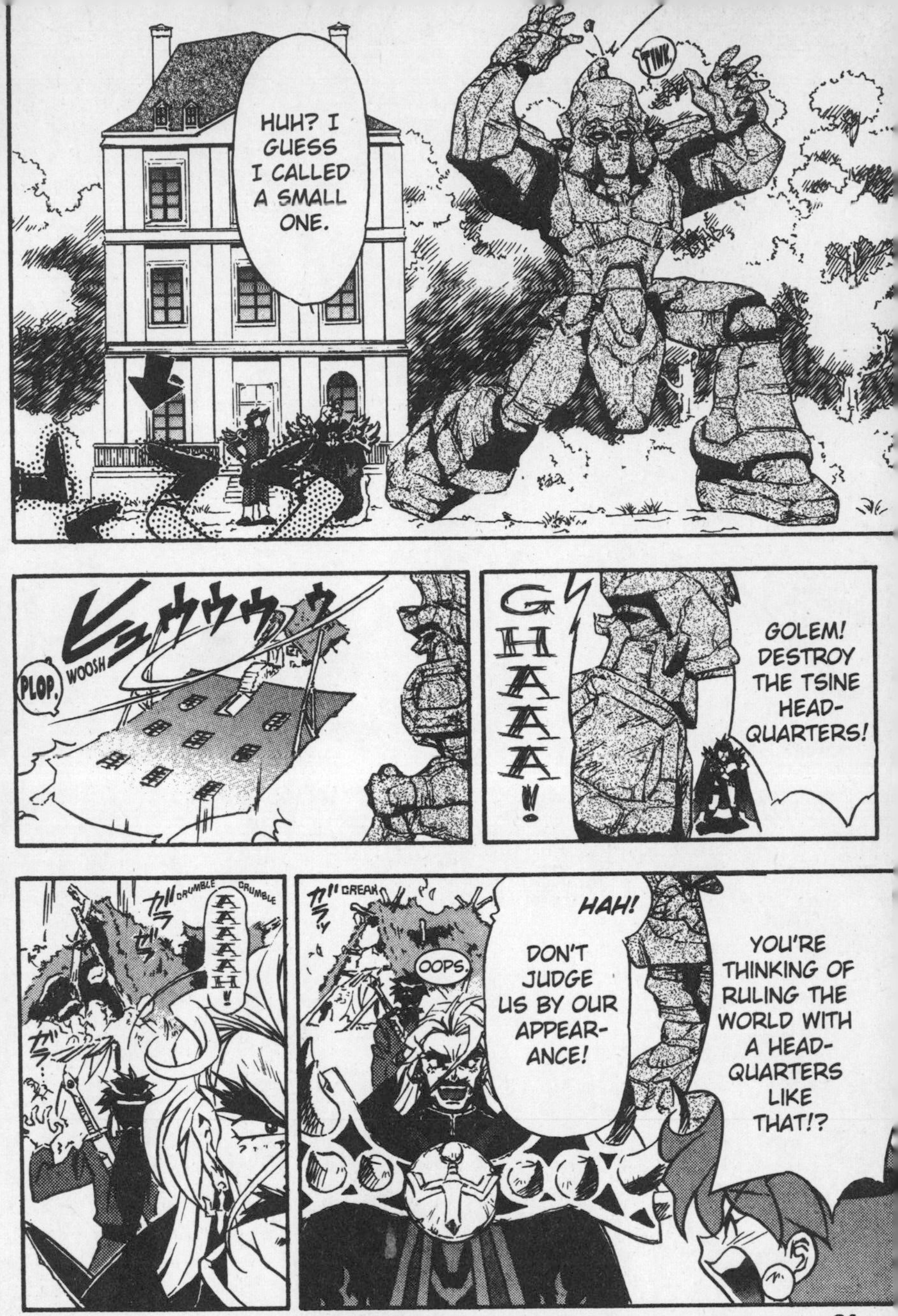
TINK
HUH? I GUESS I CALLED A SMALL ONE.
GOLEM! DESTROY THE TSINE HEAD-QUARTERS!
GHAAAA!!
ヒュウウウウ
WOOSH
PLOP,
YOU'RE THINKING OF RULING THE WORLD WITH A HEAD-QUARTERS LIKE THAT!?
HAH!
DON'T JUDGE US BY OUR APPEAR-ANCE!
OOPS.
CREAK
CRUMBLE CRUMBLE
AAAAAAH!!

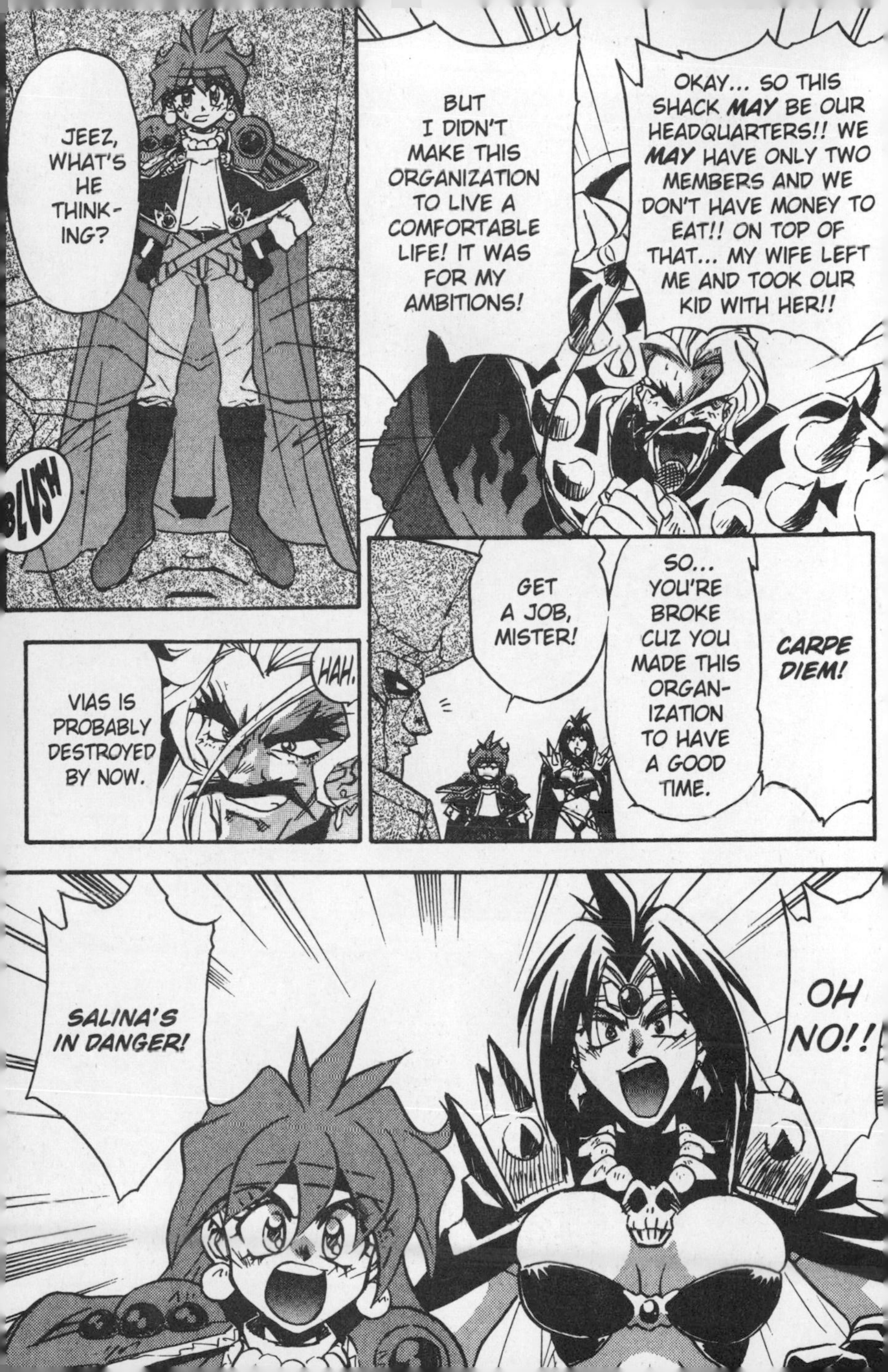
OKAY... SO THIS SHACK **MAY** BE OUR HEADQUARTERS!! WE **MAY** HAVE ONLY TWO MEMBERS AND WE DON'T HAVE MONEY TO EAT!! ON TOP OF THAT... MY WIFE LEFT ME AND TOOK OUR KID WITH HER!!
BUT I DIDN'T MAKE THIS ORGANIZATION TO LIVE A COMFORTABLE LIFE! IT WAS FOR MY AMBITIONS!
JEEZ, WHAT'S HE THINKING?
BLUSH
CARPE DIEM!
SO... YOU'RE BROKE CUZ YOU MADE THIS ORGANIZATION TO HAVE A GOOD TIME.
GET A JOB, MISTER!
HAH.
VIAS IS PROBABLY DESTROYED BY NOW.
OH NO!!
SALINA'S IN DANGER!

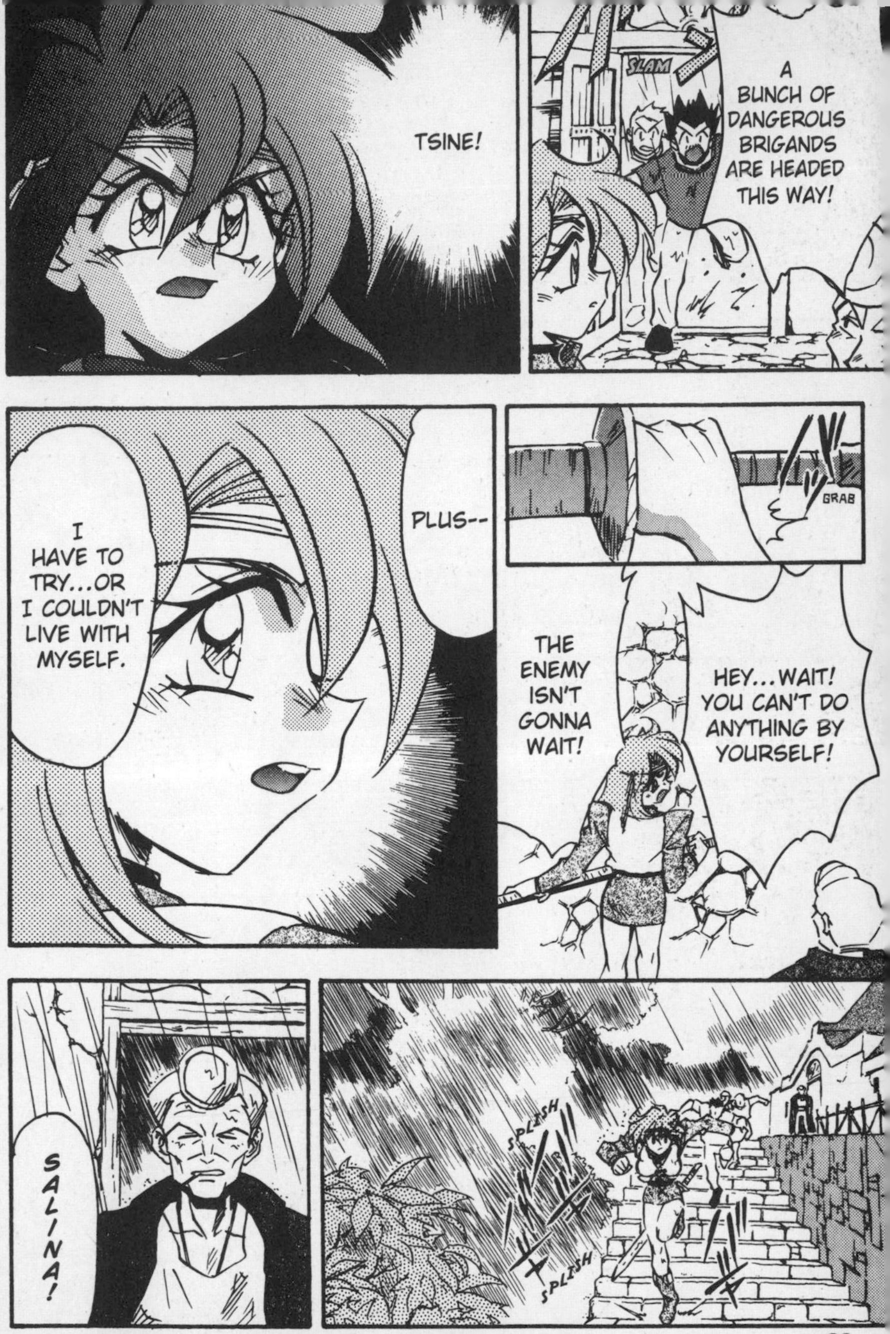
SLAM
A BUNCH OF DANGEROUS BRIGANDS ARE HEADED THIS WAY!
TSINE!
GRAB
HEY...WAIT! YOU CAN'T DO ANYTHING BY YOURSELF!
THE ENEMY ISN'T GONNA WAIT!
PLUS--
I HAVE TO TRY...OR I COULDN'T LIVE WITH MYSELF.
SPLISH
SPLISH
SALINA!

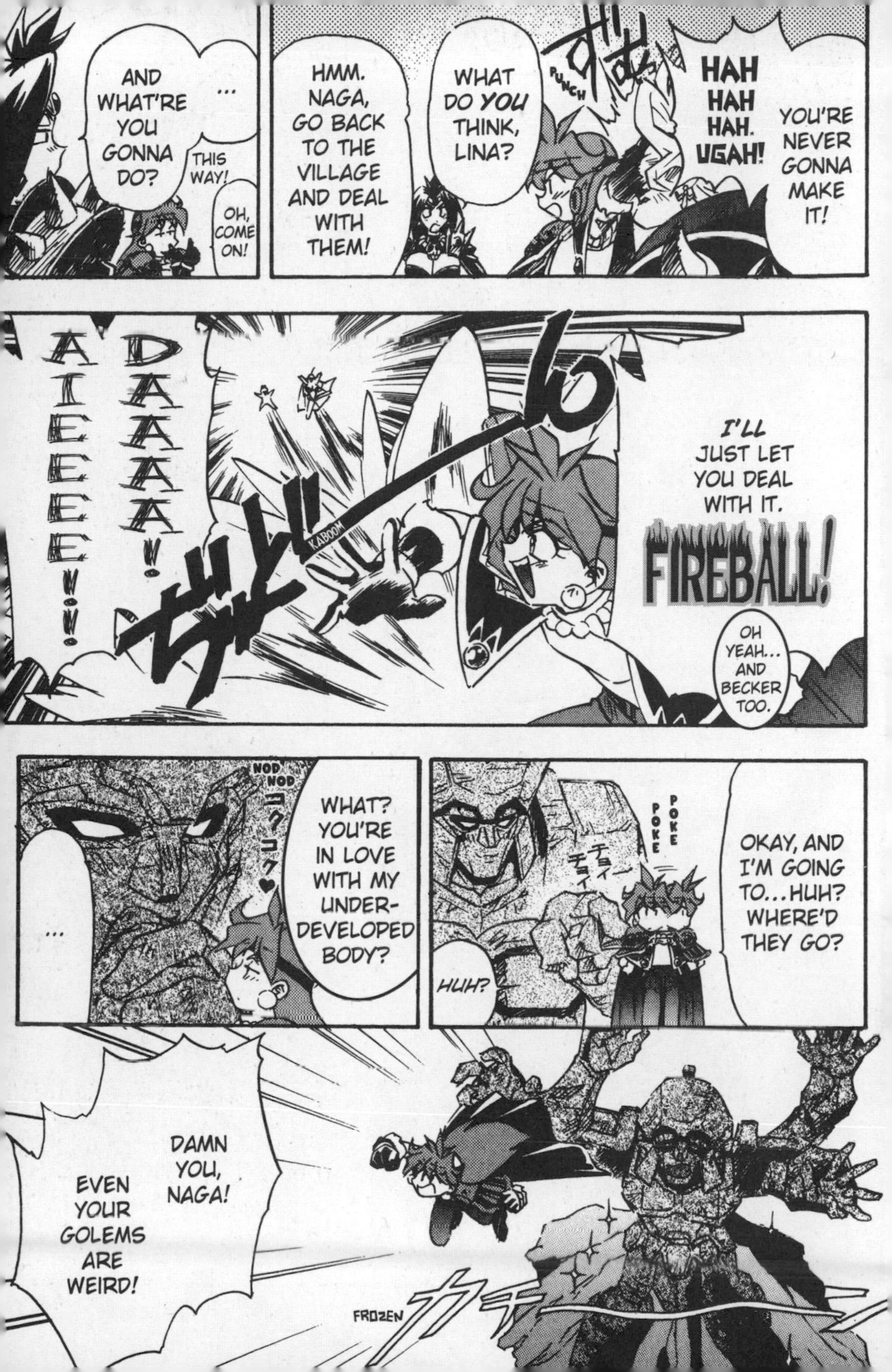
HAH HAH HAH. UGAH!
YOU'RE NEVER GONNA MAKE IT!
PUNCH
WHAT DO YOU THINK, LINA?
HMM. NAGA, GO BACK TO THE VILLAGE AND DEAL WITH THEM!
...
AND WHAT'RE YOU GONNA DO?
THIS WAY!
OH, COME ON!
I'LL JUST LET YOU DEAL WITH IT.
FIREBALL!
OH YEAH... AND BECKER TOO.
KABOOM
DAAAAA!!
AIEEEEE!!!
OKAY, AND I'M GOING TO...HUH? WHERE'D THEY GO?
POKE POKE
HUH?
NOD NOD
WHAT? YOU'RE IN LOVE WITH MY UNDER-DEVELOPED BODY?
...
DAMN YOU, NAGA!
EVEN YOUR GOLEMS ARE WEIRD!
FROZEN

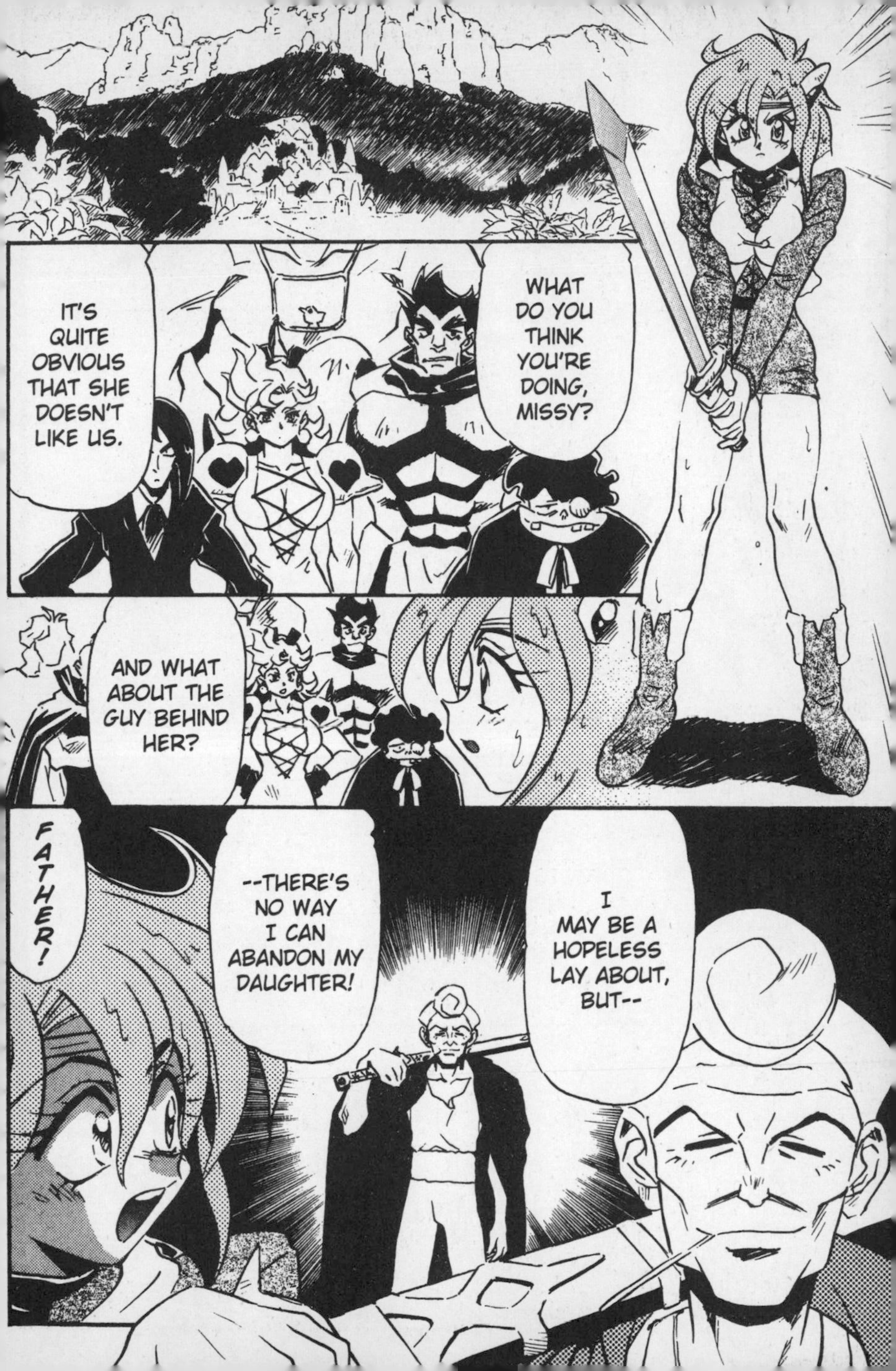
WHAT DO YOU THINK YOU'RE DOING, MISSY?
IT'S QUITE OBVIOUS THAT SHE DOESN'T LIKE US.
AND WHAT ABOUT THE GUY BEHIND HER?
I MAY BE A HOPELESS LAY ABOUT, BUT--
--THERE'S NO WAY I CAN ABANDON MY DAUGHTER!
FATHER!

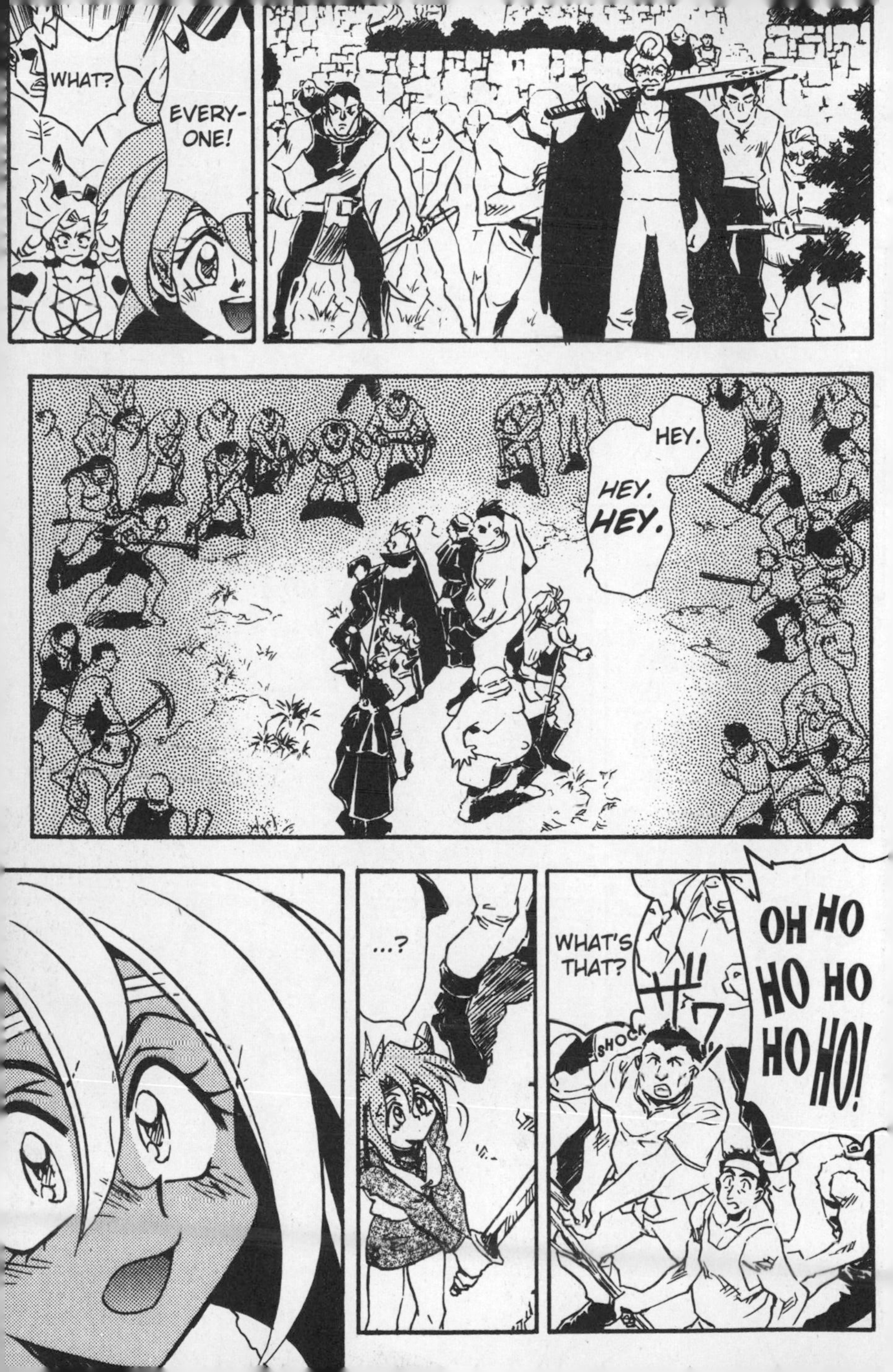
EVERY-ONE!
WHAT?
HEY.
HEY. HEY.
OH HO HO HO HO HO HO!
WHAT'S THAT?
SHOCK
...?

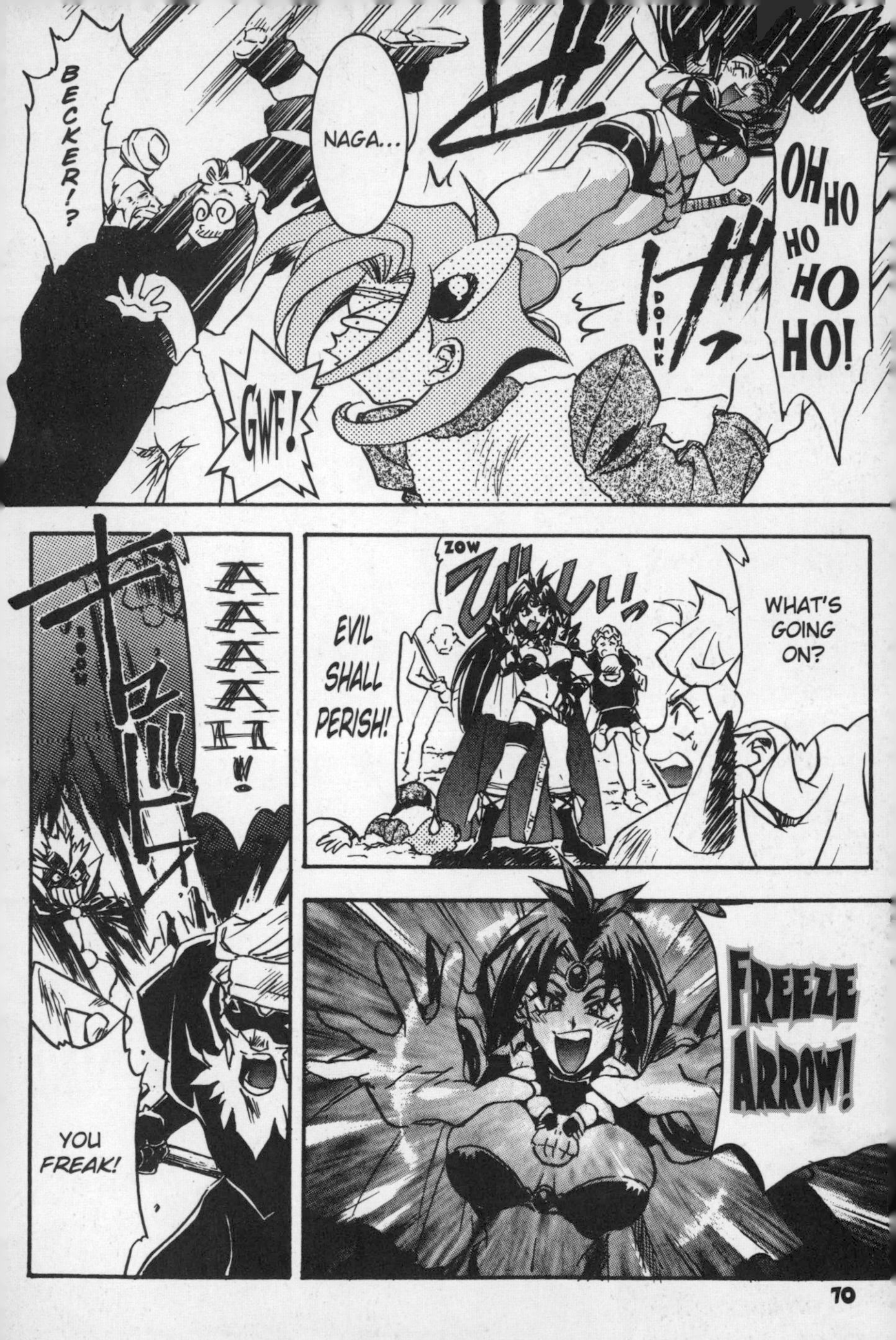
OH HO HO HO HO!
DOINK
NAGA...
GWF!
BECKER!?
WHAT'S GOING ON?
ZOW
EVIL SHALL PERISH!
FREEZE ARROW!
AAAAAH!!
BOOM
YOU FREAK!

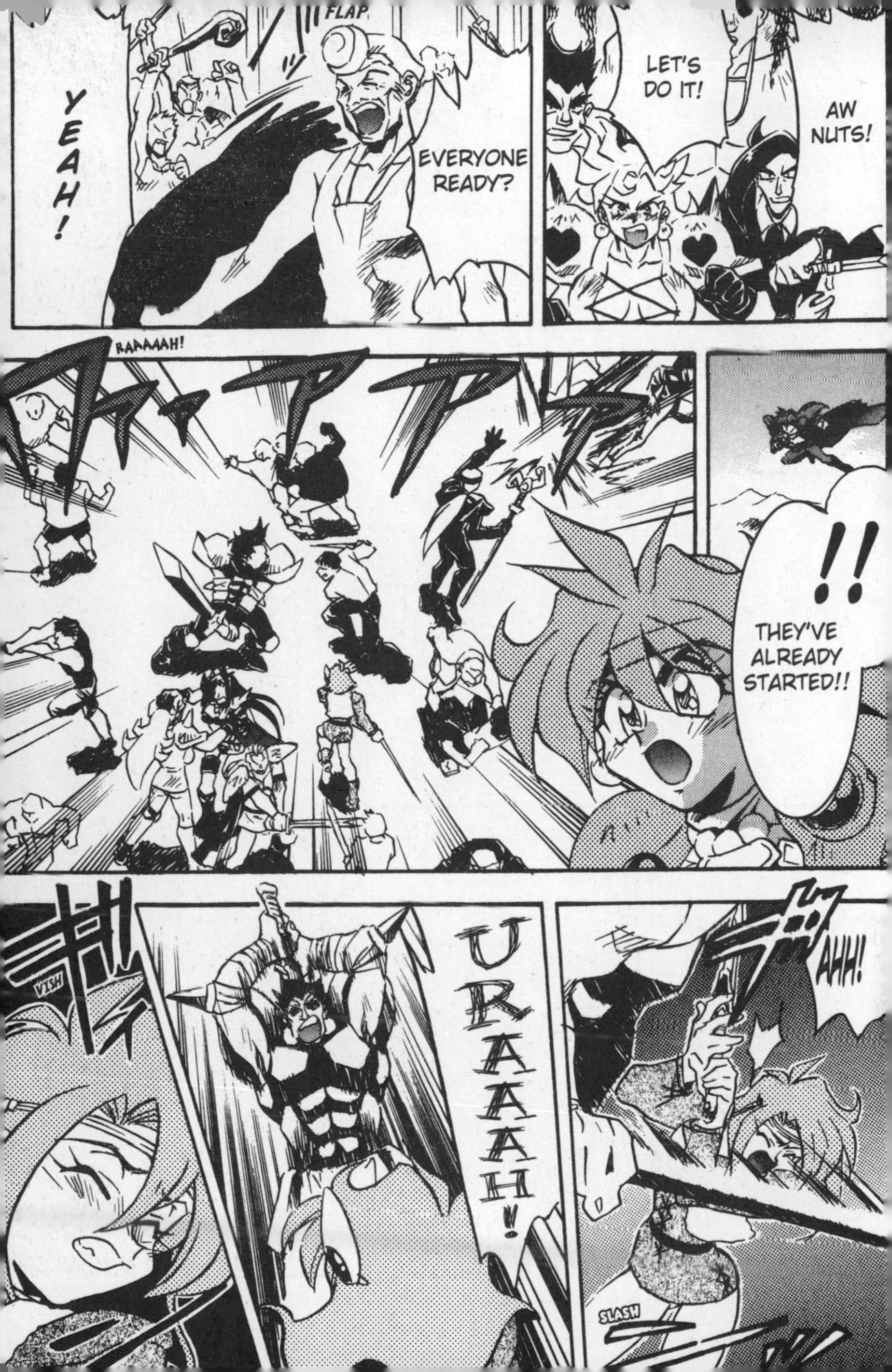

LET'S DO IT!
AW NUTS!
FLAP
EVERYONE READY?
YEAH!
!!
THEY'VE ALREADY STARTED!!
RAAAAAH!
AHH!
SLASH
URAAAAH!!
VISH

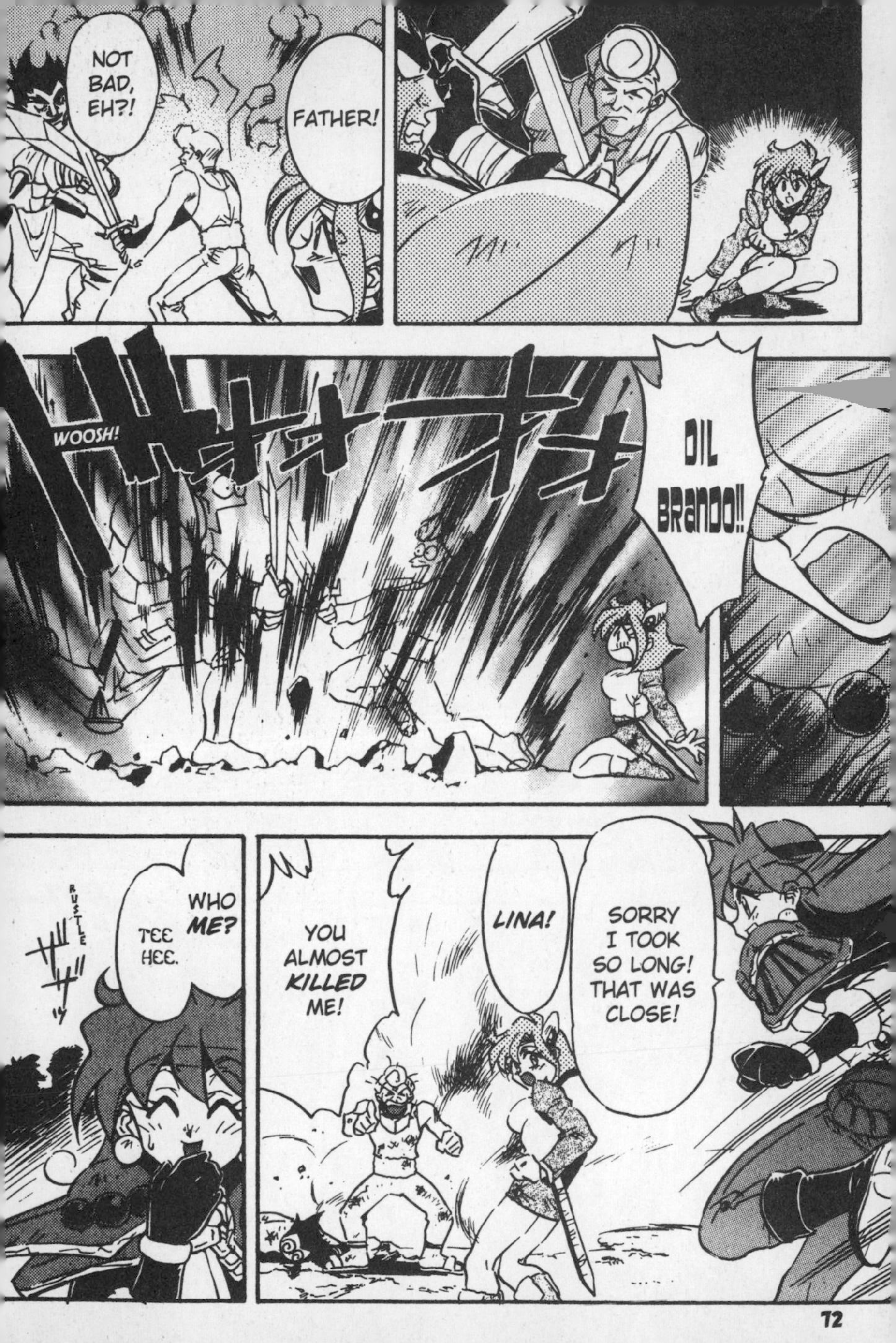
FATHER!
NOT BAD, EH?!
DIL BRANDO!!
WOOSH!
SORRY I TOOK SO LONG! THAT WAS CLOSE!
LINA!
YOU ALMOST KILLED ME!
WHO ME?
TEE HEE.
RUSTLE

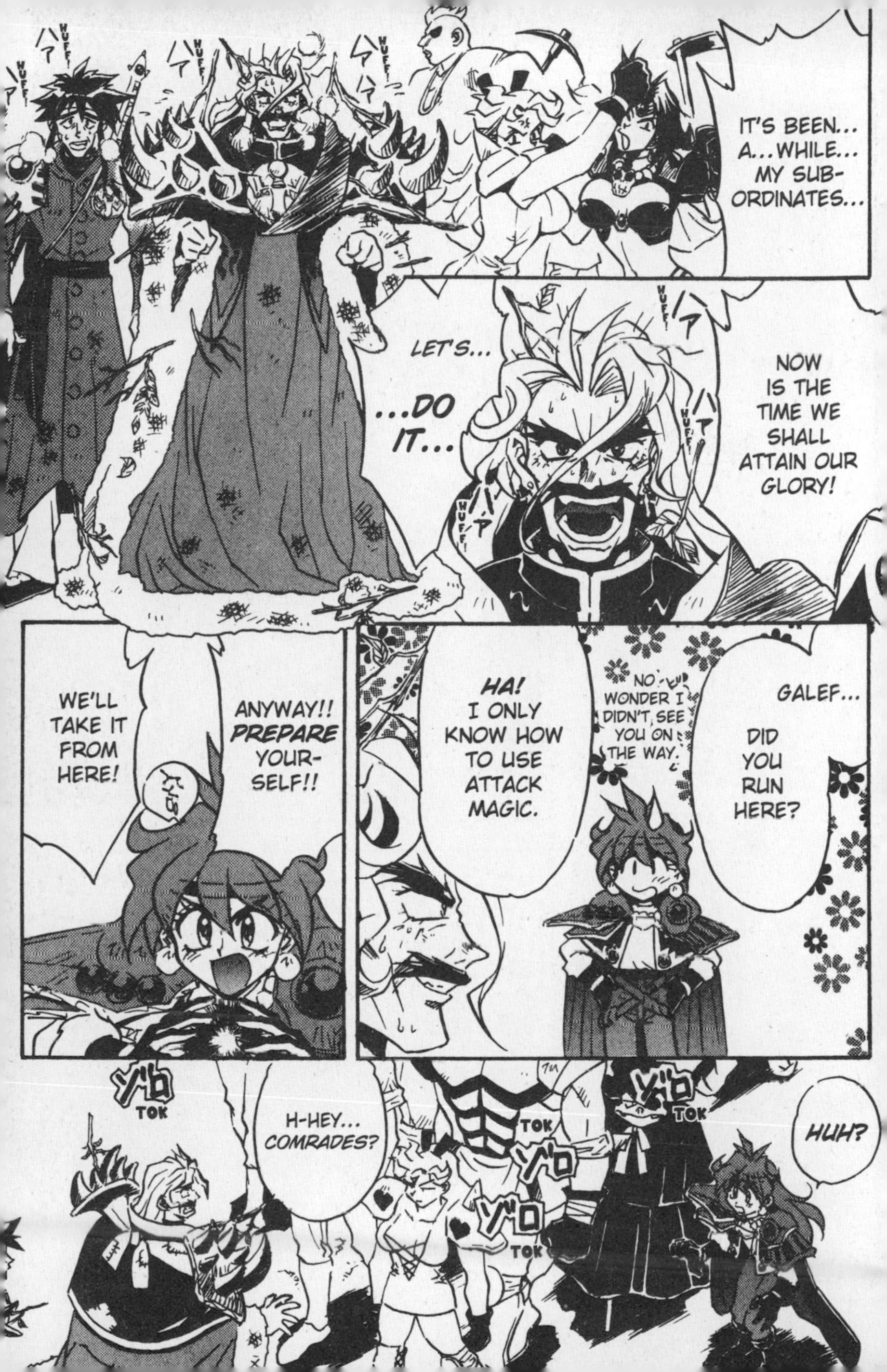
HUFF!
HUFF!
HUFF!
HUFF!
IT'S BEEN... A...WHILE... MY SUB-ORDINATES...
HUFF!
HUFF!
HUFF!
NOW IS THE TIME WE SHALL ATTAIN OUR GLORY!
LET'S...
...DO IT...
GALEF...
DID YOU RUN HERE?
NO WONDER I DIDN'T SEE YOU ON THE WAY.
HA! I ONLY KNOW HOW TO USE ATTACK MAGIC.
ANYWAY!! PREPARE YOURSELF!!
WE'LL TAKE IT FROM HERE!
HUH?
TOK
TOK
TOK
H-HEY... COMRADES?
TOK

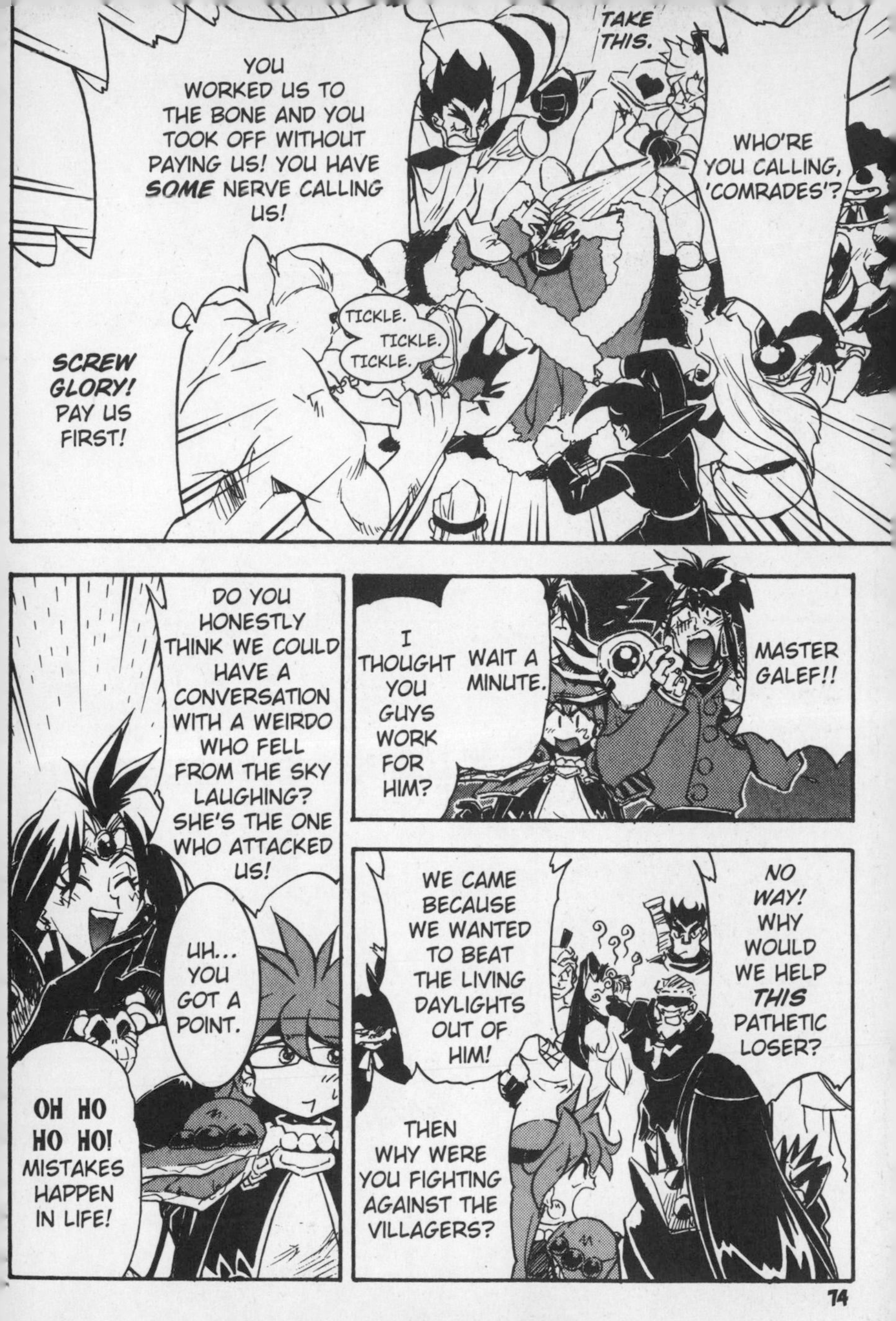
TAKE THIS.
WHO'RE YOU CALLING, 'COMRADES'?
YOU WORKED US TO THE BONE AND YOU TOOK OFF WITHOUT PAYING US! YOU HAVE *SOME* NERVE CALLING US!
TICKLE. TICKLE. TICKLE.
SCREW GLORY! PAY US FIRST!
MASTER GALEF!!
WAIT A MINUTE.
I THOUGHT YOU GUYS WORK FOR HIM?
NO WAY! WHY WOULD WE HELP *THIS* PATHETIC LOSER?
WE CAME BECAUSE WE WANTED TO BEAT THE LIVING DAYLIGHTS OUT OF HIM!
THEN WHY WERE YOU FIGHTING AGAINST THE VILLAGERS?
DO YOU HONESTLY THINK WE COULD HAVE A CONVERSATION WITH A WEIRDO WHO FELL FROM THE SKY LAUGHING? SHE'S THE ONE WHO ATTACKED US!
UH... YOU GOT A POINT.
OH HO HO HO! MISTAKES HAPPEN IN LIFE!

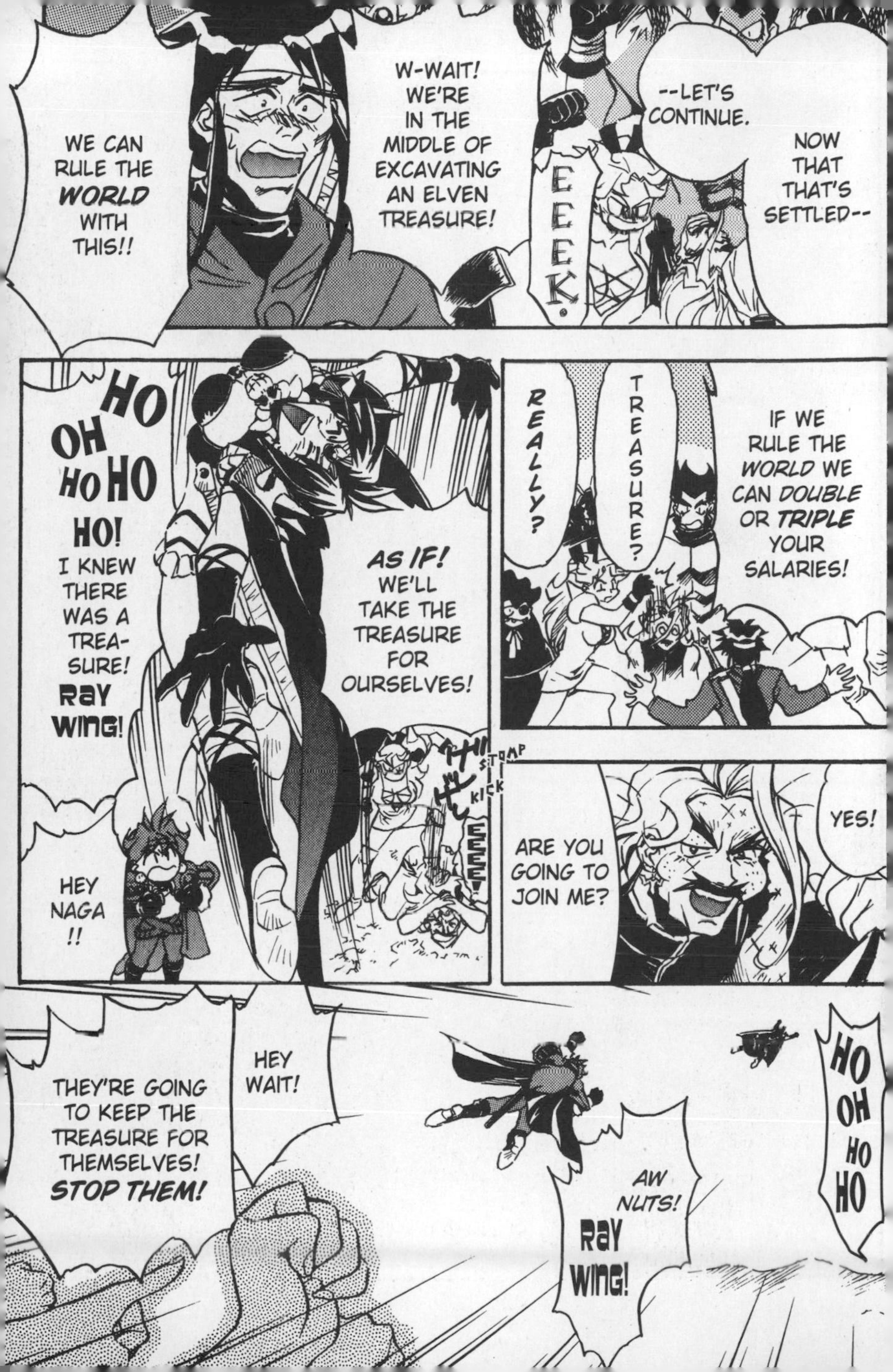

NOW THAT THAT'S SETTLED--
--LET'S CONTINUE.
EEEK.
W-WAIT! WE'RE IN THE MIDDLE OF EXCAVATING AN ELVEN TREASURE!
WE CAN RULE THE WORLD WITH THIS!!
IF WE RULE THE WORLD WE CAN DOUBLE OR TRIPLE YOUR SALARIES!
TREASURE?
REALLY?
YES!
ARE YOU GOING TO JOIN ME?
HO OH HO HO HO! I KNEW THERE WAS A TREA-SURE! RAY WING!
AS IF! WE'LL TAKE THE TREASURE FOR OURSELVES!
STOMP
KICK
EEEE!
HEY NAGA!!
HO OH HO HO
AW NUTS!
RAY WING!
HEY WAIT!
THEY'RE GOING TO KEEP THE TREASURE FOR THEMSELVES! STOP THEM!

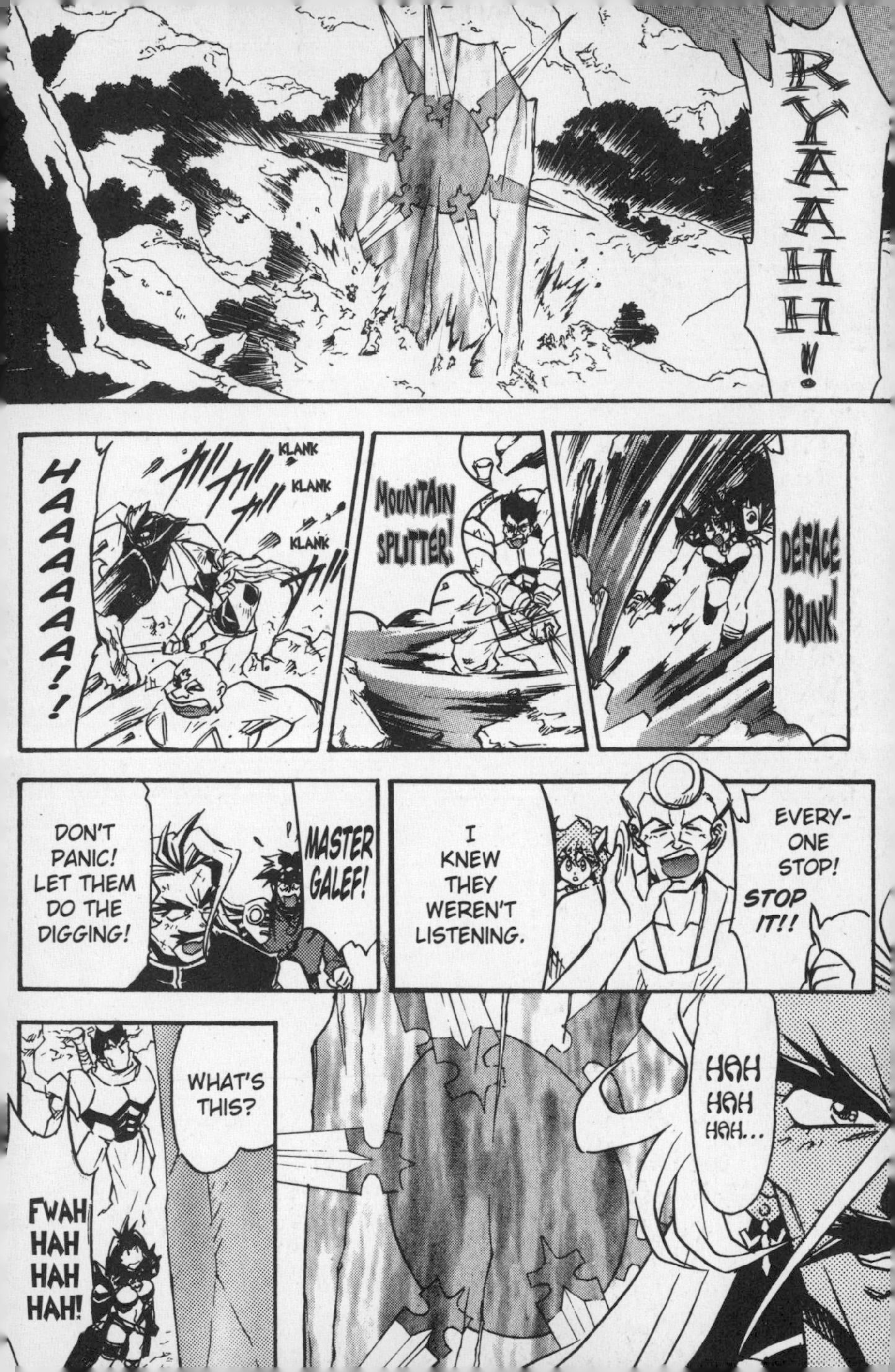
RYAAHH!!
DEFACE BRINK!
MOUNTAIN SPLITTER!
KLANK
KLANK
KLANK
HAAAAAAA!!
EVERY-ONE STOP!
STOP IT!!
I KNEW THEY WEREN'T LISTENING.
MASTER GALEF!
DON'T PANIC! LET THEM DO THE DIGGING!
HAH HAH HAH...
WHAT'S THIS?
FWAH HAH HAH HAH!

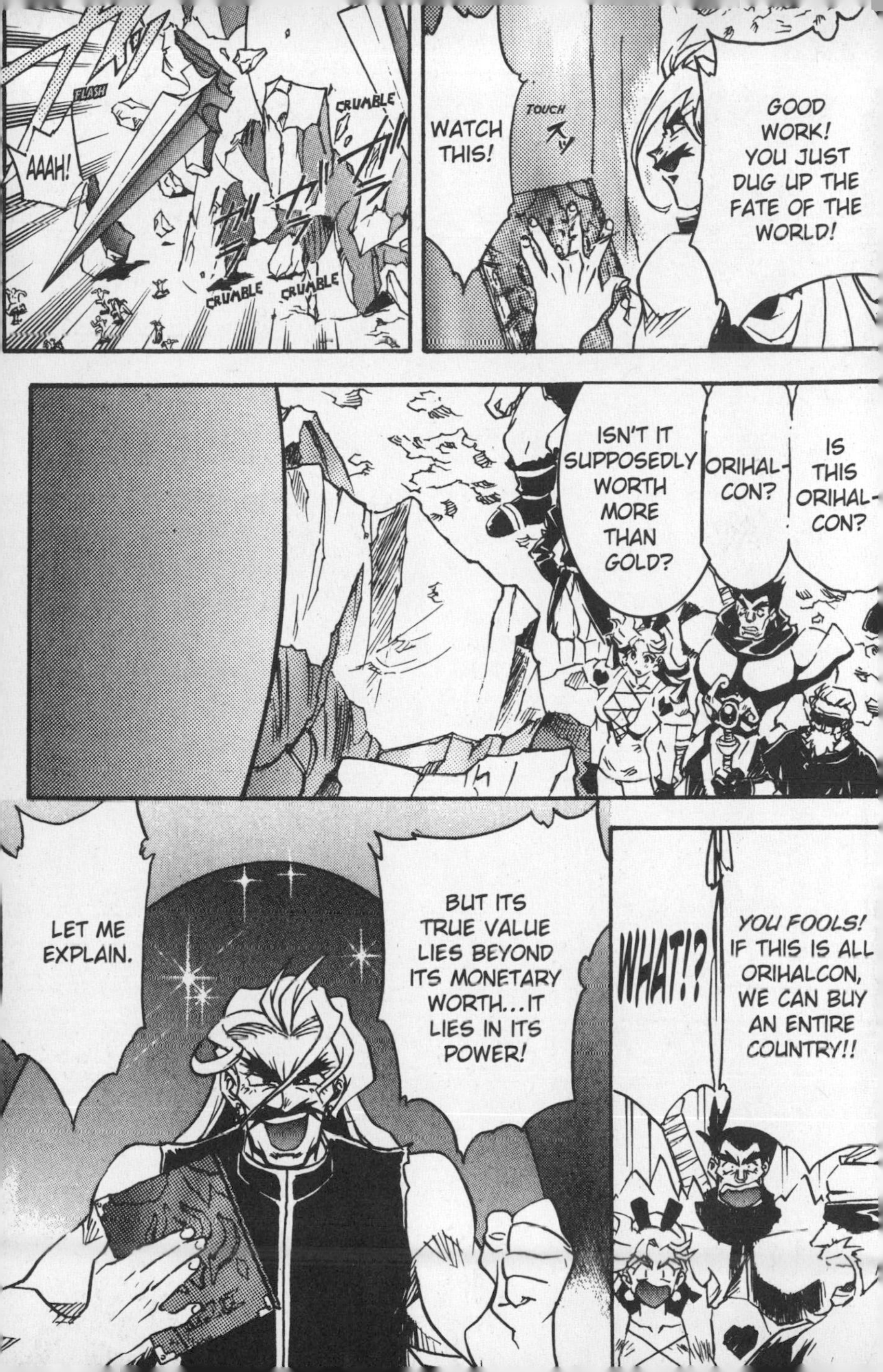
GOOD WORK! YOU JUST DUG UP THE FATE OF THE WORLD!
TOUCH
スッ
WATCH THIS!
FLASH
CRUMBLE
AAAH!
CRUMBLE
CRUMBLE
IS THIS ORIHAL-CON?
ORIHAL-CON?
ISN'T IT SUPPOSEDLY WORTH MORE THAN GOLD?
YOU FOOLS! IF THIS IS ALL ORIHALCON, WE CAN BUY AN ENTIRE COUNTRY!!
WHAT!?
BUT ITS TRUE VALUE LIES BEYOND ITS MONETARY WORTH...IT LIES IN ITS POWER!
LET ME EXPLAIN.

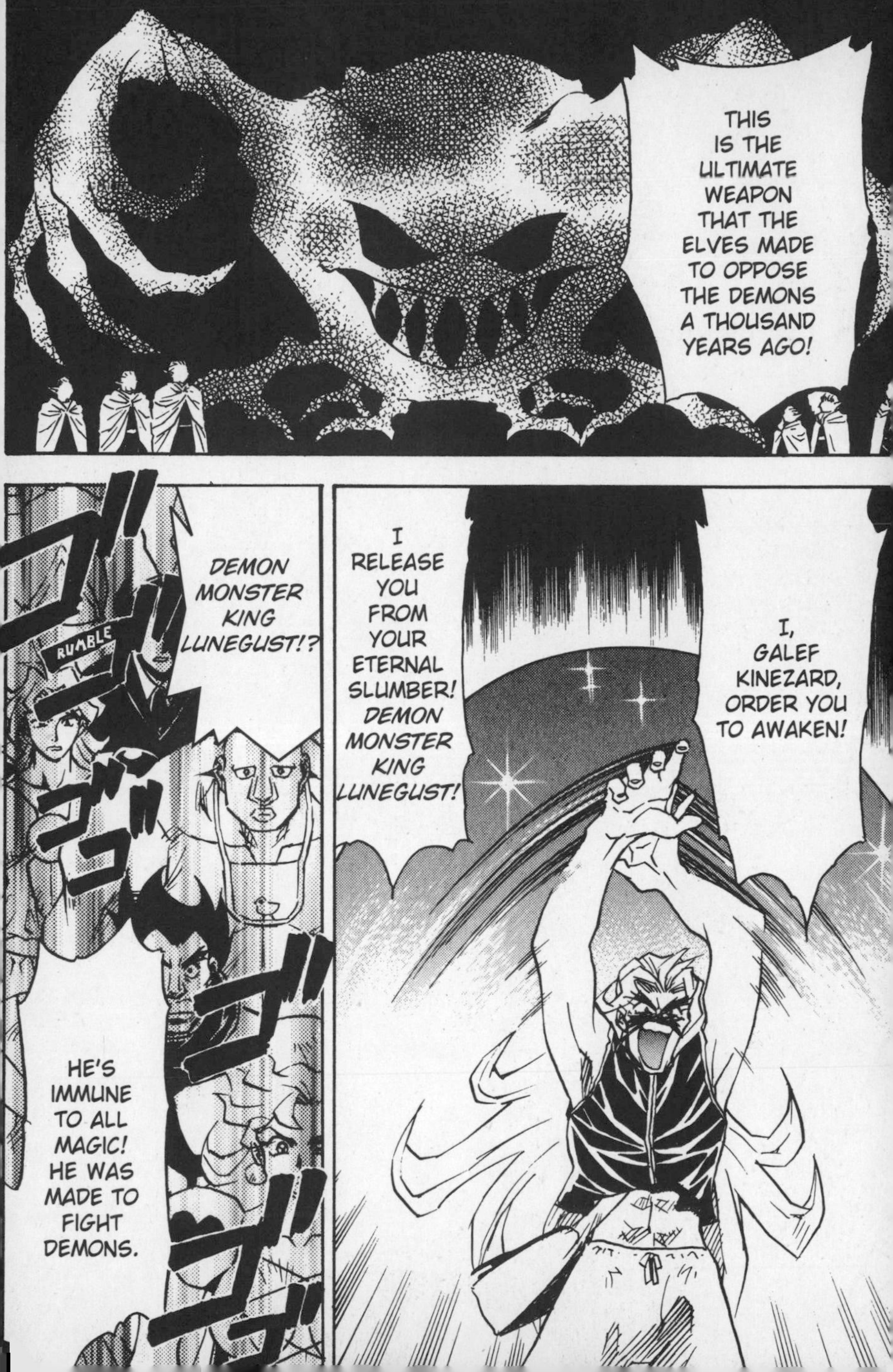
THIS IS THE ULTIMATE WEAPON THAT THE ELVES MADE TO OPPOSE THE DEMONS A THOUSAND YEARS AGO!
I, GALEF KINEZARD, ORDER YOU TO AWAKEN!
I RELEASE YOU FROM YOUR ETERNAL SLUMBER! DEMON MONSTER KING LUNEGUST!
DEMON MONSTER KING LUNEGUST!?
RUMBLE
HE'S IMMUNE TO ALL MAGIC! HE WAS MADE TO FIGHT DEMONS.

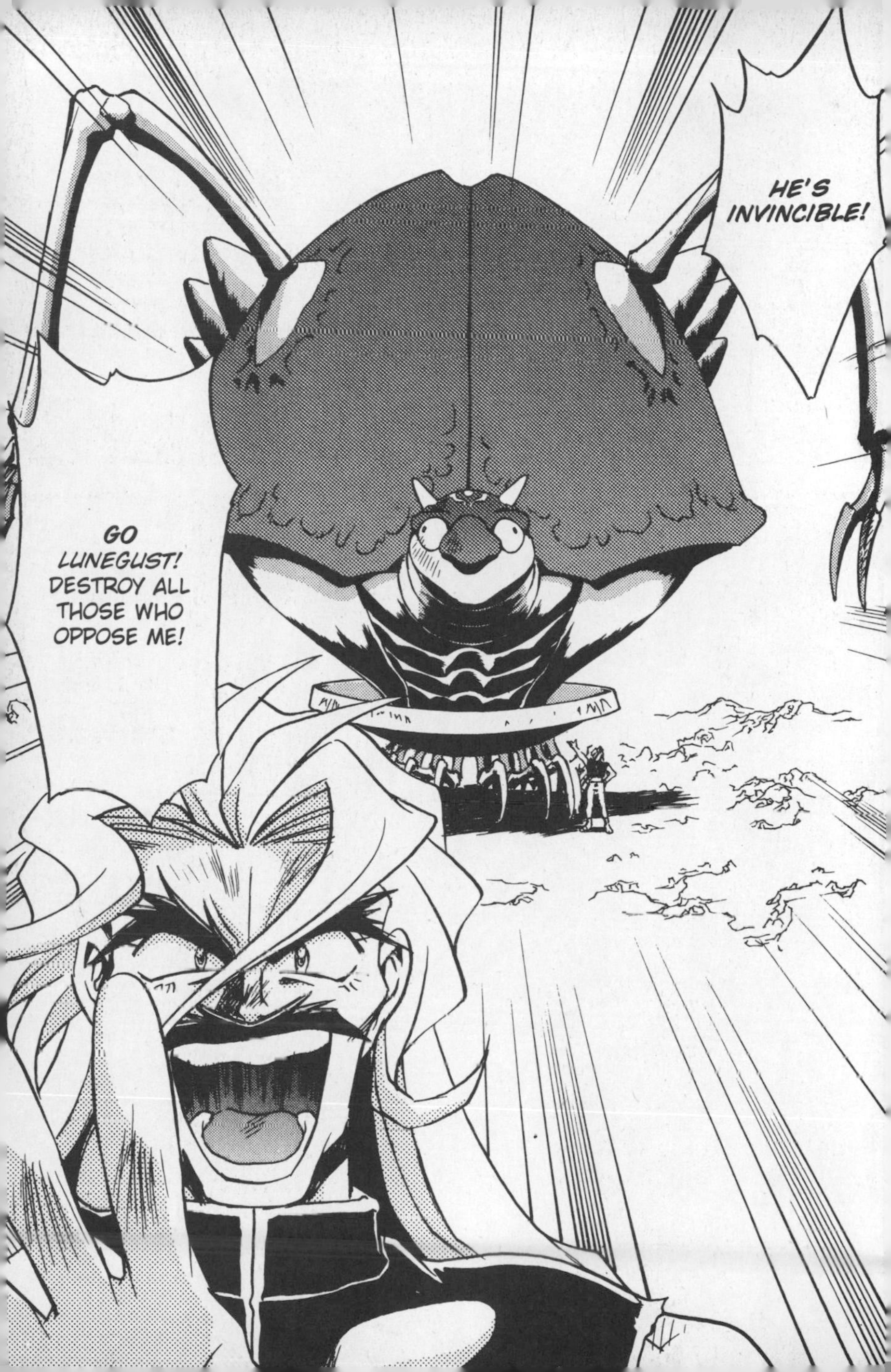
HE'S INVINCIBLE!
GO LUNEGUST! DESTROY ALL THOSE WHO OPPOSE ME!

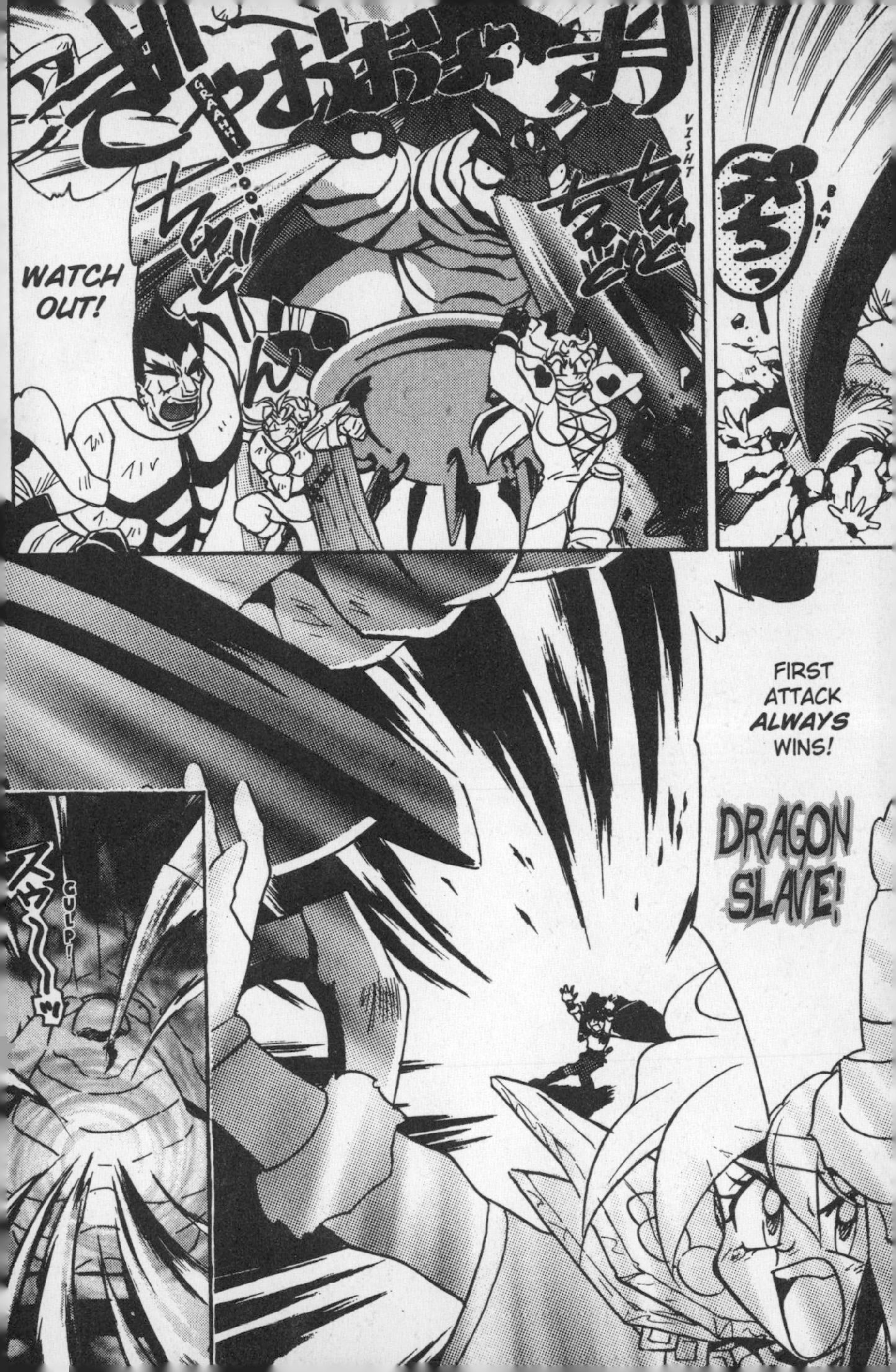

BAM!
VISHT
GRAAHH!
BOOM!
WATCH OUT!
FIRST ATTACK ALWAYS WINS!
DRAGON SLAVE!
GULP!

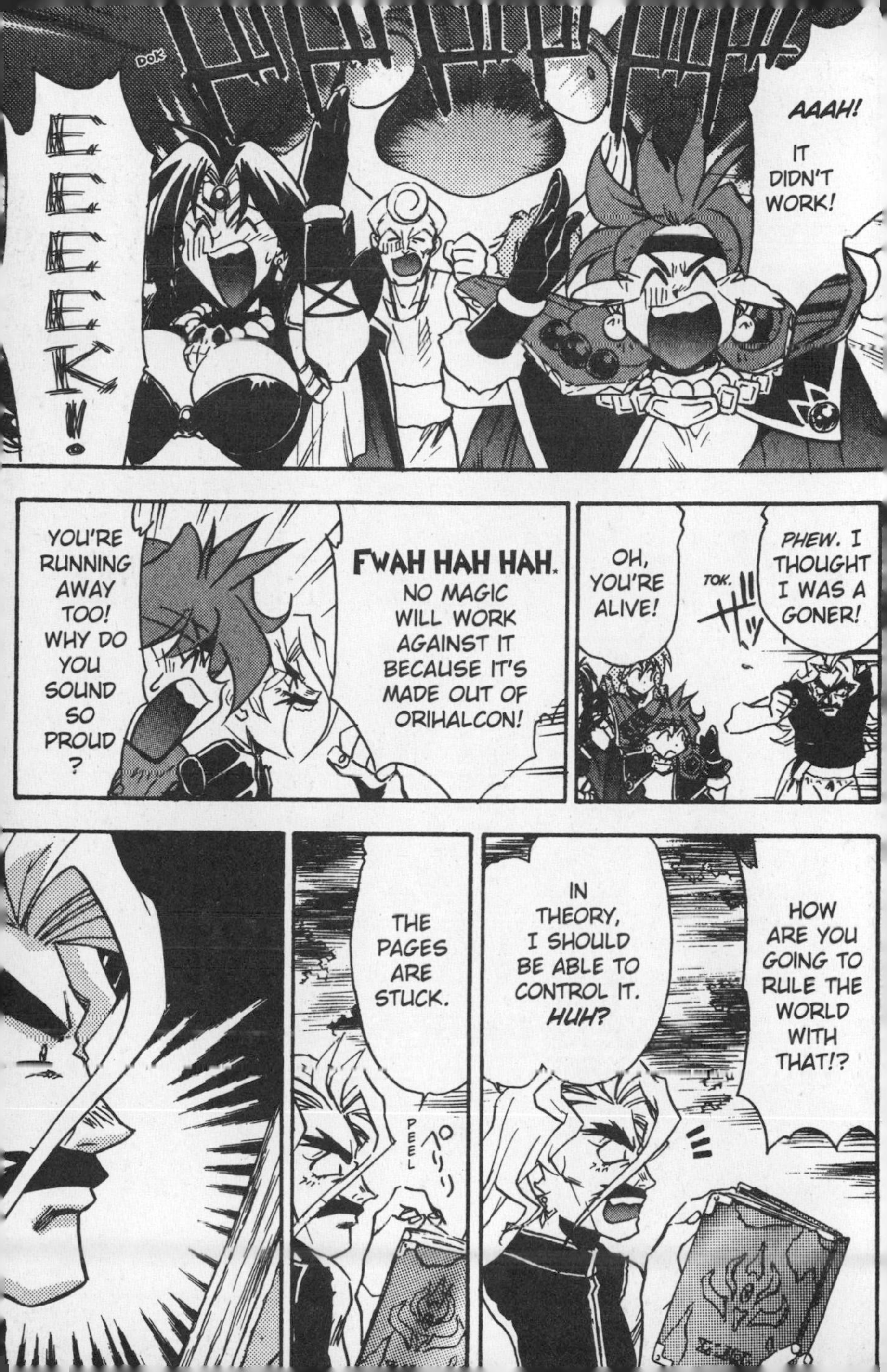
AAAH!
IT DIDN'T WORK!
DoK
EEEEK!!
PHEW. I THOUGHT I WAS A GONER!
TOK.
OH, YOU'RE ALIVE!
FWAH HAH HAH. NO MAGIC WILL WORK AGAINST IT BECAUSE IT'S MADE OUT OF ORIHALCON!
YOU'RE RUNNING AWAY TOO! WHY DO YOU SOUND SO PROUD?
HOW ARE YOU GOING TO RULE THE WORLD WITH THAT!?
IN THEORY, I SHOULD BE ABLE TO CONTROL IT. HUH?
THE PAGES ARE STUCK.
PEEL

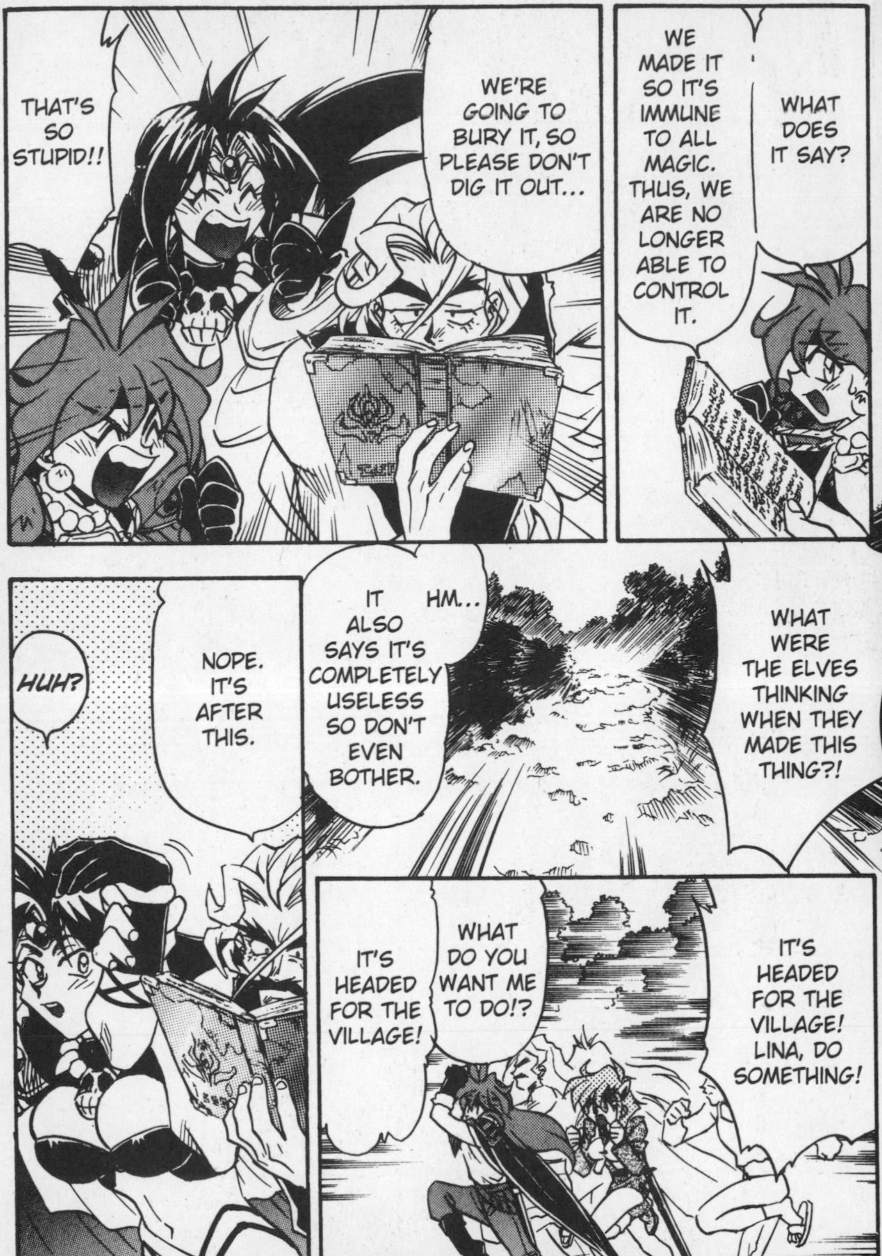
WHAT DOES IT SAY?
WE MADE IT SO IT'S IMMUNE TO ALL MAGIC. THUS, WE ARE NO LONGER ABLE TO CONTROL IT.
WE'RE GOING TO BURY IT, SO PLEASE DON'T DIG IT OUT...
THAT'S SO STUPID!!
WHAT WERE THE ELVES THINKING WHEN THEY MADE THIS THING?!
HM...
IT ALSO SAYS IT'S COMPLETELY USELESS SO DON'T EVEN BOTHER.
IT'S HEADED FOR THE VILLAGE! LINA, DO SOMETHING!
WHAT DO YOU WANT ME TO DO!?
IT'S HEADED FOR THE VILLAGE!
NOPE. IT'S AFTER THIS.
HUH?

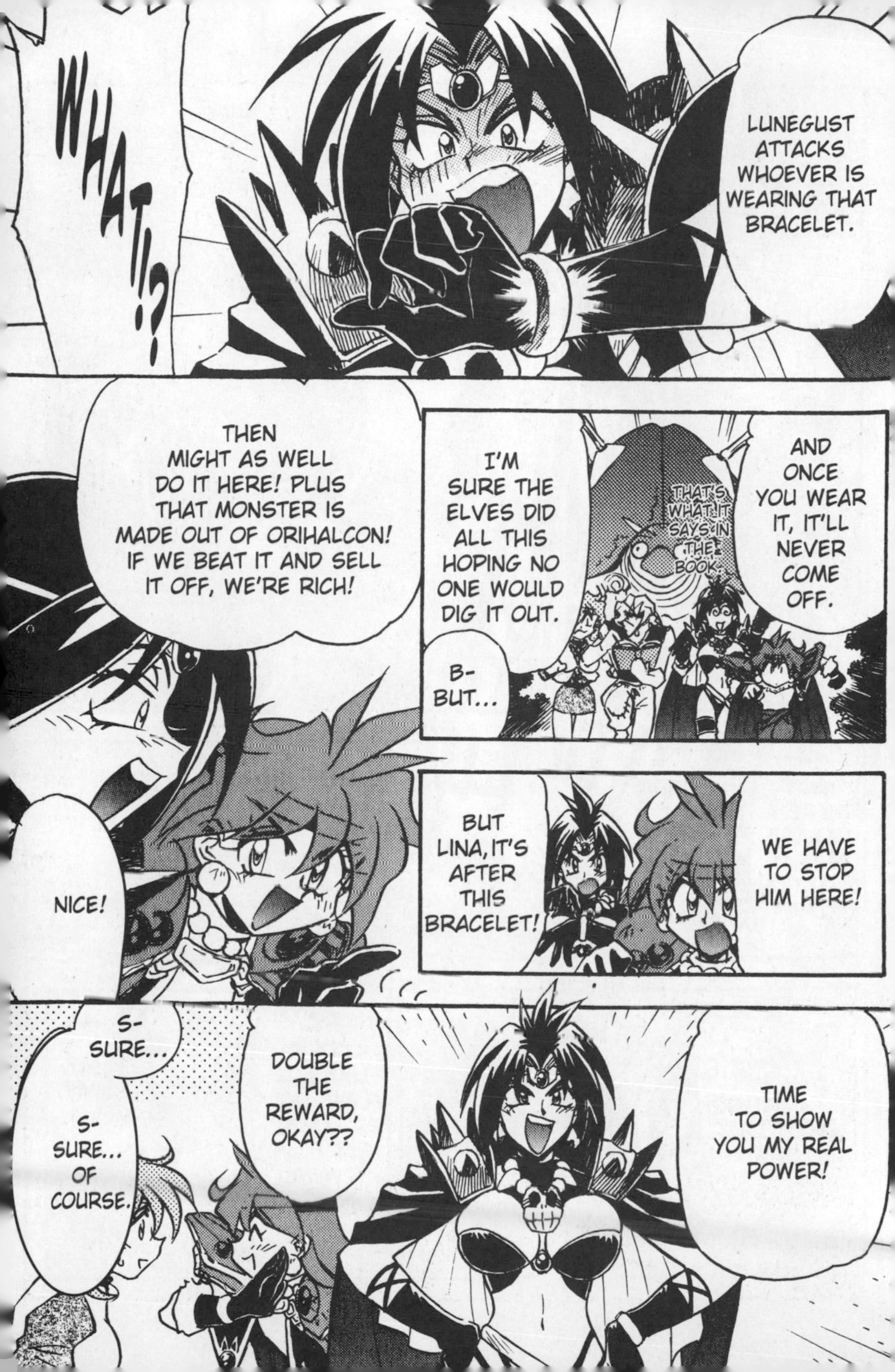

LUNEGUST ATTACKS WHOEVER IS WEARING THAT BRACELET.
WHAT!!?
AND ONCE YOU WEAR IT, IT'LL NEVER COME OFF.
THAT'S WHAT IT SAYS IN THE BOOK.
I'M SURE THE ELVES DID ALL THIS HOPING NO ONE WOULD DIG IT OUT.
B-BUT...
WE HAVE TO STOP HIM HERE!
BUT LINA, IT'S AFTER THIS BRACELET!
THEN MIGHT AS WELL DO IT HERE! PLUS THAT MONSTER IS MADE OUT OF ORIHALCON! IF WE BEAT IT AND SELL IT OFF, WE'RE RICH!
NICE!
TIME TO SHOW YOU MY REAL POWER!
DOUBLE THE REWARD, OKAY??
S-SURE...
S-SURE... OF COURSE.

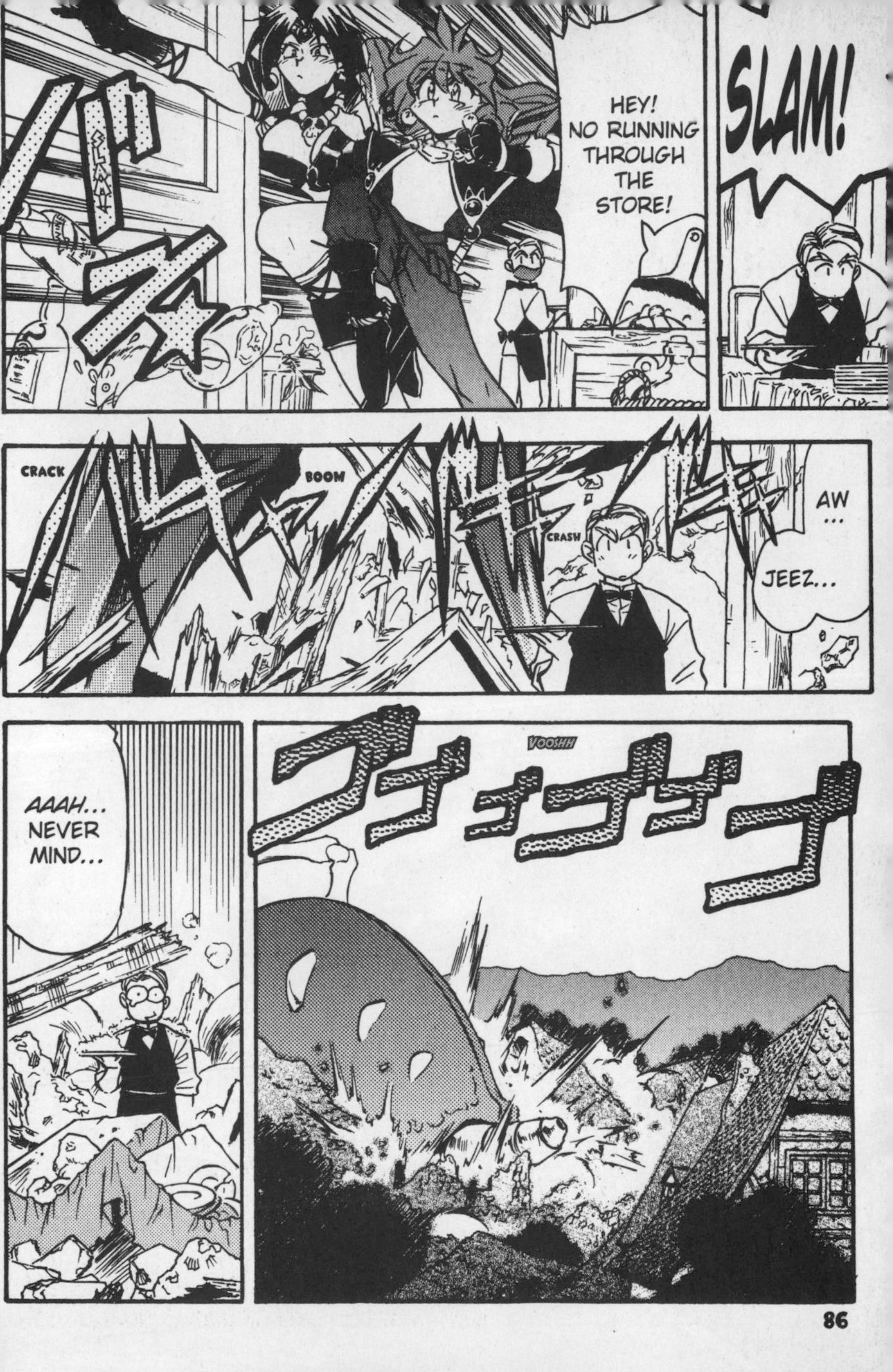
SLAM!
HEY! NO RUNNING THROUGH THE STORE!
AW ...
JEEZ...
CRASH
BOOM
CRACK
VOOSHH
AAAH... NEVER MIND...

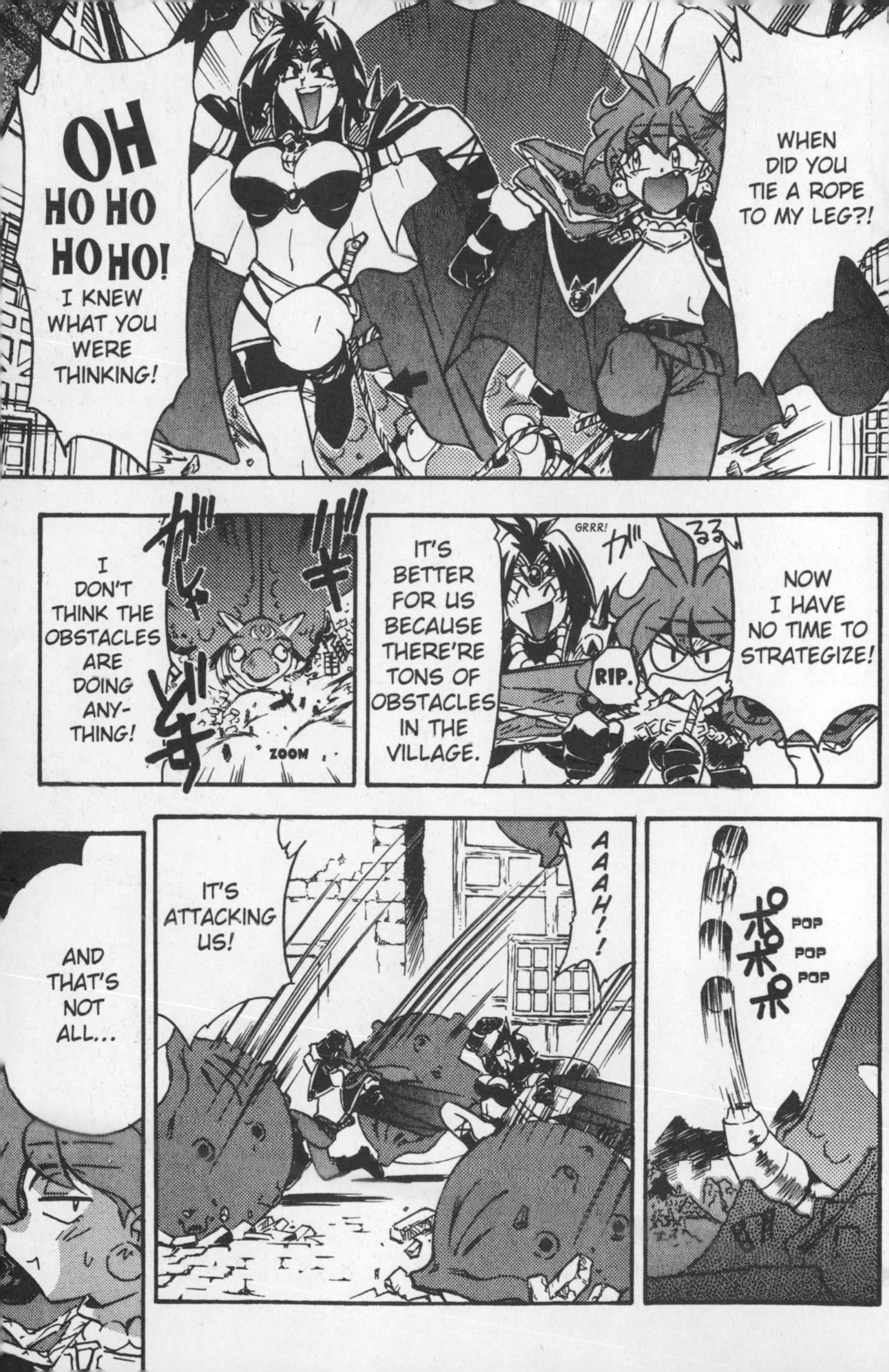

WHEN DID YOU TIE A ROPE TO MY LEG?!
OH HO HO HO HO!
I KNEW WHAT YOU WERE THINKING!
GRRR!
NOW I HAVE NO TIME TO STRATEGIZE!
RIP.
IT'S BETTER FOR US BECAUSE THERE'RE TONS OF OBSTACLES IN THE VILLAGE.
I DON'T THINK THE OBSTACLES ARE DOING ANYTHING!
ZOOM
POP
POP
POP
AAAAH!!
IT'S ATTACKING US!
AND THAT'S NOT ALL...

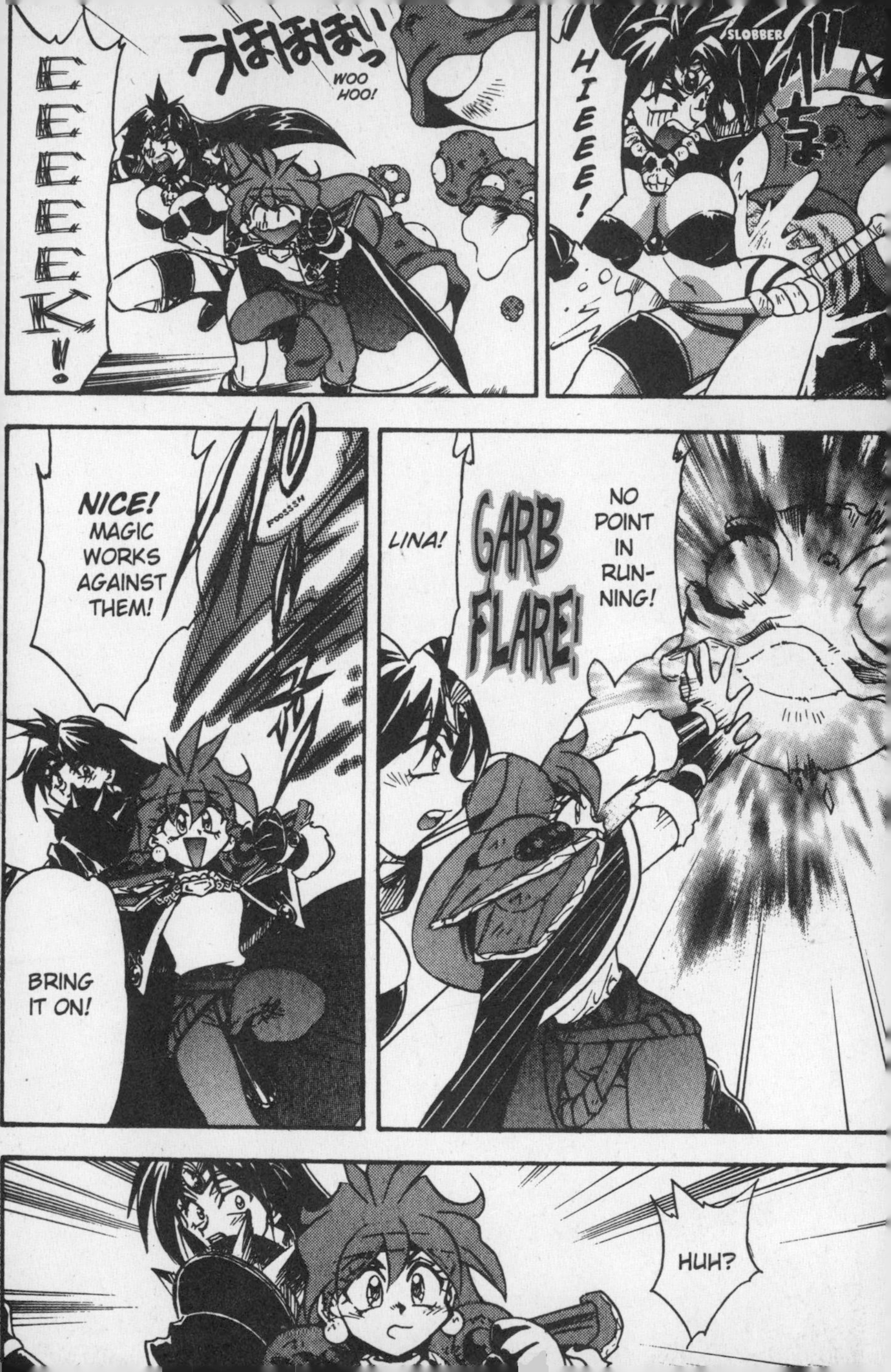
SLOBBER
HIEEEE!
うほほほっ
WOO HOO!
EEEEEEK!!
NO POINT IN RUN-NING!
GARB FLARE!
LINA!
FOOSSSH
NICE! MAGIC WORKS AGAINST THEM!
BRING IT ON!
HUH?

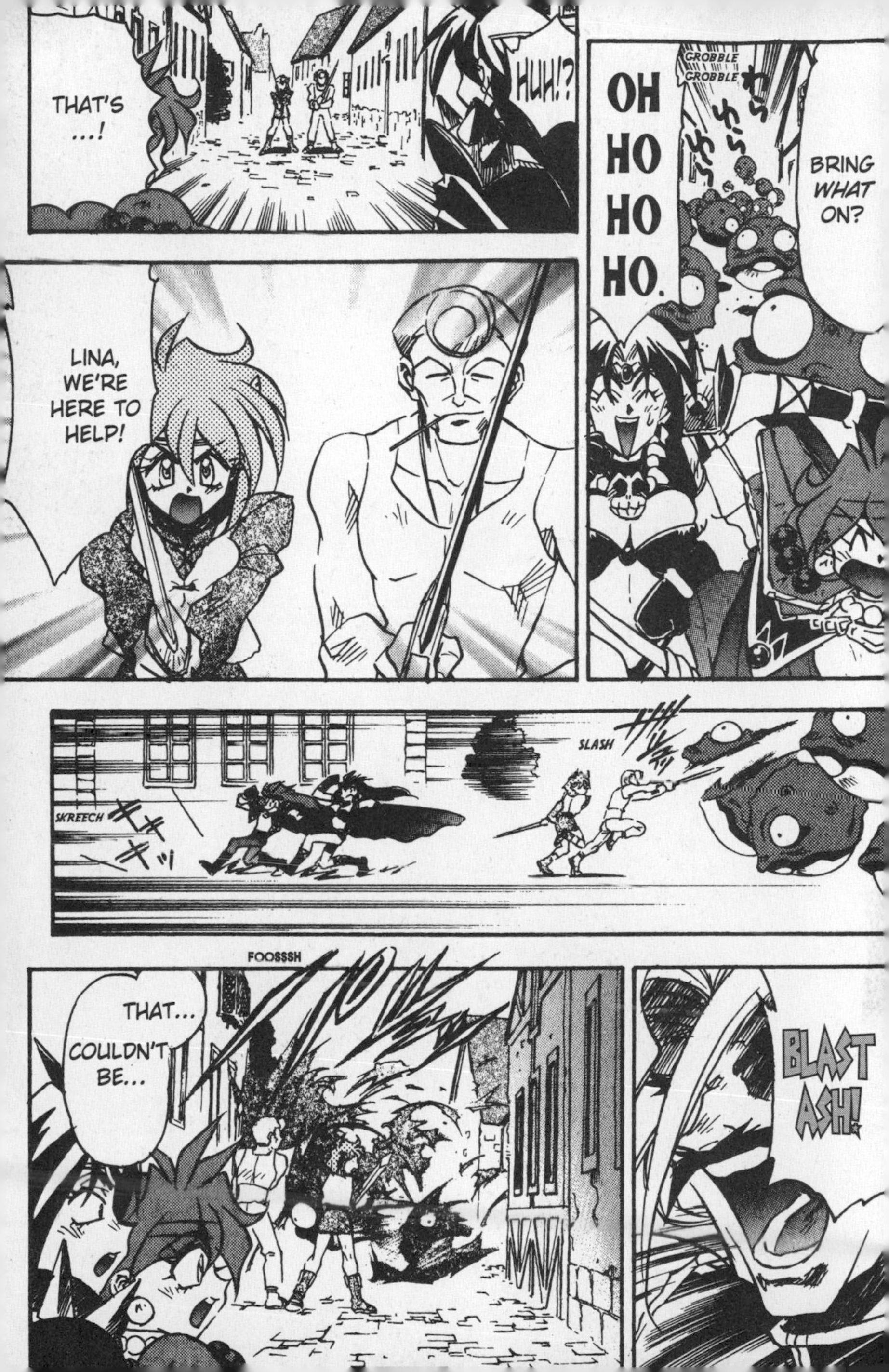
GROBBLE GROBBLE
OH HO HO HO.
BRING WHAT ON?
HUH!?
THAT'S ...!
LINA, WE'RE HERE TO HELP!
SLASH
SKREECH
BLAST ASH!
FOOSSSH
THAT... COULDN'T BE...

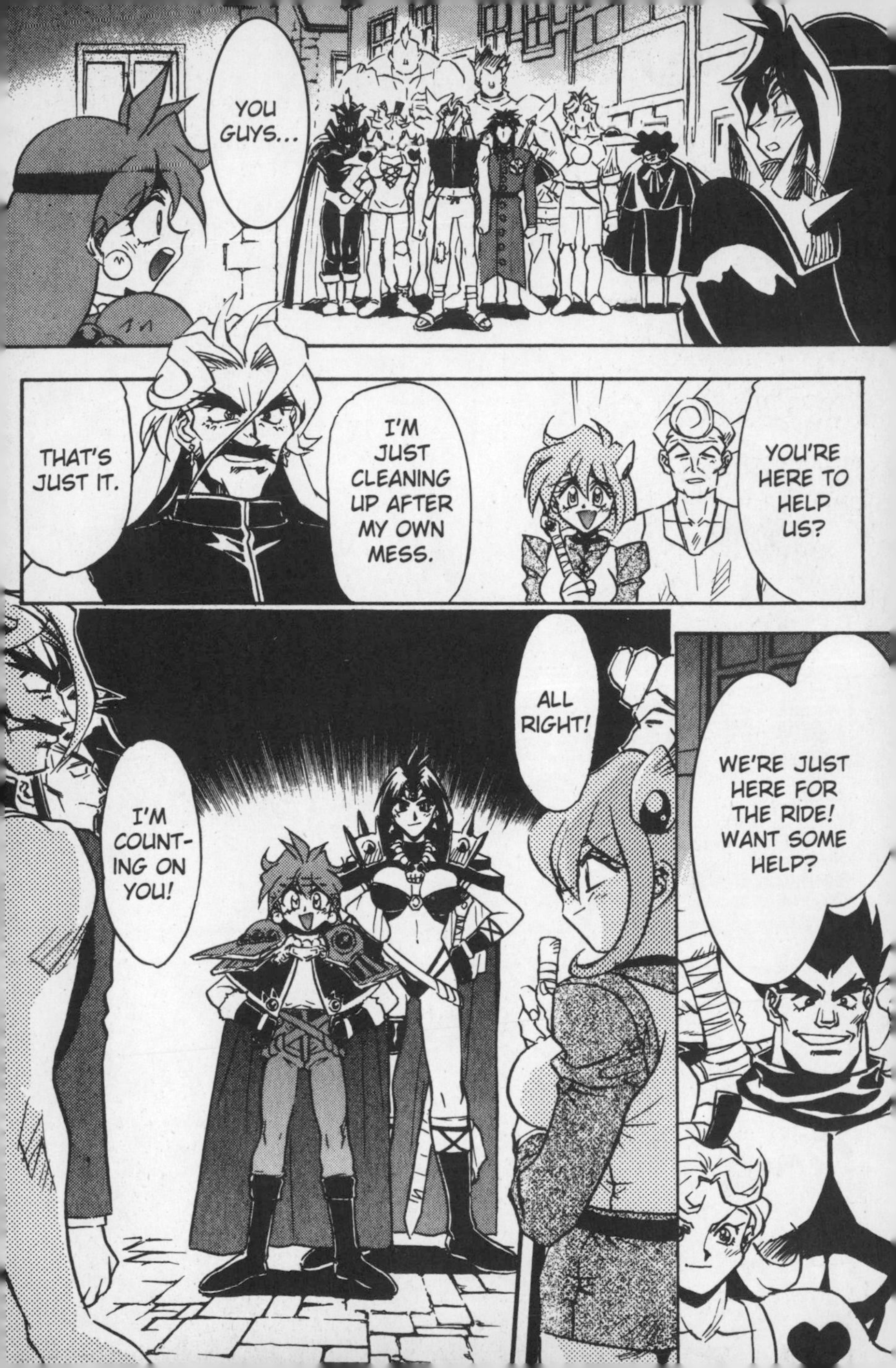
YOU GUYS...
YOU'RE HERE TO HELP US?
I'M JUST CLEANING UP AFTER MY OWN MESS.
THAT'S JUST IT.
WE'RE JUST HERE FOR THE RIDE! WANT SOME HELP?
ALL RIGHT!
I'M COUNTING ON YOU!

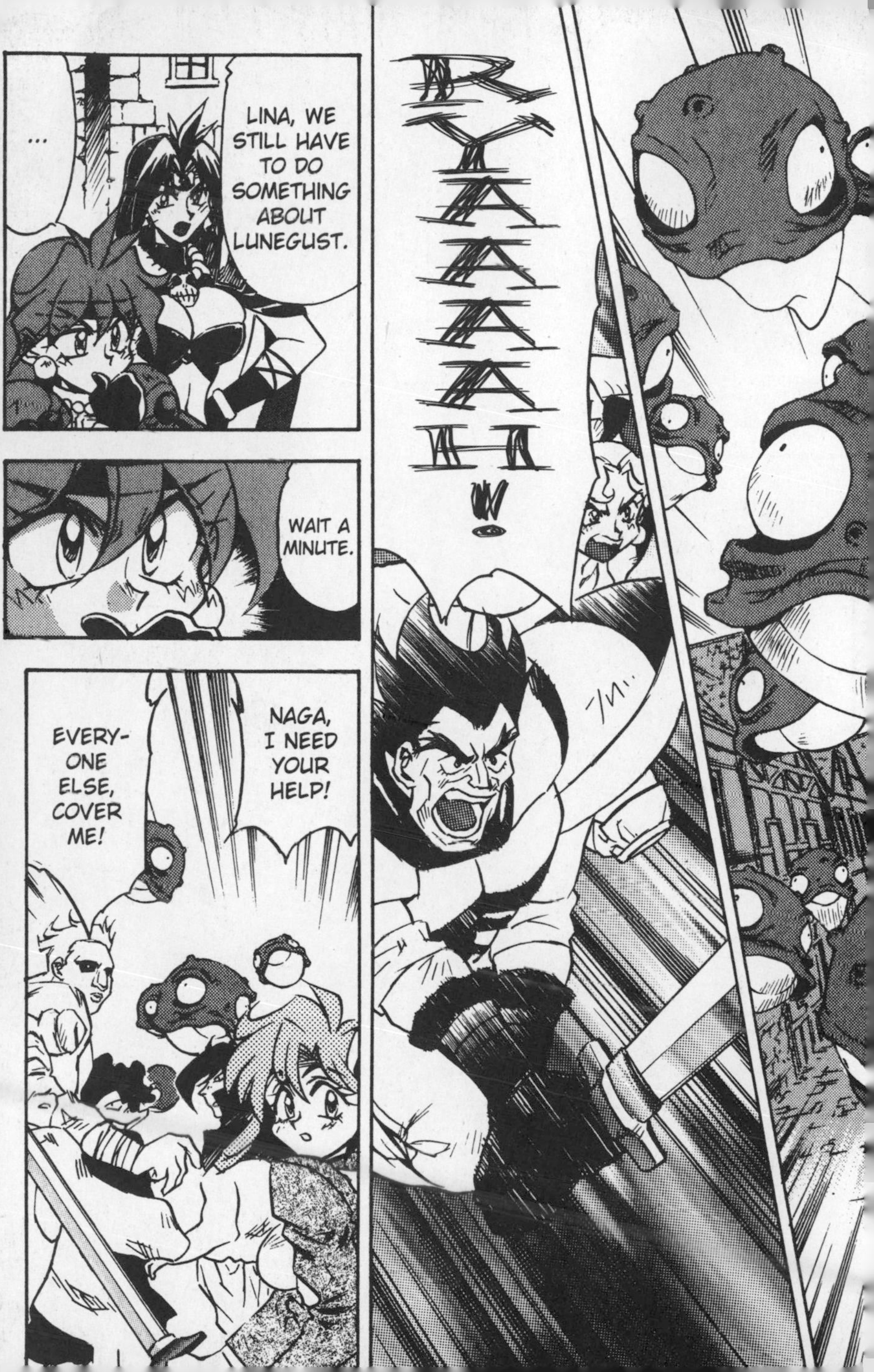
RYAAAAAH!!
LINA, WE STILL HAVE TO DO SOMETHING ABOUT LUNEGUST.
...
WAIT A MINUTE.
NAGA, I NEED YOUR HELP!
EVERY-ONE ELSE, COVER ME!

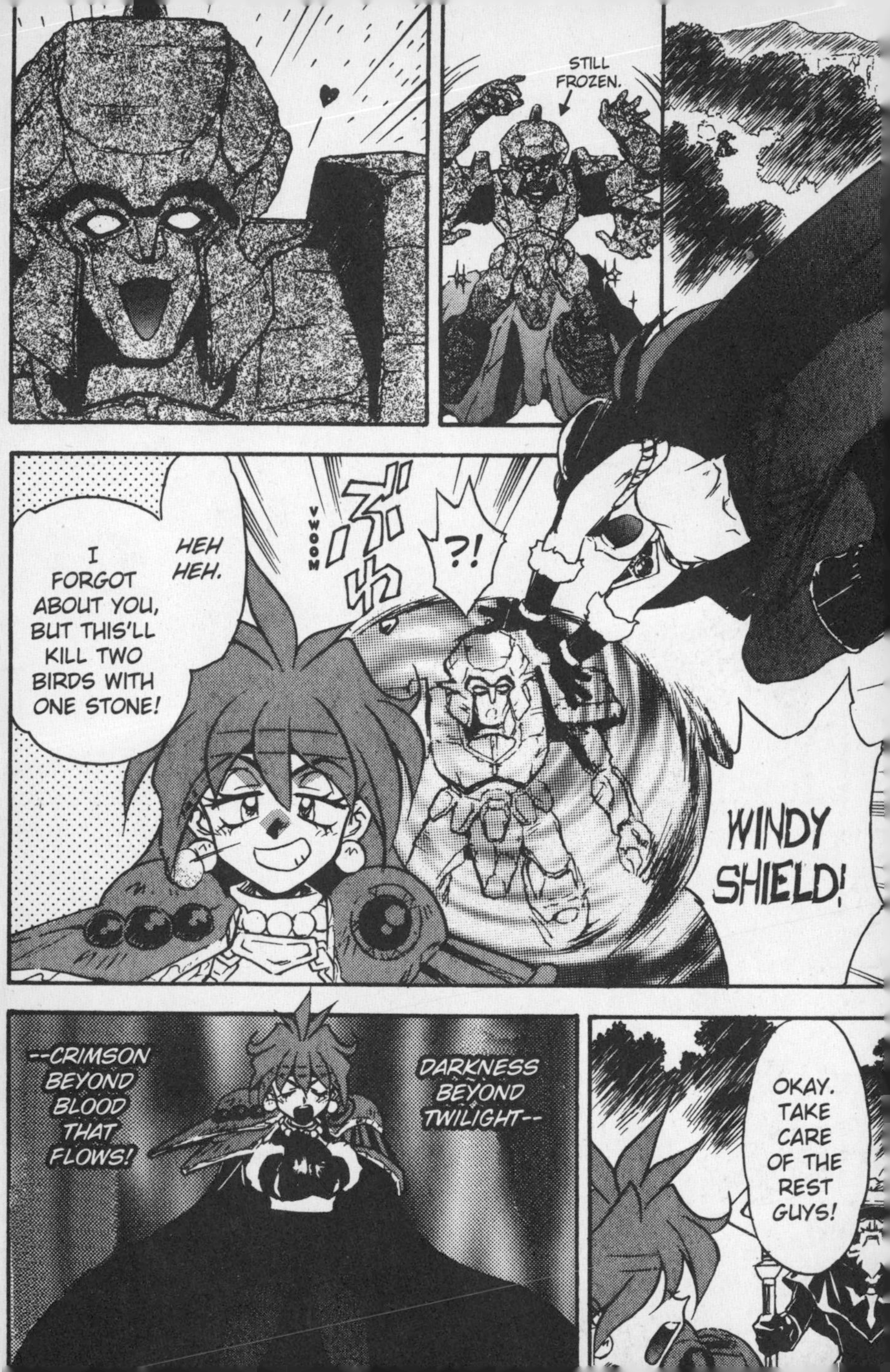
STILL FROZEN.
WINDY SHIELD!
?!
VWOOM
HEH HEH.
I FORGOT ABOUT YOU, BUT THIS'LL KILL TWO BIRDS WITH ONE STONE!
OKAY. TAKE CARE OF THE REST GUYS!
DARKNESS BEYOND TWILIGHT--
--CRIMSON BEYOND BLOOD THAT FLOWS!

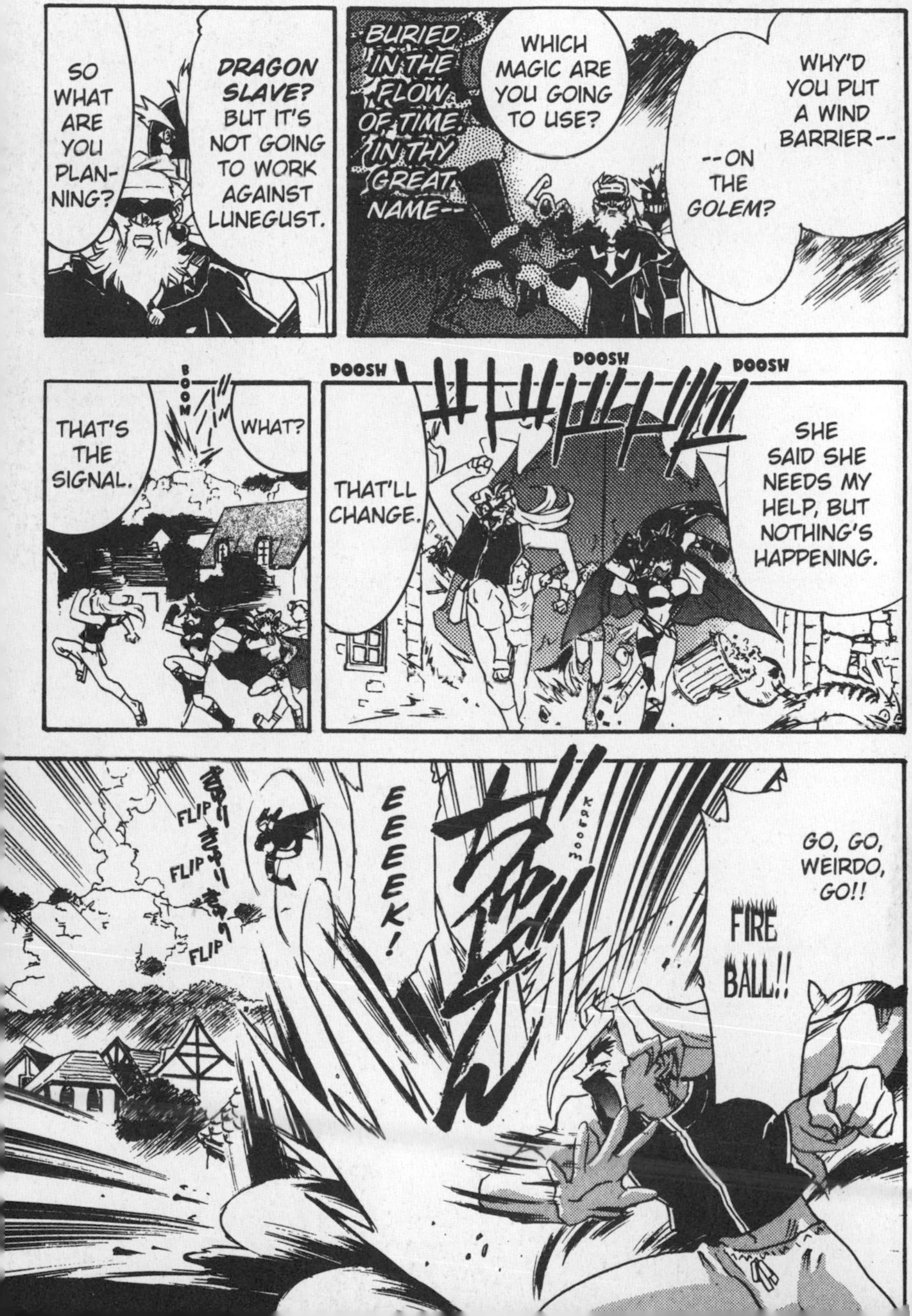
WHY'D YOU PUT A WIND BARRIER--
--ON THE GOLEM?
WHICH MAGIC ARE YOU GOING TO USE?
BURIED IN THE FLOW OF TIME, IN THY GREAT NAME--
DRAGON SLAVE? BUT IT'S NOT GOING TO WORK AGAINST LUNEGUST.
SO WHAT ARE YOU PLANNING?
DOOSH
DOOSH
DOOSH
SHE SAID SHE NEEDS MY HELP, BUT NOTHING'S HAPPENING.
THAT'LL CHANGE.
BOOM
WHAT?
THAT'S THE SIGNAL.
GO, GO, WEIRDO, GO!!
FIRE BALL!!
kaboom
EEEEK!
FLIP
FLIP
FLIP

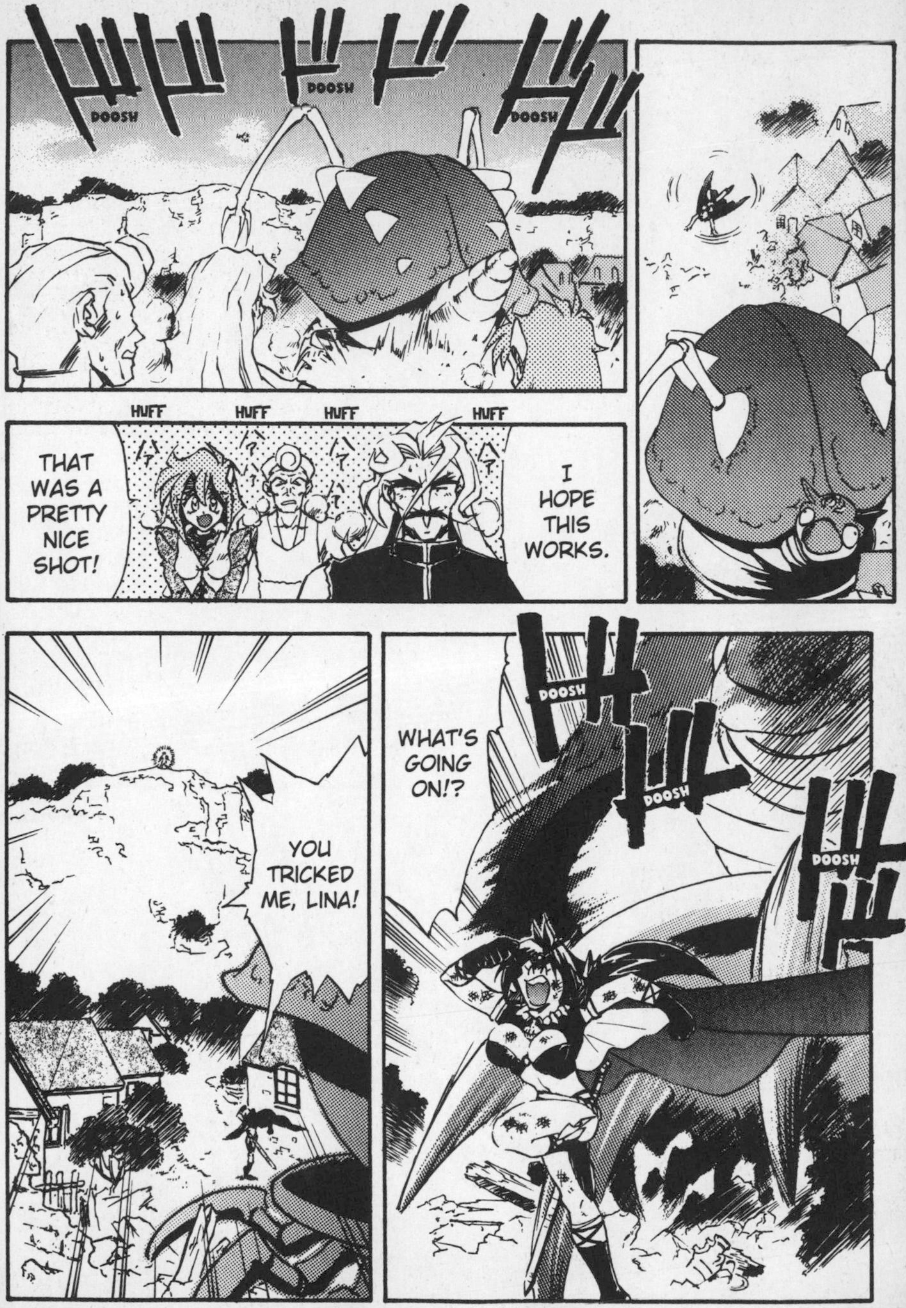
DOOSH
DOOSH
DOOSH
HUFF
HUFF
HUFF
HUFF
I HOPE THIS WORKS.
THAT WAS A PRETTY NICE SHOT!
DOOSH
DOOSH
DOOSH
WHAT'S GOING ON!?
YOU TRICKED ME, LINA!

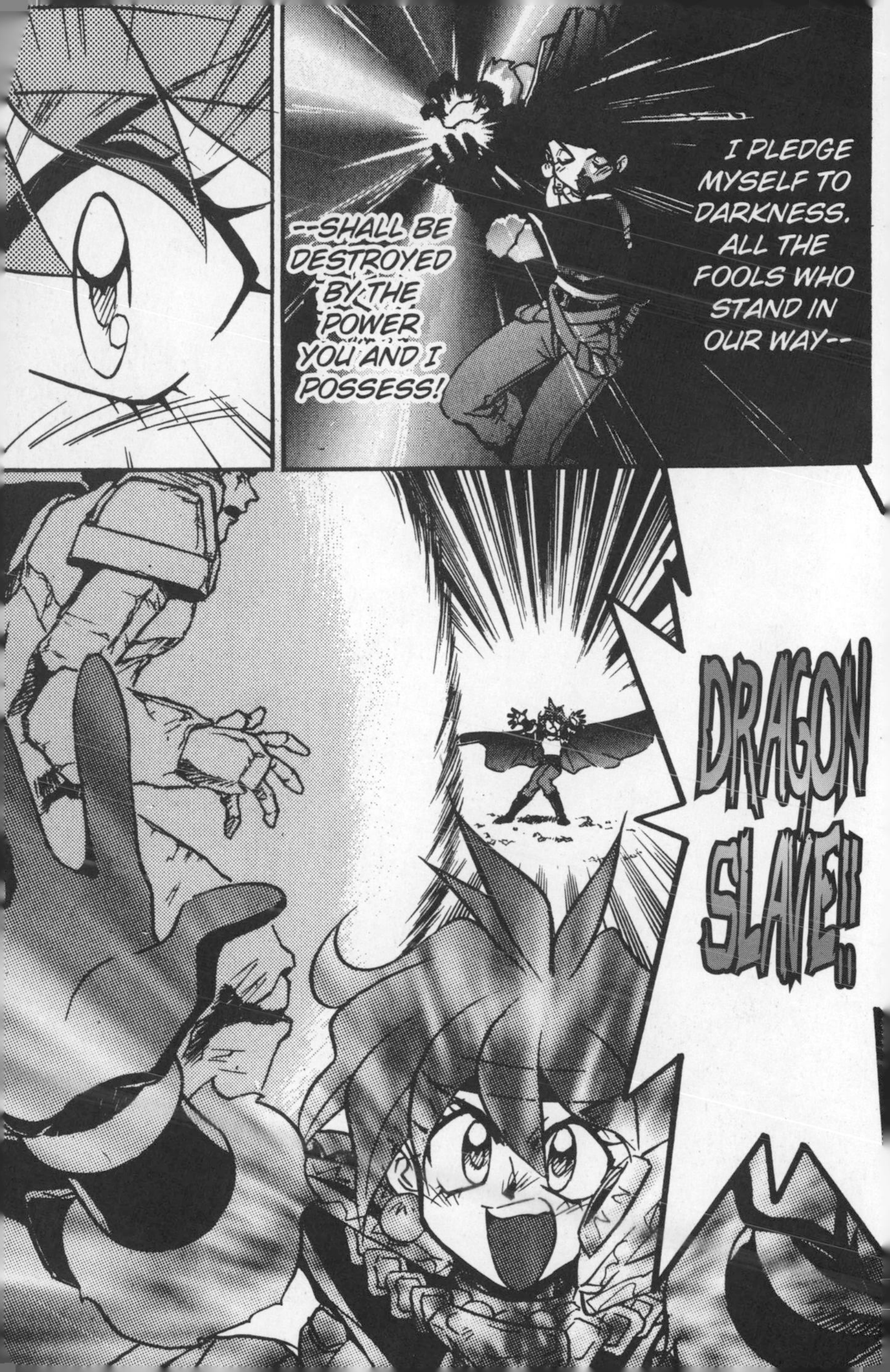
I PLEDGE MYSELF TO DARKNESS. ALL THE FOOLS WHO STAND IN OUR WAY--
--SHALL BE DESTROYED BY THE POWER YOU AND I POSSESS!
DRAGON SLAVE!!

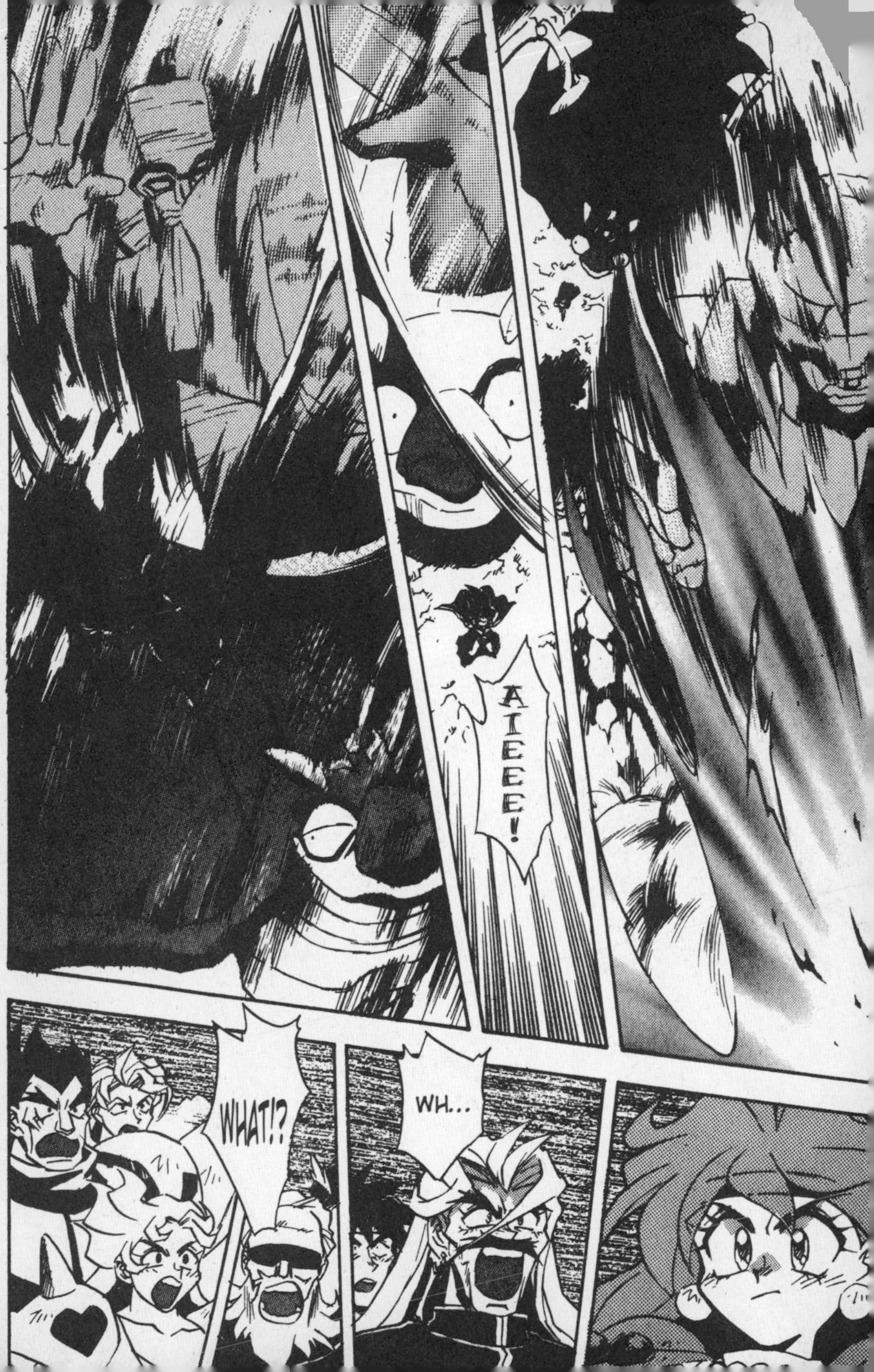
AIEEE!
WH...
WHAT!?

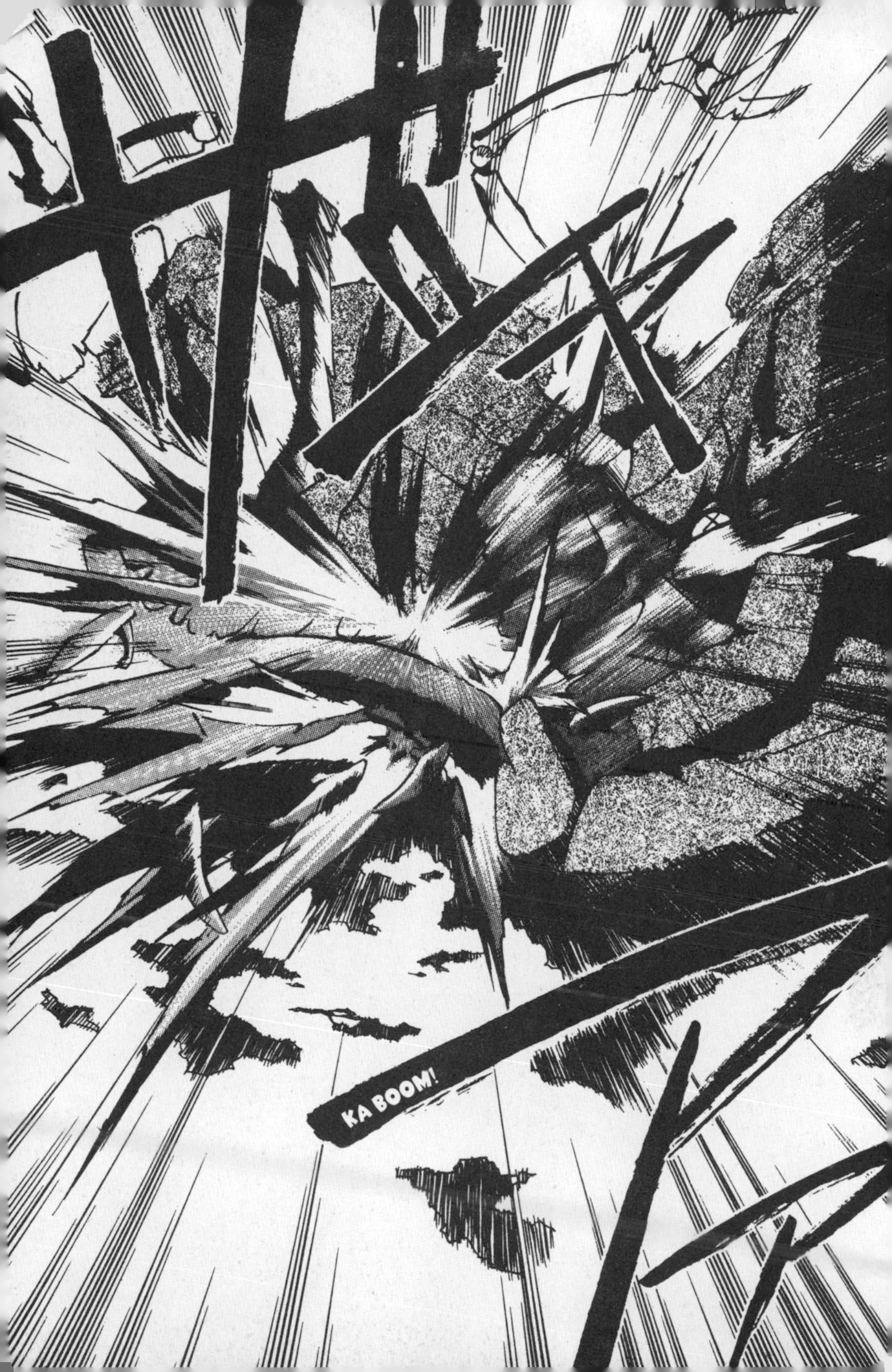
KA BOOM!

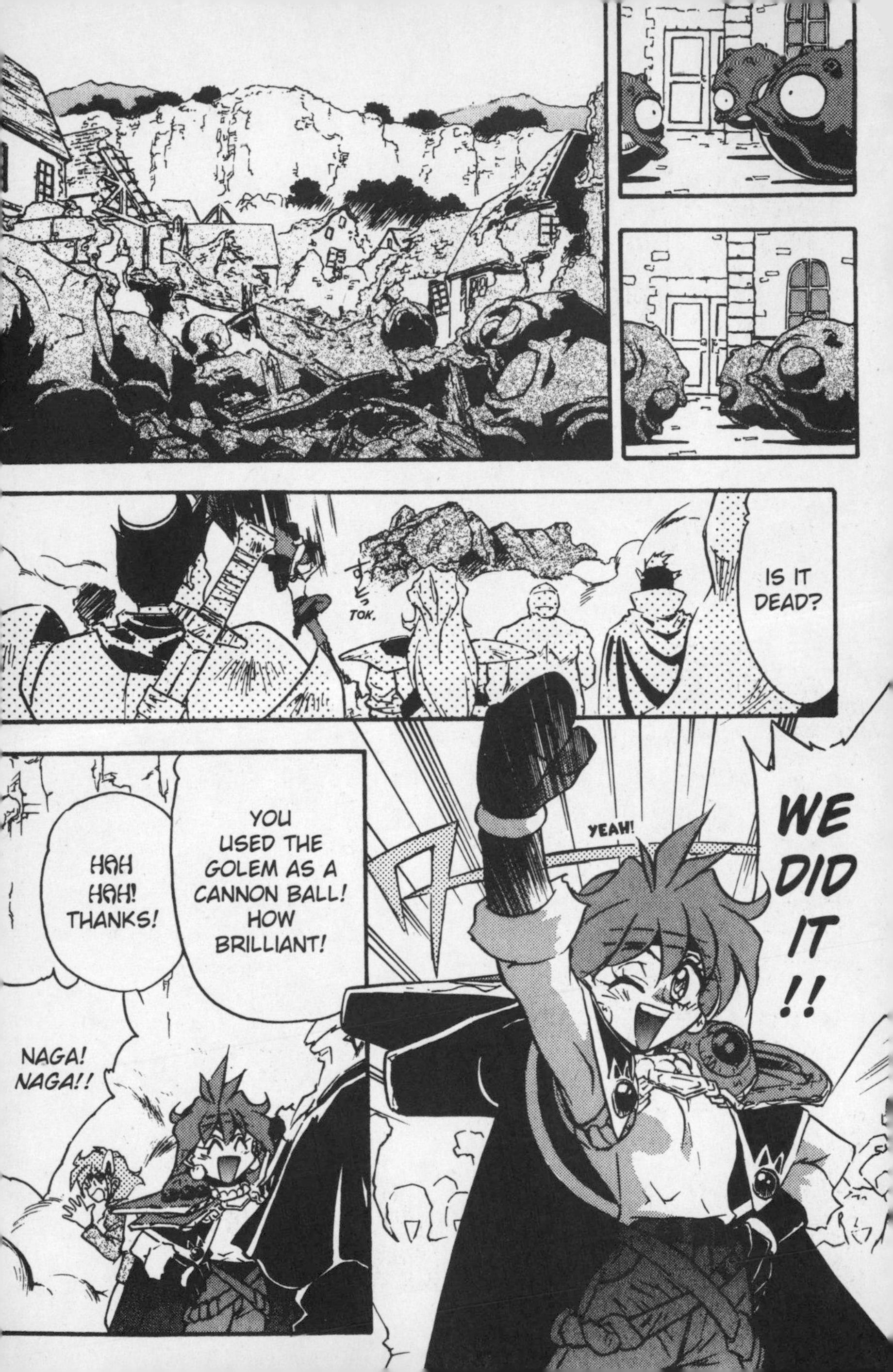
IS IT DEAD?
TOK.
WE DID IT!!
YEAH!
YOU USED THE GOLEM AS A CANNON BALL! HOW BRILLIANT!
HAH HAH! THANKS!
NAGA! NAGA!!

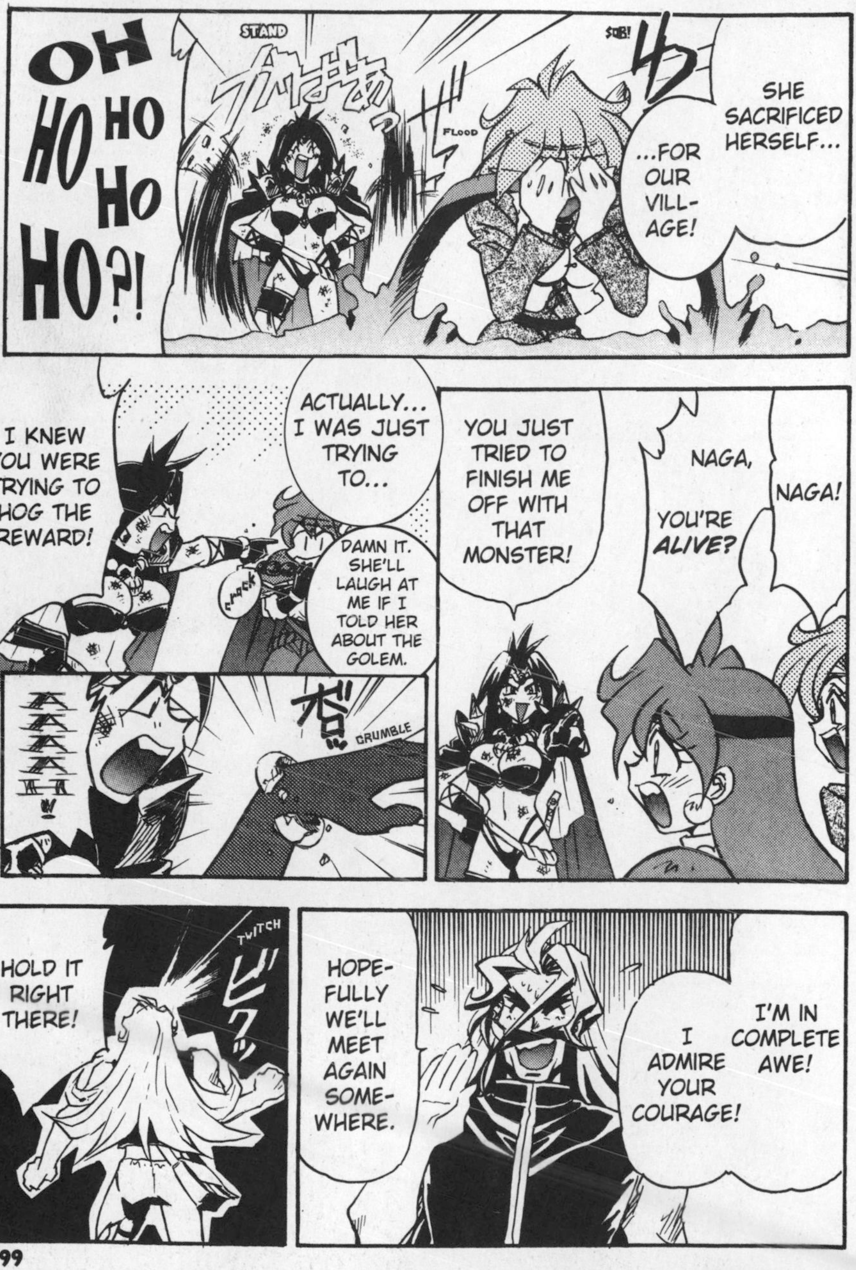
SOB!
SHE SACRIFICED HERSELF...
...FOR OUR VILL-AGE!
FLOOD
STAND
OH HO HO HO HO HO?!
NAGA!
NAGA, YOU'RE *ALIVE?*
YOU JUST TRIED TO FINISH ME OFF WITH THAT MONSTER!
ACTUALLY... I WAS JUST TRYING TO...
DAMN IT. SHE'LL LAUGH AT ME IF I TOLD HER ABOUT THE GOLEM.
CRACK
I KNEW YOU WERE TRYING TO HOG THE REWARD!
CRUMBLE
AAAAAH!!
I'M IN COMPLETE AWE!
I ADMIRE YOUR COURAGE!
HOPE-FULLY WE'LL MEET AGAIN SOME-WHERE.
TWITCH
HOLD IT RIGHT THERE!

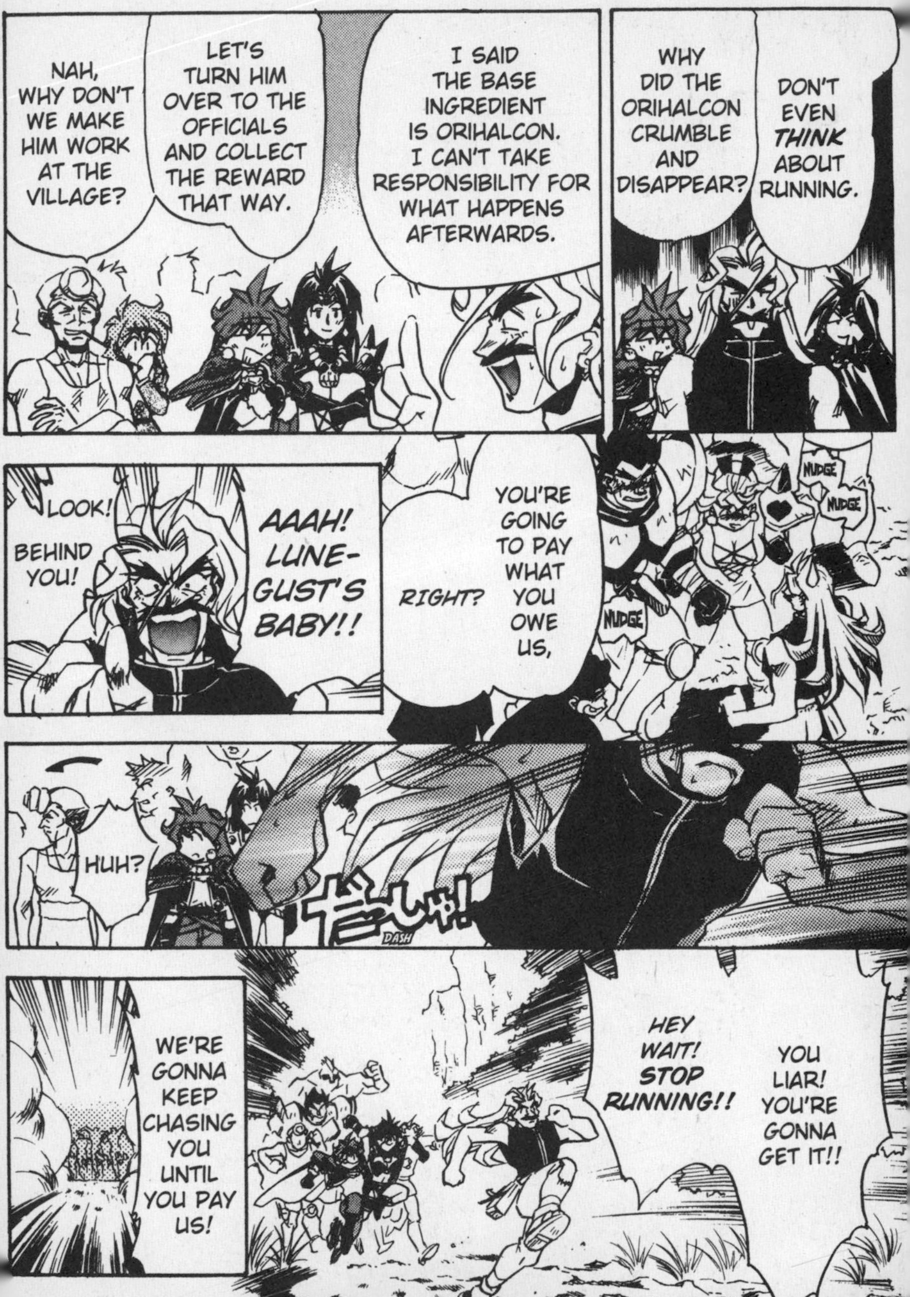
DON'T EVEN THINK ABOUT RUNNING.
WHY DID THE ORIHALCON CRUMBLE AND DISAPPEAR?
I SAID THE BASE INGREDIENT IS ORIHALCON. I CAN'T TAKE RESPONSIBILITY FOR WHAT HAPPENS AFTERWARDS.
LET'S TURN HIM OVER TO THE OFFICIALS AND COLLECT THE REWARD THAT WAY.
NAH, WHY DON'T WE MAKE HIM WORK AT THE VILLAGE?
NUDGE
NUDGE
YOU'RE GOING TO PAY WHAT YOU OWE US,
RIGHT?
NUDGE
AAAH! LUNE-GUST'S BABY!!
LOOK!
BEHIND YOU!
HUH?
DASH
YOU LIAR! YOU'RE GONNA GET IT!!
HEY WAIT! STOP RUNNING!!
WE'RE GONNA KEEP CHASING YOU UNTIL YOU PAY US!

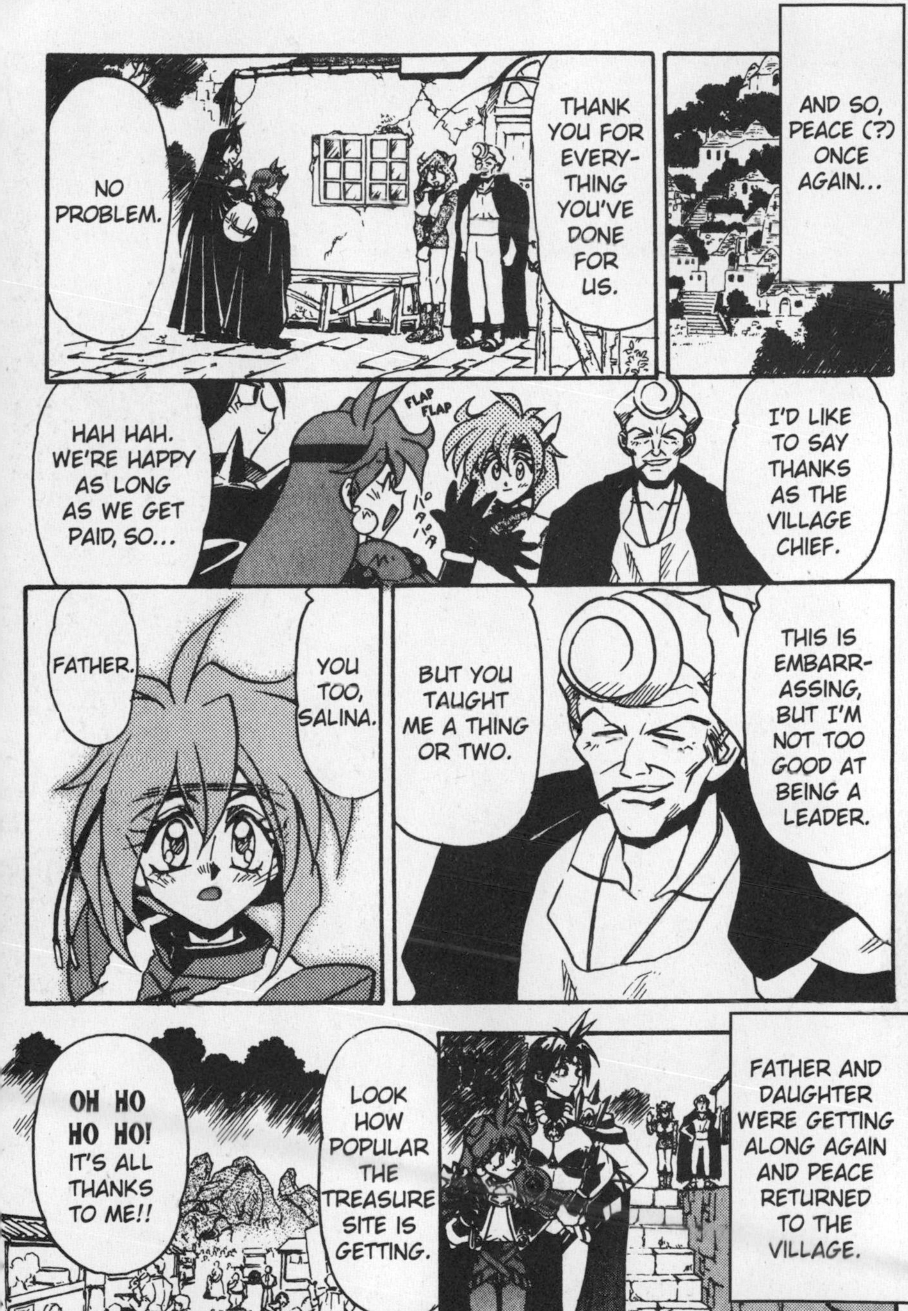
AND SO, PEACE (?) ONCE AGAIN...
THANK YOU FOR EVERYTHING YOU'VE DONE FOR US.
NO PROBLEM.
I'D LIKE TO SAY THANKS AS THE VILLAGE CHIEF.
FLAP FLAP
HAH HAH. WE'RE HAPPY AS LONG AS WE GET PAID, SO...
THIS IS EMBARRASSING, BUT I'M NOT TOO GOOD AT BEING A LEADER.
BUT YOU TAUGHT ME A THING OR TWO.
YOU TOO, SALINA.
FATHER.
FATHER AND DAUGHTER WERE GETTING ALONG AGAIN AND PEACE RETURNED TO THE VILLAGE.
LOOK HOW POPULAR THE TREASURE SITE IS GETTING.
OH HO HO HO! IT'S ALL THANKS TO ME!!

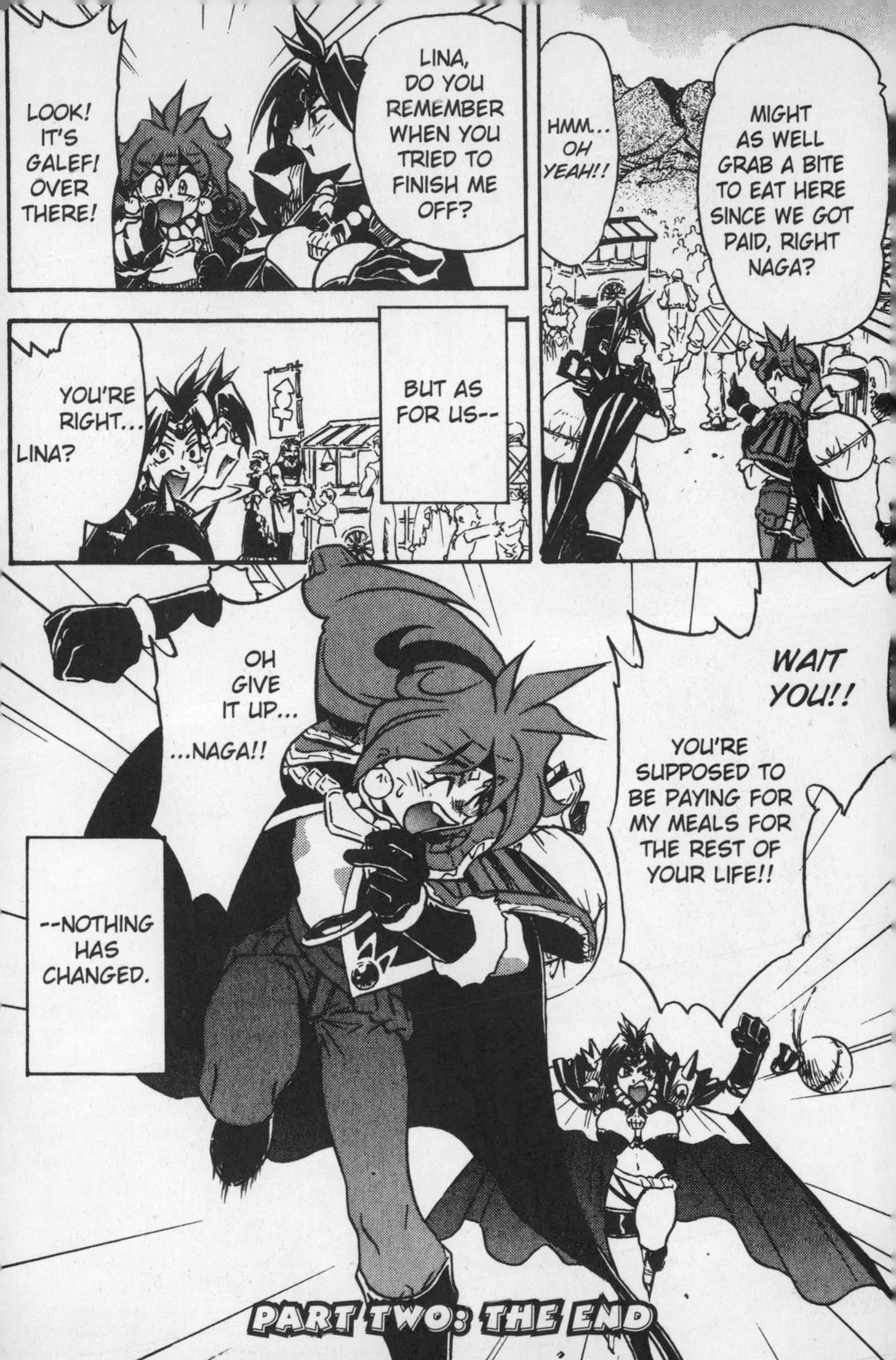
MIGHT AS WELL GRAB A BITE TO EAT HERE SINCE WE GOT PAID, RIGHT NAGA?
HMM... OH YEAH!!
LINA, DO YOU REMEMBER WHEN YOU TRIED TO FINISH ME OFF?
LOOK! IT'S GALEF! OVER THERE!
BUT AS FOR US--
YOU'RE RIGHT... LINA?
WAIT YOU!!
YOU'RE SUPPOSED TO BE PAYING FOR MY MEALS FOR THE REST OF YOUR LIFE!!
OH GIVE IT UP...
...NAGA!!
--NOTHING HAS CHANGED.
PART TWO: THE END

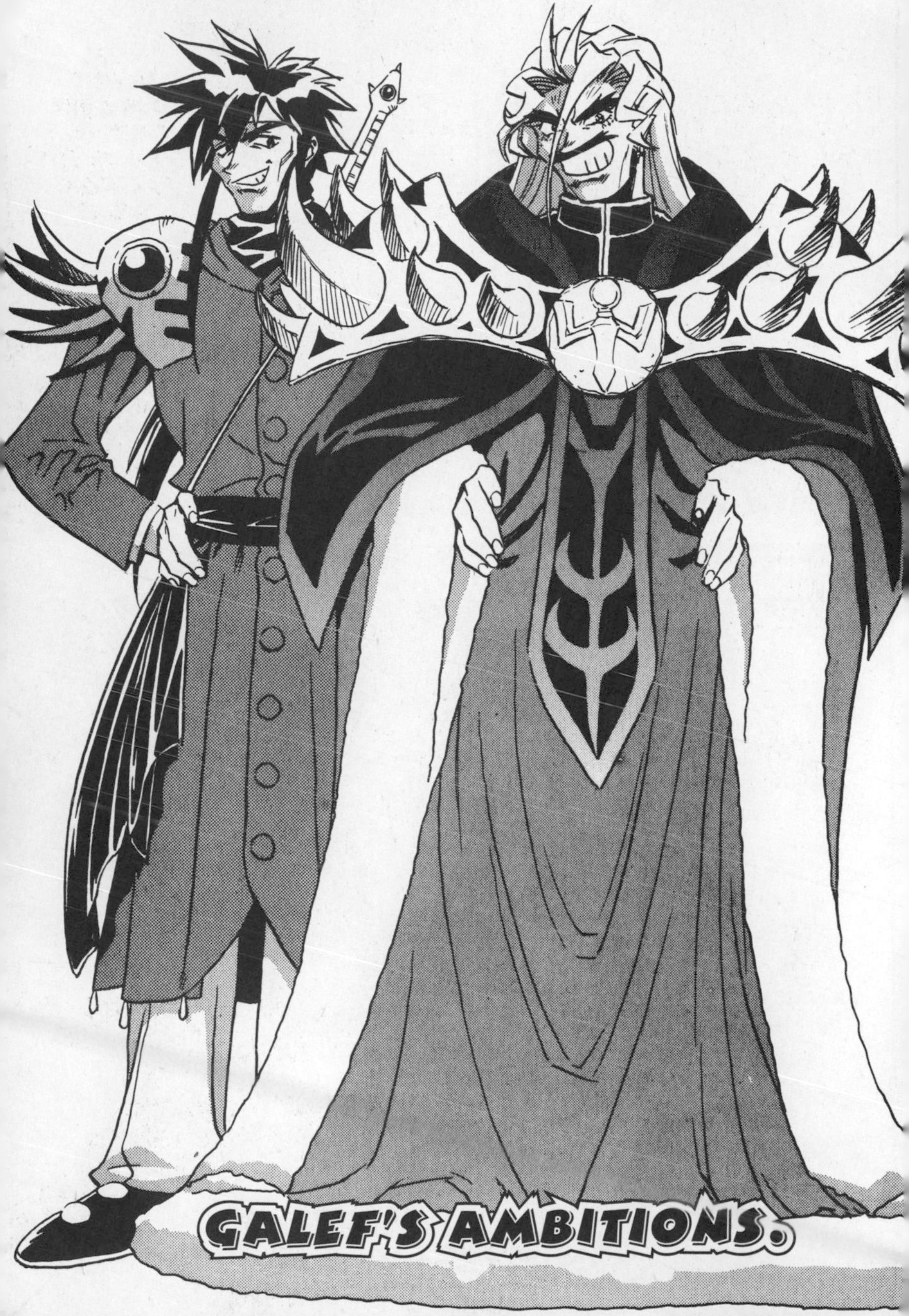
GALEF'S AMBITIONS.

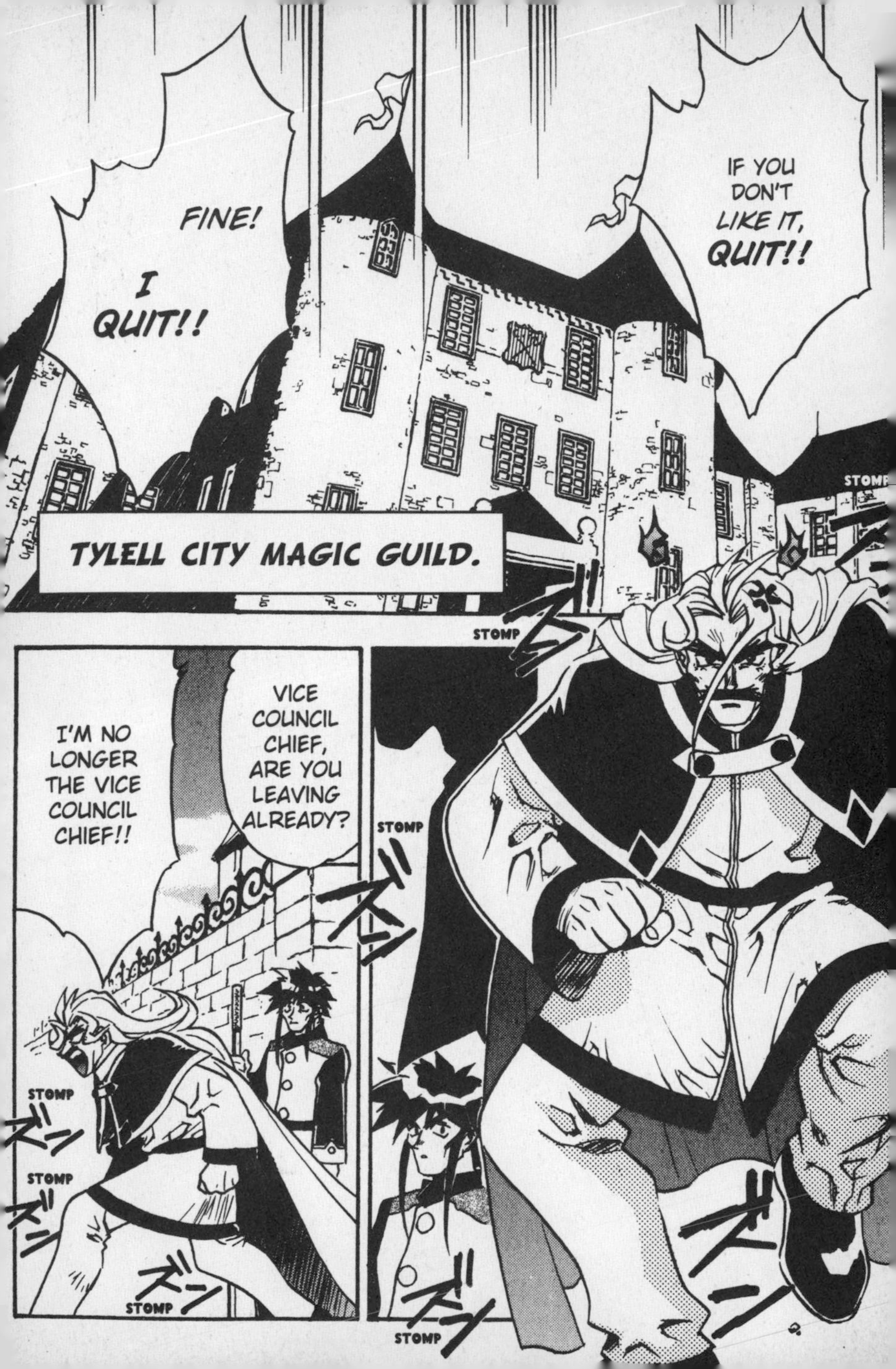
IF YOU DON'T LIKE IT, QUIT!!
FINE! I QUIT!!
TYLELL CITY MAGIC GUILD.
STOMP
STOMP
STOMP
STOMP
VICE COUNCIL CHIEF, ARE YOU LEAVING ALREADY?
I'M NO LONGER THE VICE COUNCIL CHIEF!!
STOMP
STOMP
STOMP

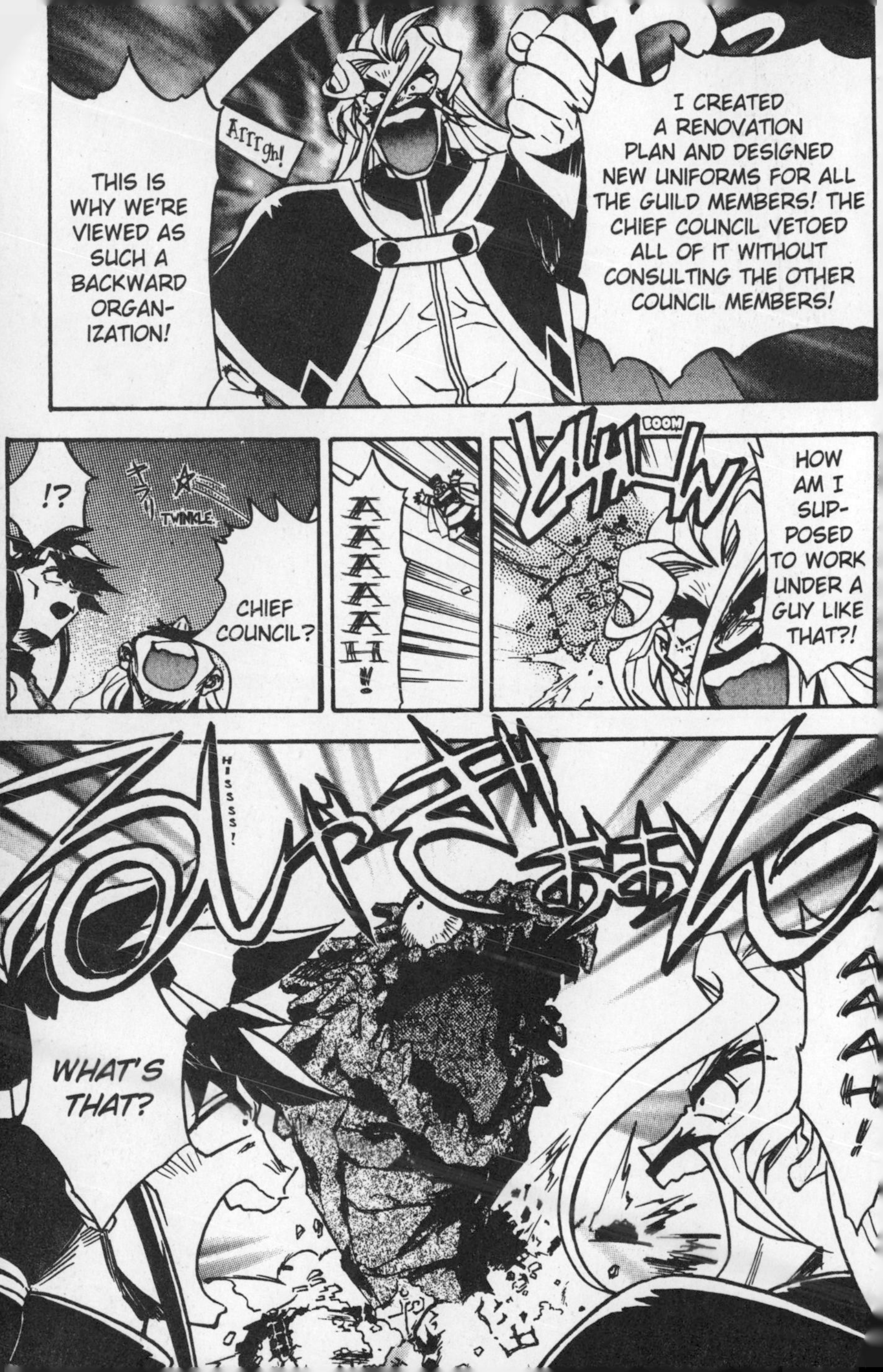
I CREATED A RENOVATION PLAN AND DESIGNED NEW UNIFORMS FOR ALL THE GUILD MEMBERS! THE CHIEF COUNCIL VETOED ALL OF IT WITHOUT CONSULTING THE OTHER COUNCIL MEMBERS!
Arrrgh!
THIS IS WHY WE'RE VIEWED AS SUCH A BACKWARD ORGAN-IZATION!
BOOM
HOW AM I SUP-POSED TO WORK UNDER A GUY LIKE THAT?!
AAAAAAH!
!?
TWINKLE
CHIEF COUNCIL?
AAAA!
HISSSSS!
WHAT'S THAT?

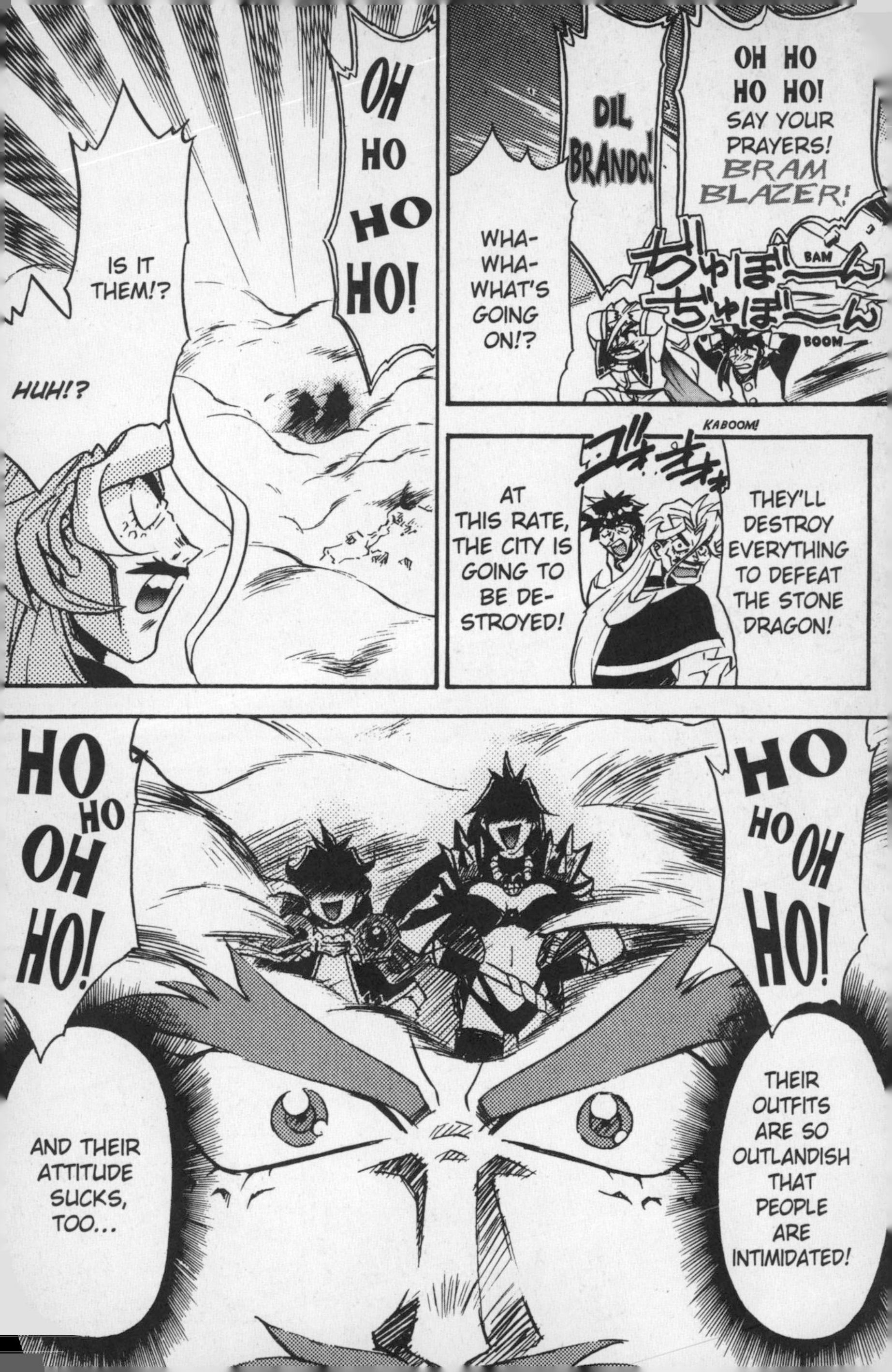
OH HO HO HO! SAY YOUR PRAYERS! BRAM BLAZER!
DIL BRANDO!
BAM
BOOM
WHA-WHA-WHAT'S GOING ON!?
KABOOM!
THEY'LL DESTROY EVERYTHING TO DEFEAT THE STONE DRAGON!
AT THIS RATE, THE CITY IS GOING TO BE DESTROYED!
OH HO HO HO!
IS IT THEM!?
HUH!?
HO HO OH HO!
HO HO OH HO!
THEIR OUTFITS ARE SO OUTLANDISH THAT PEOPLE ARE INTIMIDATED!
AND THEIR ATTITUDE SUCKS, TOO...

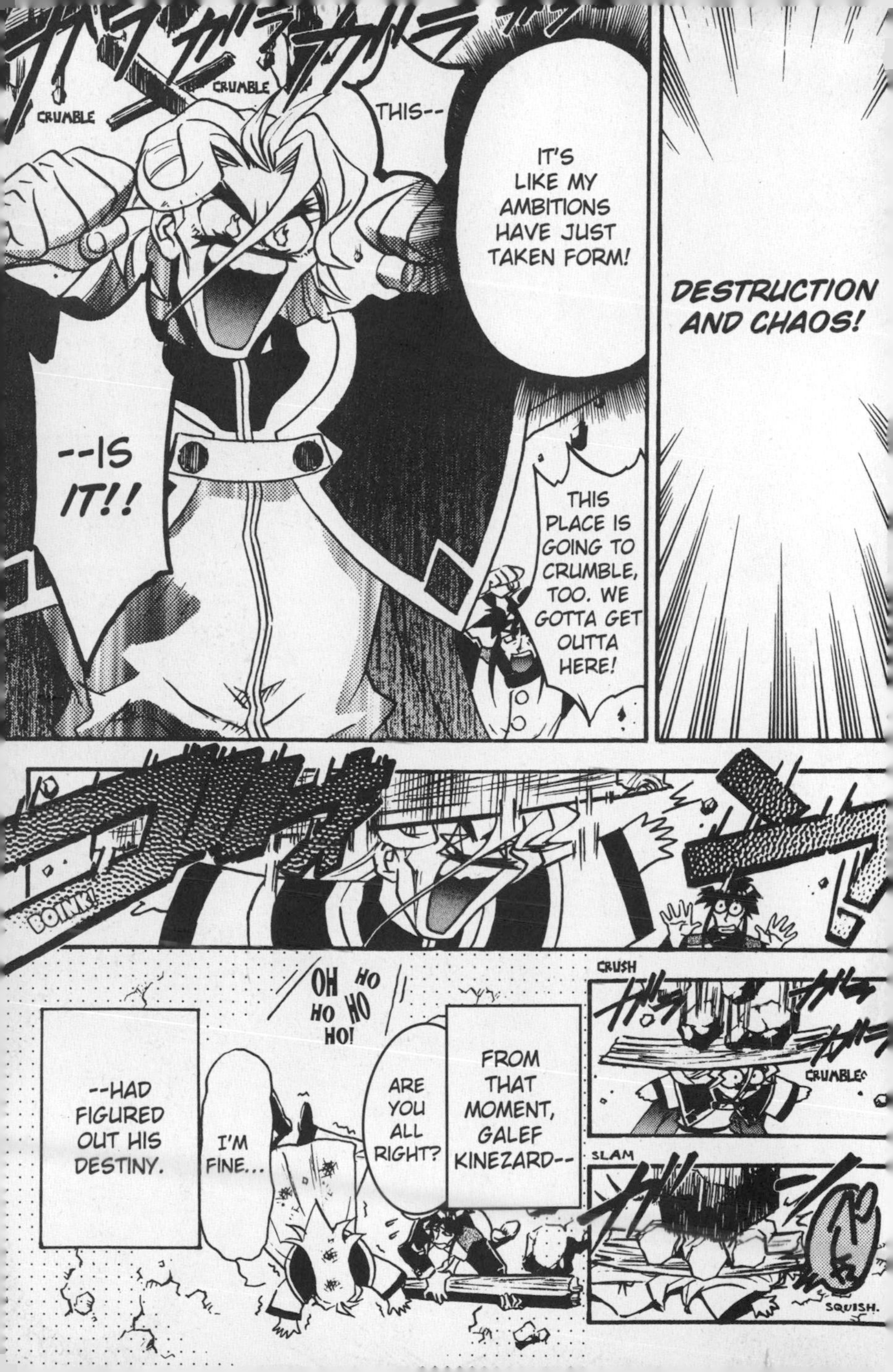
DESTRUCTION AND CHAOS!
CRUMBLE
CRUMBLE
THIS--
IT'S LIKE MY AMBITIONS HAVE JUST TAKEN FORM!
--IS IT!!
THIS PLACE IS GOING TO CRUMBLE, TOO. WE GOTTA GET OUTTA HERE!
BOINK!
CRUSH
CRUMBLE
SLAM
SQUISH.
FROM THAT MOMENT, GALEF KINEZARD--
ARE YOU ALL RIGHT?
OH HO HO HO HO!
I'M FINE...
--HAD FIGURED OUT HIS DESTINY.

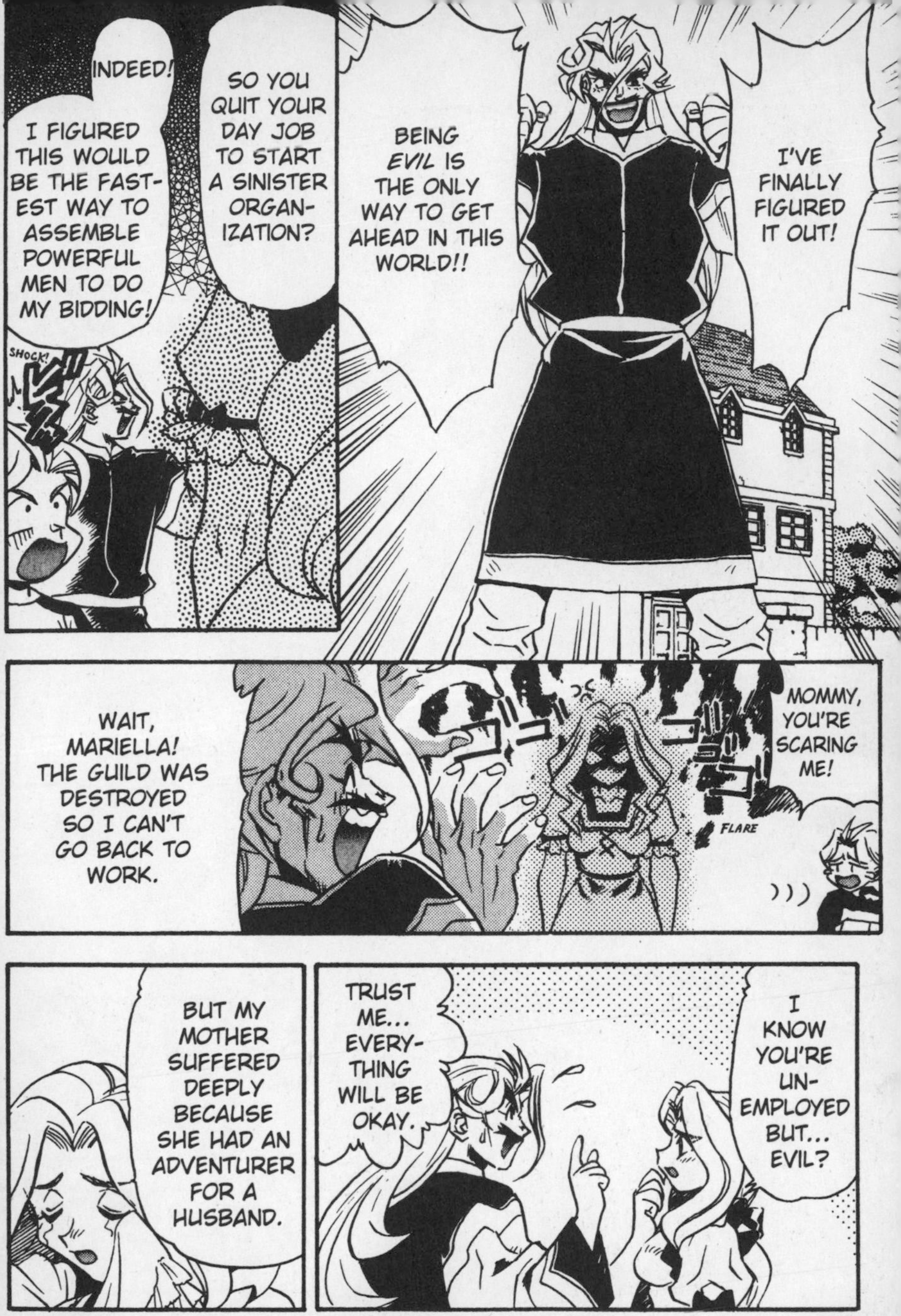
I'VE FINALLY FIGURED IT OUT!
BEING *EVIL* IS THE ONLY WAY TO GET AHEAD IN THIS WORLD!!
SO YOU QUIT YOUR DAY JOB TO START A SINISTER ORGANIZATION?
INDEED!
I FIGURED THIS WOULD BE THE FASTEST WAY TO ASSEMBLE POWERFUL MEN TO DO MY BIDDING!
SHOCK!
MOMMY, YOU'RE SCARING ME!
FLARE
WAIT, MARIELLA! THE GUILD WAS DESTROYED SO I CAN'T GO BACK TO WORK.
I KNOW YOU'RE UNEMPLOYED BUT... EVIL?
TRUST ME... EVERYTHING WILL BE OKAY.
BUT MY MOTHER SUFFERED DEEPLY BECAUSE SHE HAD AN ADVENTURER FOR A HUSBAND.

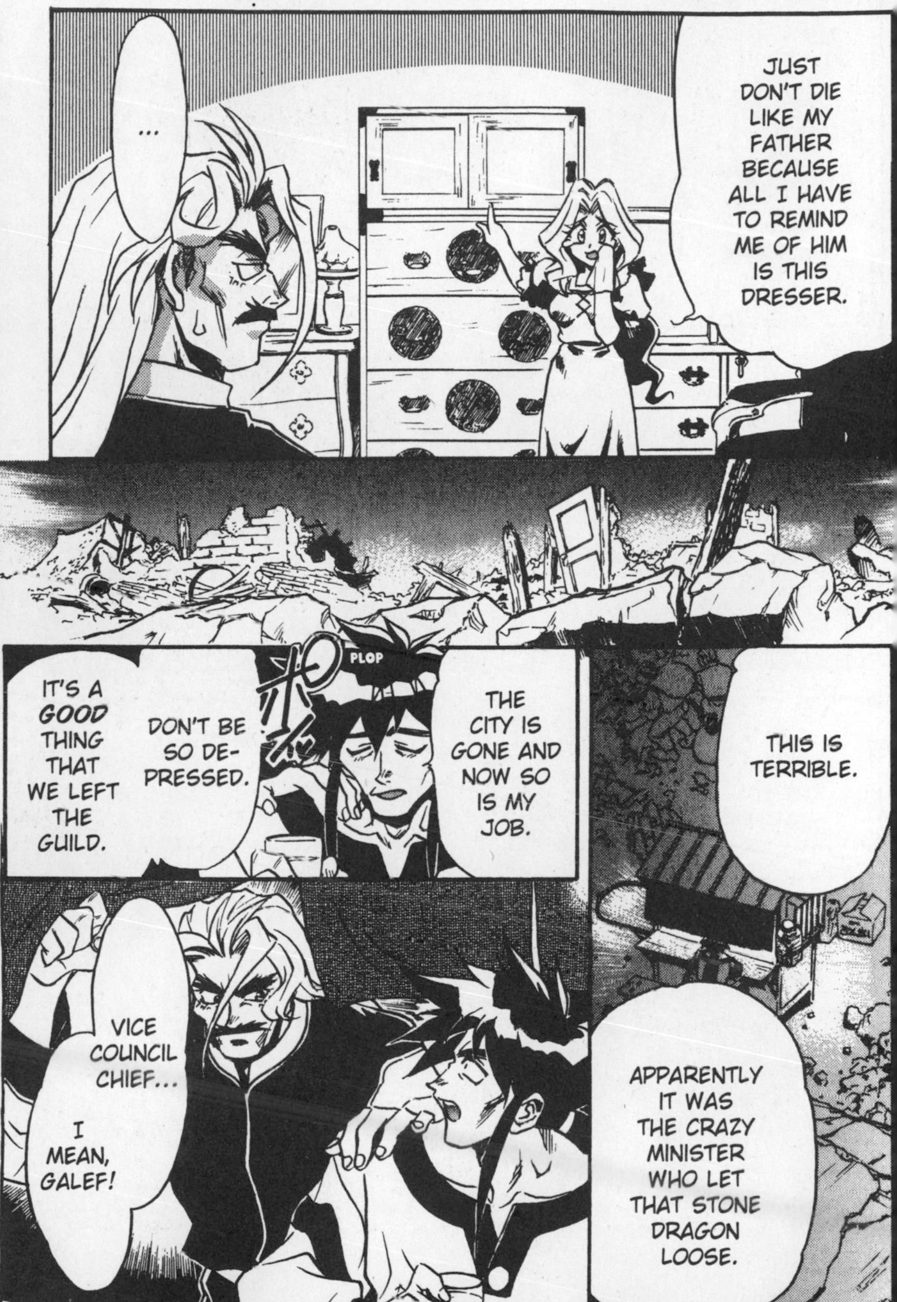
JUST DON'T DIE LIKE MY FATHER BECAUSE ALL I HAVE TO REMIND ME OF HIM IS THIS DRESSER.
...
THIS IS TERRIBLE.
APPARENTLY IT WAS THE CRAZY MINISTER WHO LET THAT STONE DRAGON LOOSE.
THE CITY IS GONE AND NOW SO IS MY JOB.
PLOP
DON'T BE SO DE-PRESSED.
IT'S A *GOOD* THING THAT WE LEFT THE GUILD.
VICE COUNCIL CHIEF...
I MEAN, GALEF!

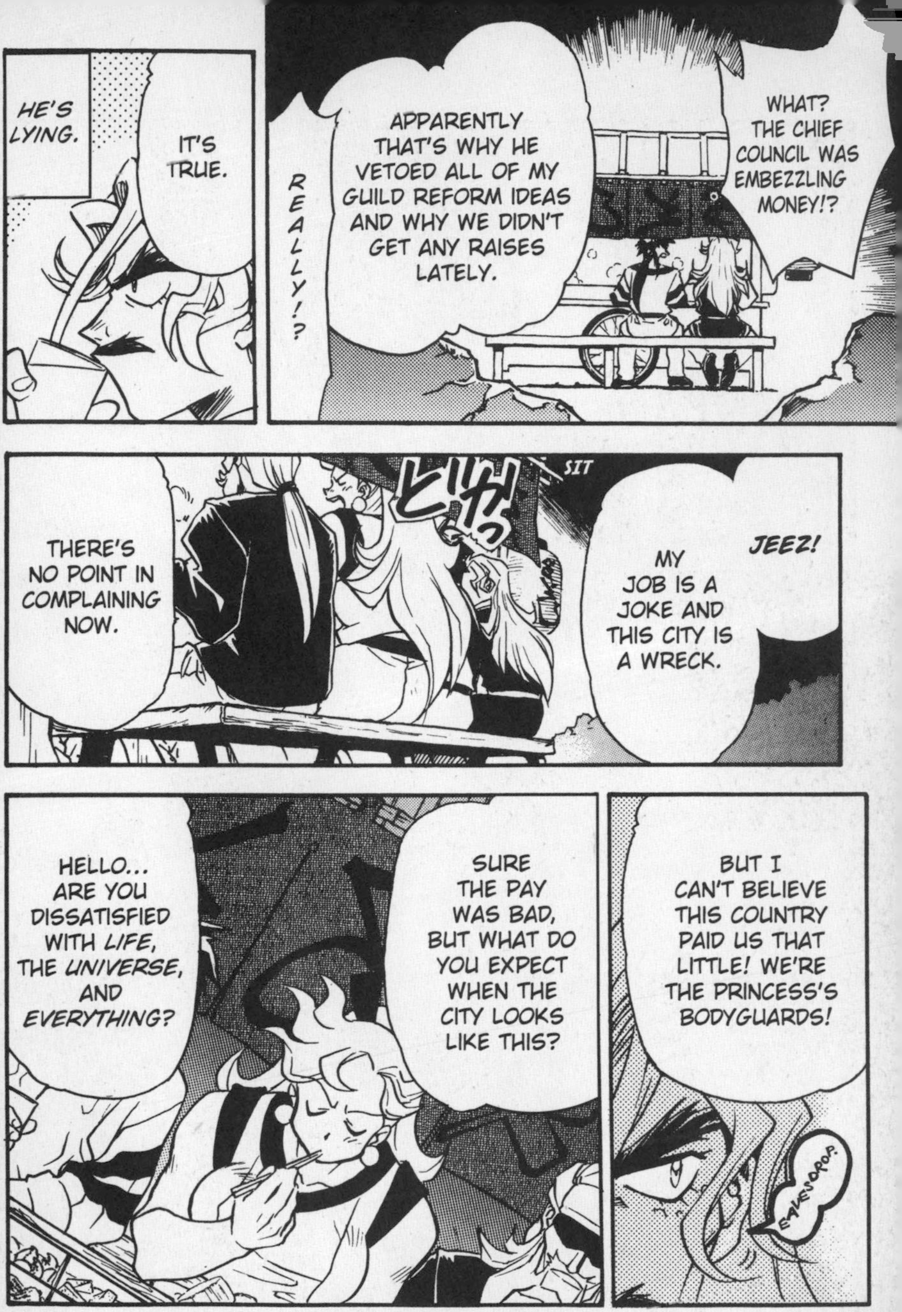
WHAT? THE CHIEF COUNCIL WAS EMBEZZLING MONEY!?
APPARENTLY THAT'S WHY HE VETOED ALL OF MY GUILD REFORM IDEAS AND WHY WE DIDN'T GET ANY RAISES LATELY.
REALLY!?
IT'S TRUE.
HE'S LYING.
JEEZ!
MY JOB IS A JOKE AND THIS CITY IS A WRECK.
SIT
THERE'S NO POINT IN COMPLAINING NOW.
BUT I CAN'T BELIEVE THIS COUNTRY PAID US THAT LITTLE! WE'RE THE PRINCESS'S BODYGUARDS!
EAVESDROP.
SURE THE PAY WAS BAD, BUT WHAT DO YOU EXPECT WHEN THE CITY LOOKS LIKE THIS?
HELLO... ARE YOU DISSATISFIED WITH *LIFE*, THE *UNIVERSE*, AND *EVERYTHING*?

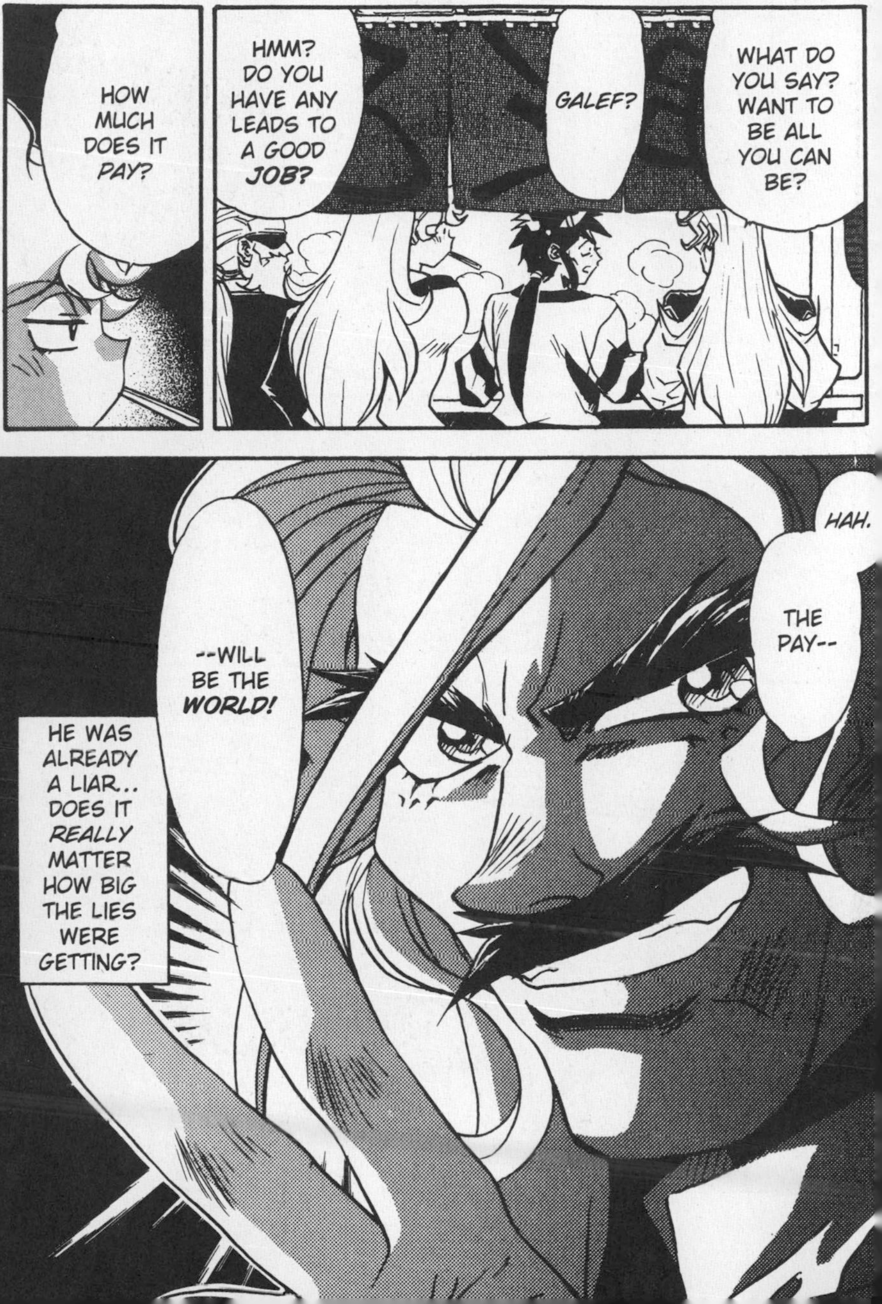
WHAT DO YOU SAY? WANT TO BE ALL YOU CAN BE?
GALEF?
HMM? DO YOU HAVE ANY LEADS TO A GOOD JOB?
HOW MUCH DOES IT PAY?
HAH.
THE PAY--
--WILL BE THE WORLD!
HE WAS ALREADY A LIAR... DOES IT REALLY MATTER HOW BIG THE LIES WERE GETTING?

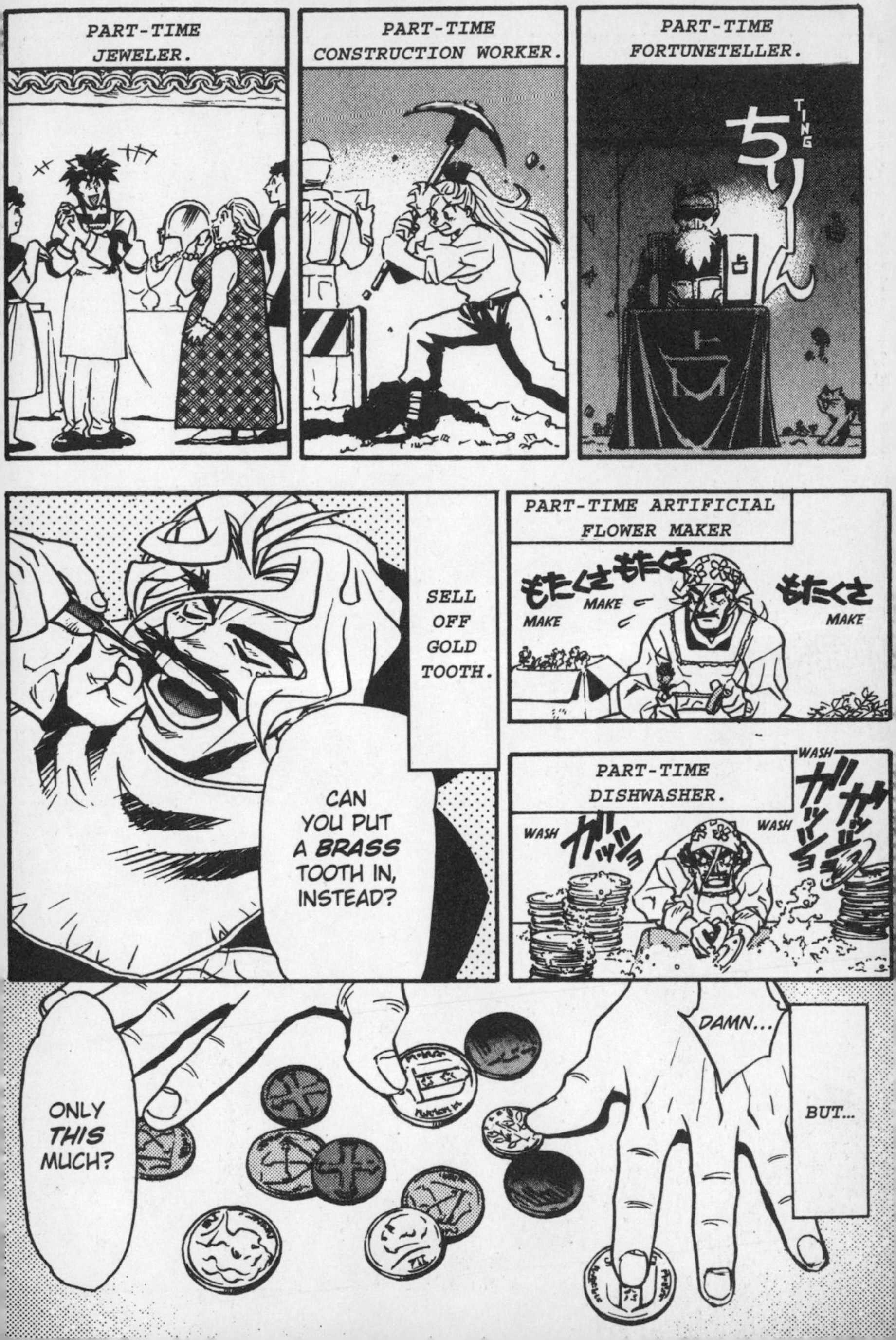

PART-TIME FORTUNETELLER.
ちりん
TING
PART-TIME CONSTRUCTION WORKER.
PART-TIME JEWELER.
PART-TIME ARTIFICIAL FLOWER MAKER
もたくさ
MAKE
もたくさ
MAKE
もたくさ
MAKE
PART-TIME DISHWASHER.
WASH
WASH
WASH
SELL OFF GOLD TOOTH.
CAN YOU PUT A *BRASS* TOOTH IN, INSTEAD?
DAMN...
BUT...
ONLY *THIS* MUCH?

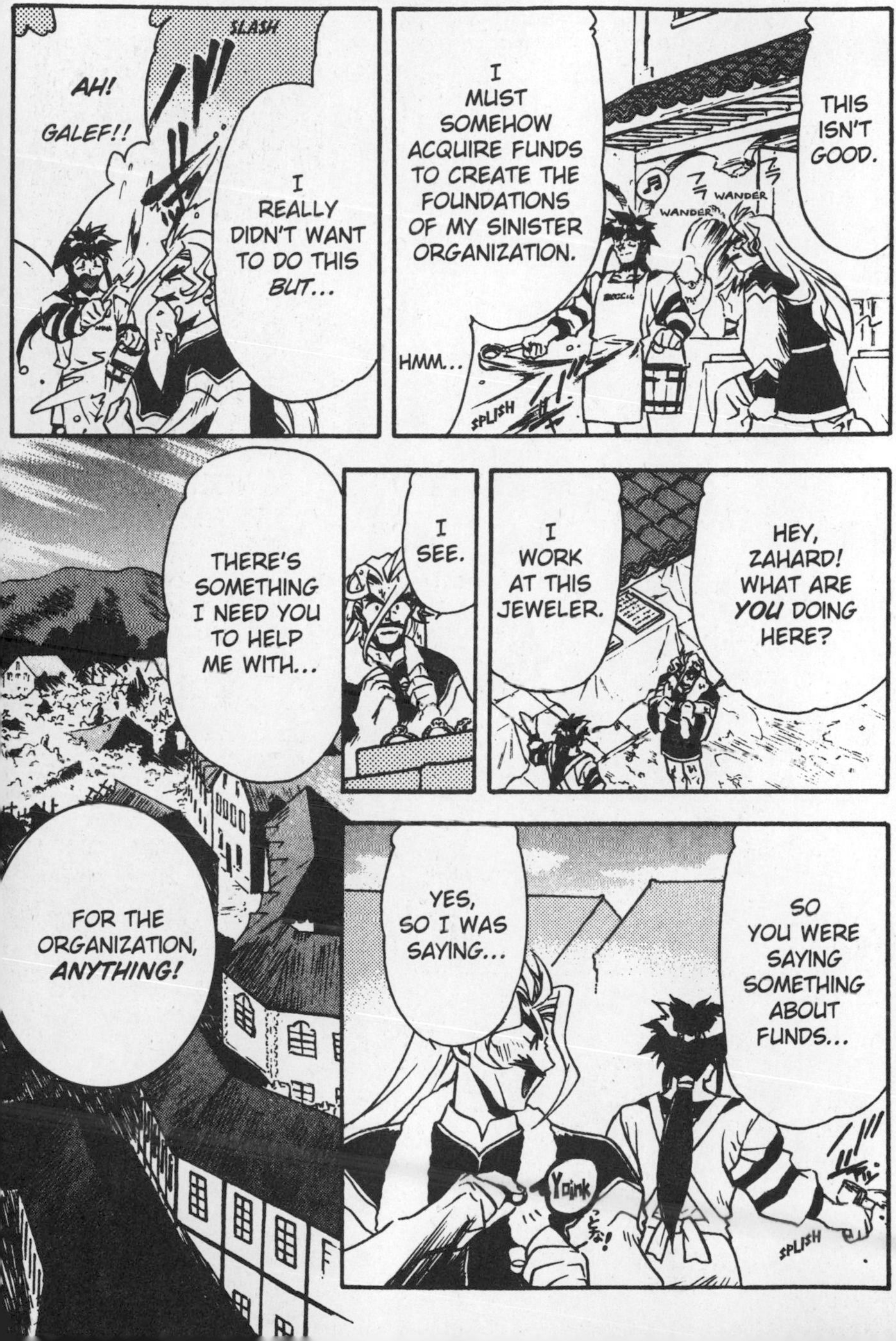

THIS ISN'T GOOD.
WANDER
WANDER
I MUST SOMEHOW ACQUIRE FUNDS TO CREATE THE FOUNDATIONS OF MY SINISTER ORGANIZATION.
HMM...
SPLISH
SLASH
I REALLY DIDN'T WANT TO DO THIS *BUT*...
AH!
GALEF!!
HEY, ZAHARD! WHAT ARE *YOU* DOING HERE?
I WORK AT THIS JEWELER.
I SEE.
SO YOU WERE SAYING SOMETHING ABOUT FUNDS...
YES, SO I WAS SAYING...
Yoink
SPLISH
THERE'S SOMETHING I NEED YOU TO HELP ME WITH...
FOR THE ORGANIZATION, *ANYTHING!*

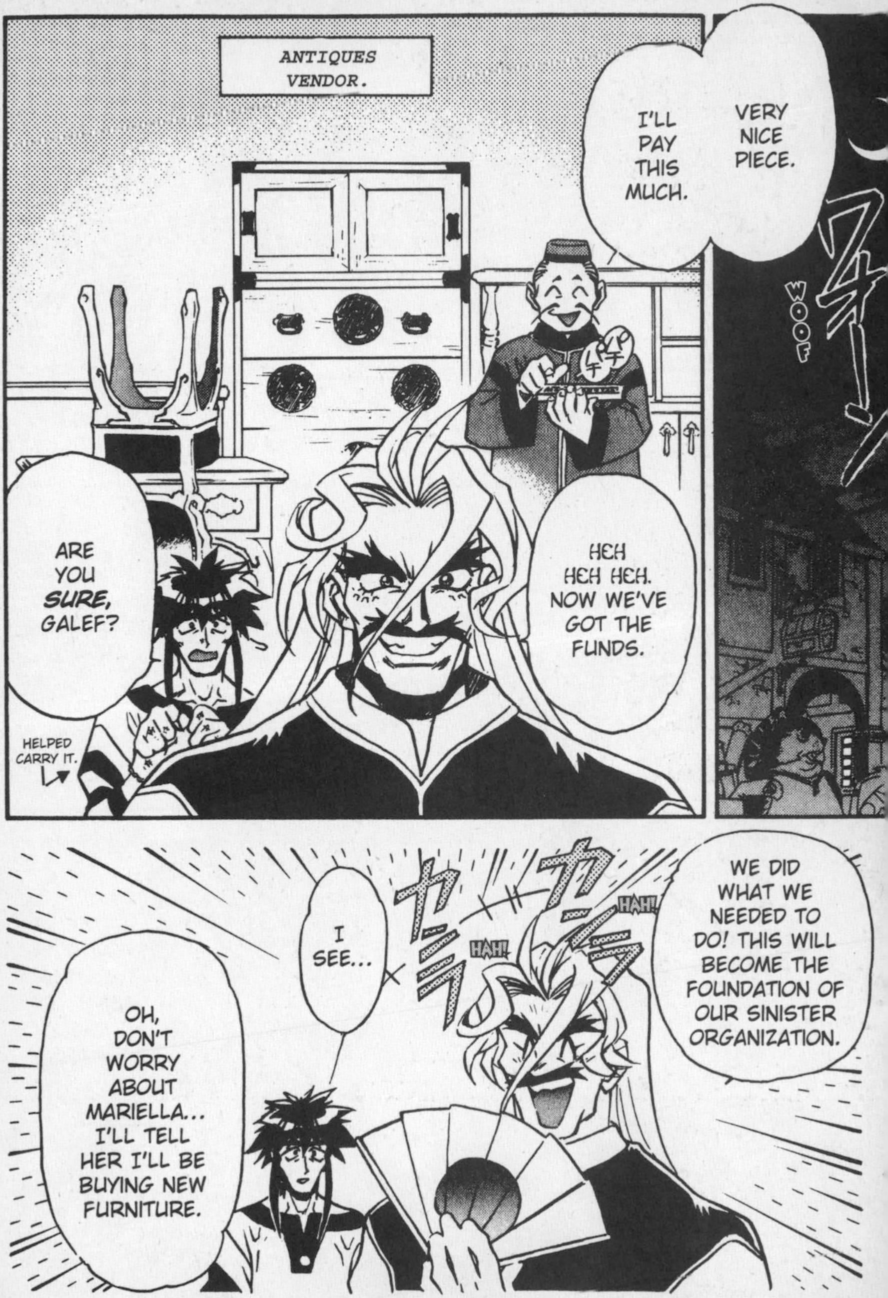
WOOF
VERY NICE PIECE.
I'LL PAY THIS MUCH.
ANTIQUES VENDOR.
HEH HEH HEH. NOW WE'VE GOT THE FUNDS.
ARE YOU **SURE,** GALEF?
HELPED CARRY IT.
WE DID WHAT WE NEEDED TO DO! THIS WILL BECOME THE FOUNDATION OF OUR SINISTER ORGANIZATION.
HAH!
HAH!
I SEE...
OH, DON'T WORRY ABOUT MARIELLA... I'LL TELL HER I'LL BE BUYING NEW FURNITURE.

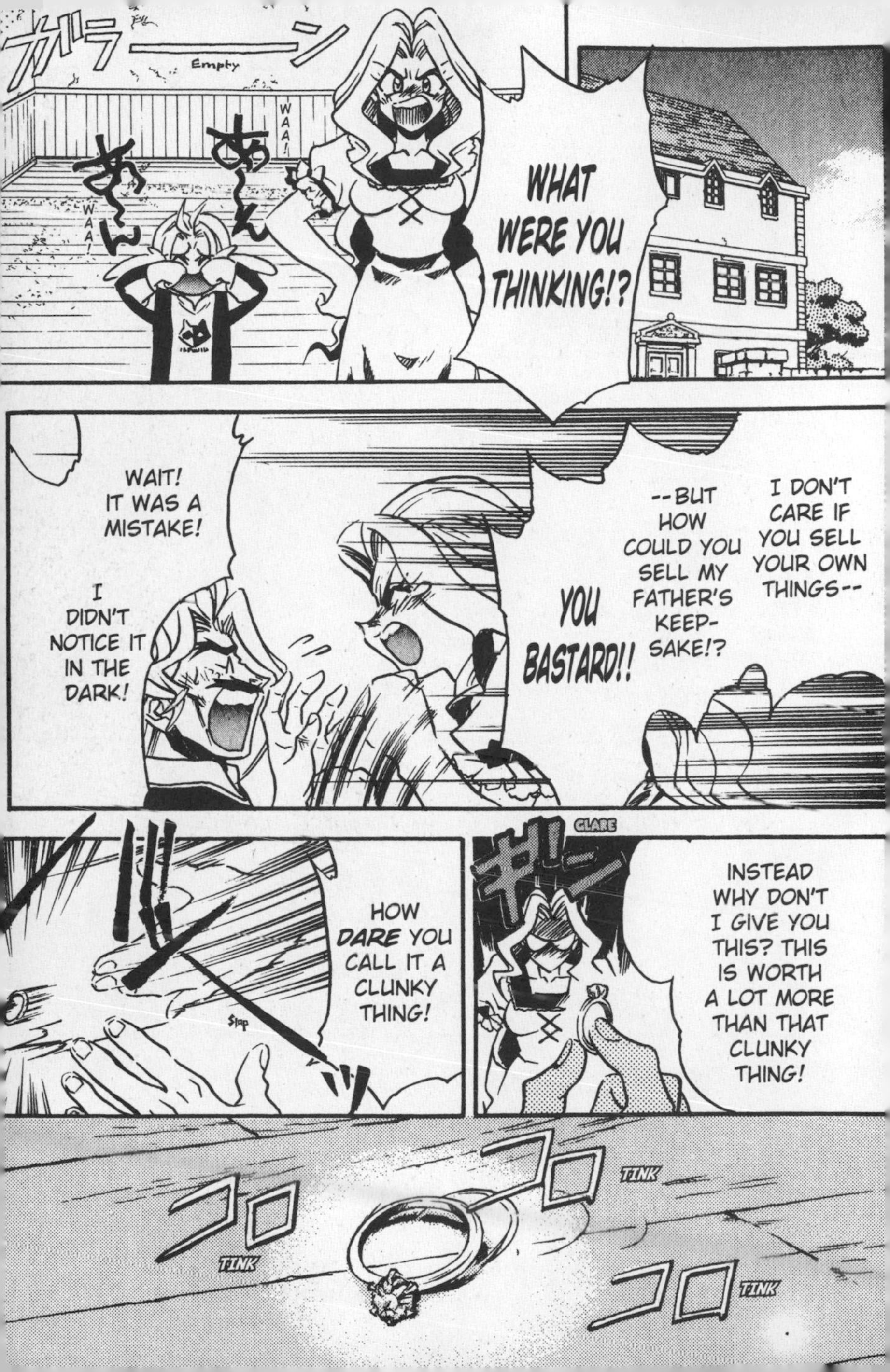

ガラーン
Empty
WAA!
あ～ん
WAA!
あ～ん
WHAT WERE YOU THINKING!?
I DON'T CARE IF YOU SELL YOUR OWN THINGS--
--BUT HOW COULD YOU SELL MY FATHER'S KEEP-SAKE!?
YOU BASTARD!!
WAIT! IT WAS A MISTAKE!
I DIDN'T NOTICE IT IN THE DARK!
GLARE
INSTEAD WHY DON'T I GIVE YOU THIS? THIS IS WORTH A LOT MORE THAN THAT CLUNKY THING!
HOW DARE YOU CALL IT A CLUNKY THING!
Slap
コロ
TINK
コロ
TINK
コロ
TINK

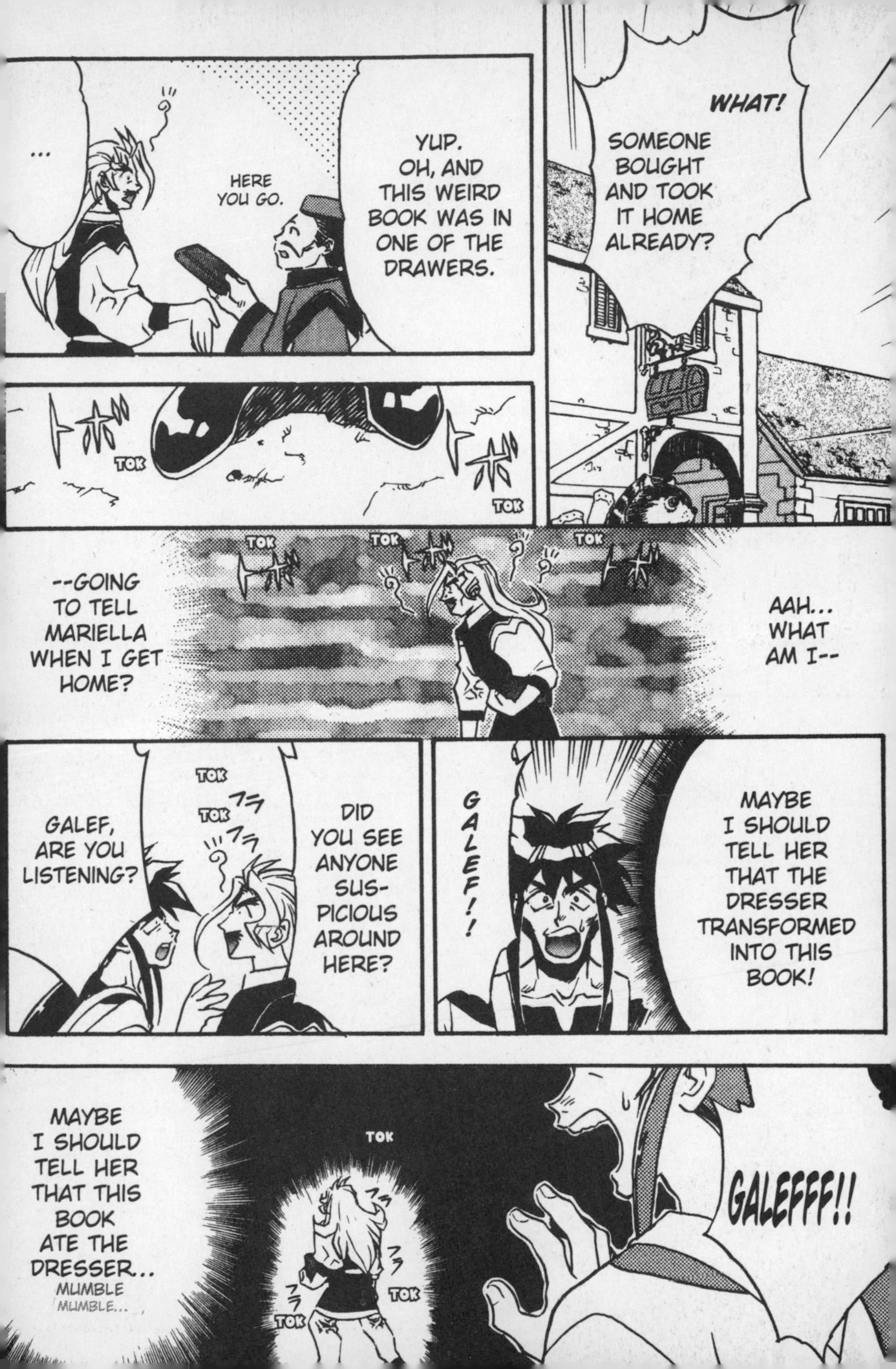

WHAT!
SOMEONE BOUGHT AND TOOK IT HOME ALREADY?
YUP. OH, AND THIS WEIRD BOOK WAS IN ONE OF THE DRAWERS.
HERE YOU GO.
...
TOK
TOK
TOK
TOK
TOK
AAH... WHAT AM I--
--GOING TO TELL MARIELLA WHEN I GET HOME?
MAYBE I SHOULD TELL HER THAT THE DRESSER TRANSFORMED INTO THIS BOOK!
GALEF!!
DID YOU SEE ANYONE SUS-PICIOUS AROUND HERE?
TOK
TOK
GALEF, ARE YOU LISTENING?
GALEFFF!!
TOK
TOK
TOK
MAYBE I SHOULD TELL HER THAT THIS BOOK ATE THE DRESSER...
MUMBLE MUMBLE...

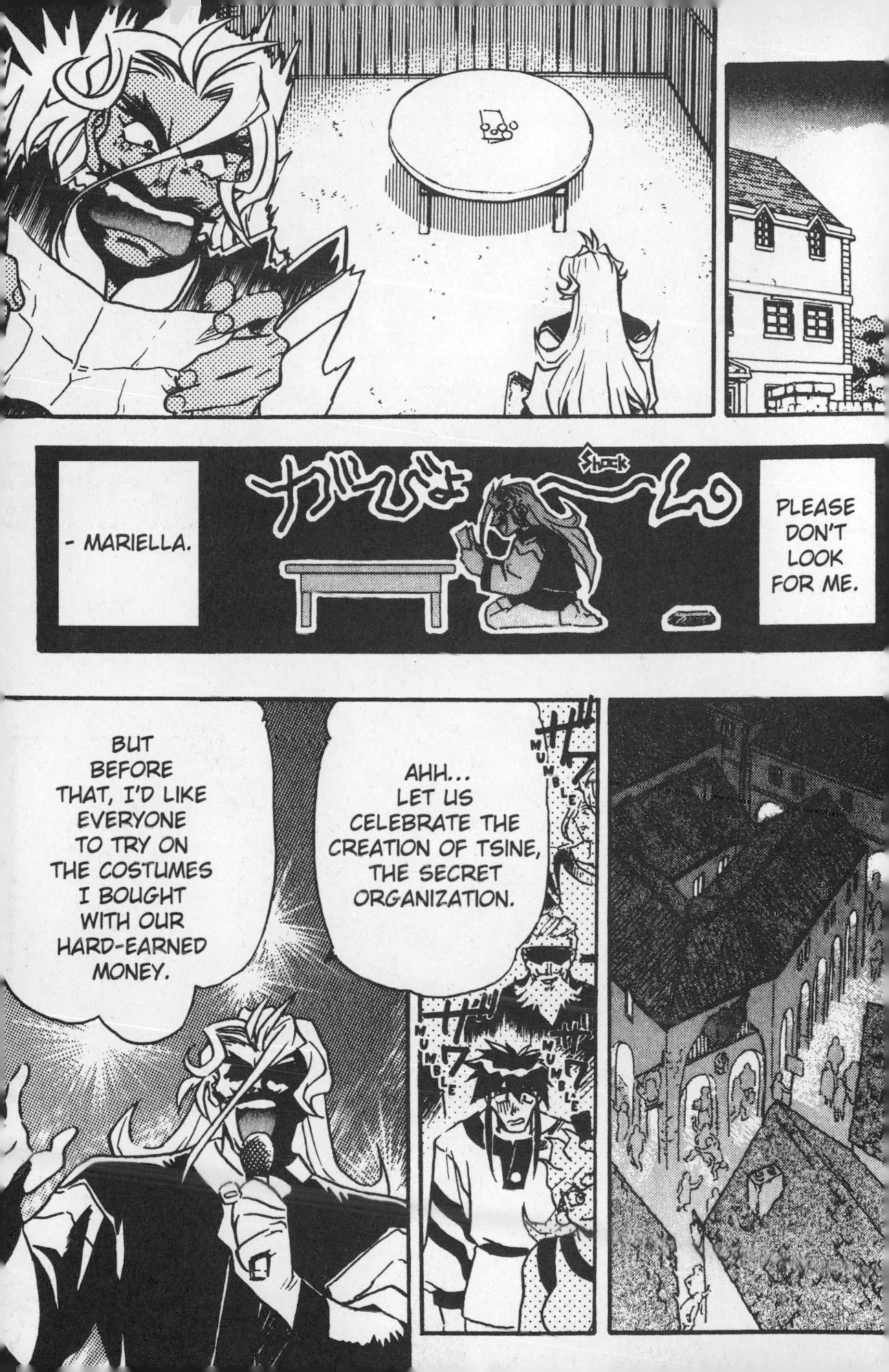
PLEASE DON'T LOOK FOR ME.
がびょーん
Shock
- MARIELLA.
MUMBLE
MUMBLE
MUMBLE
AHH... LET US CELEBRATE THE CREATION OF TSINE, THE SECRET ORGANIZATION.
BUT BEFORE THAT, I'D LIKE EVERYONE TO TRY ON THE COSTUMES I BOUGHT WITH OUR HARD-EARNED MONEY.

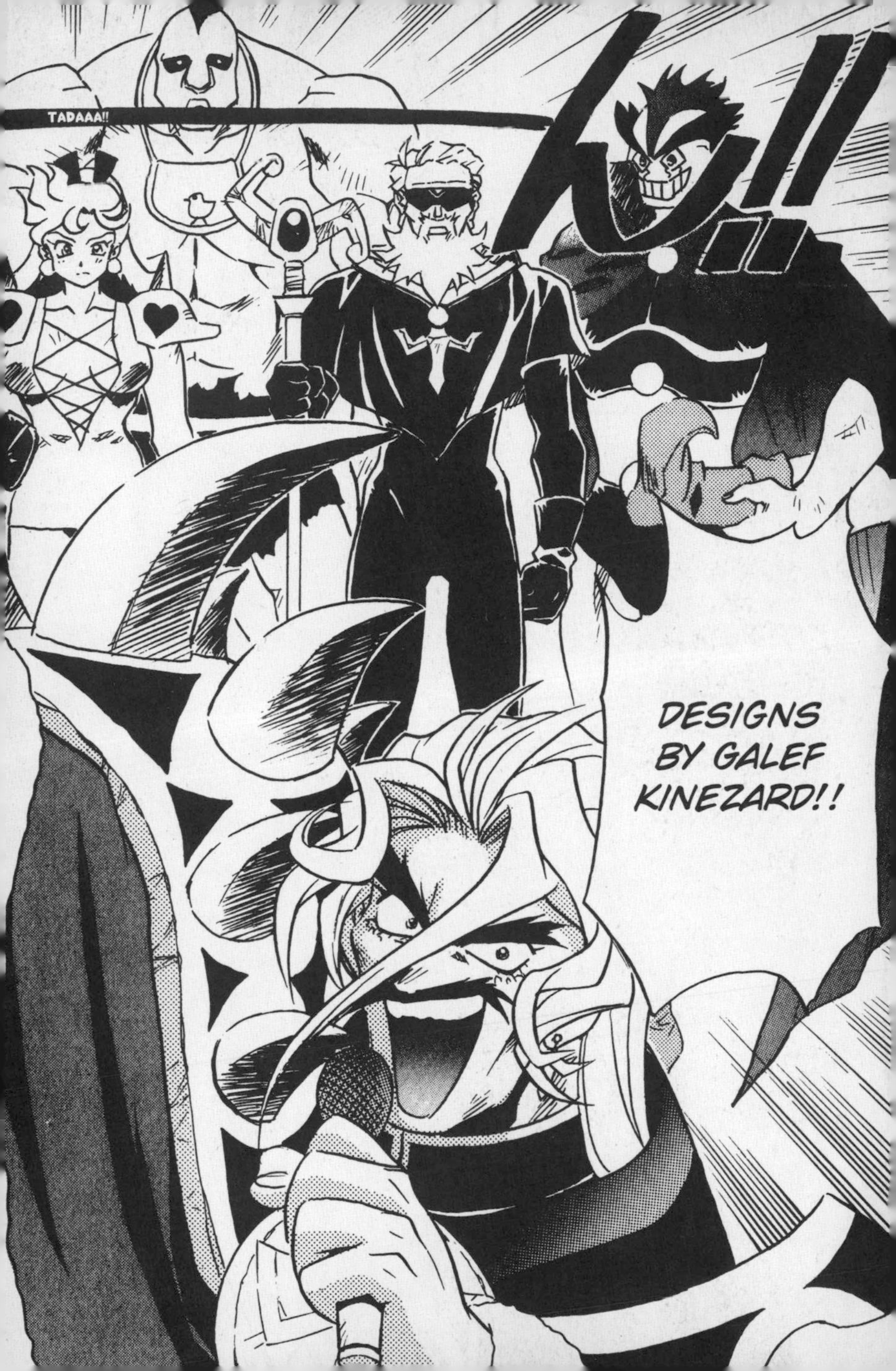
DESIGNS BY GALEF KINEZARD!!
TADAAA!!

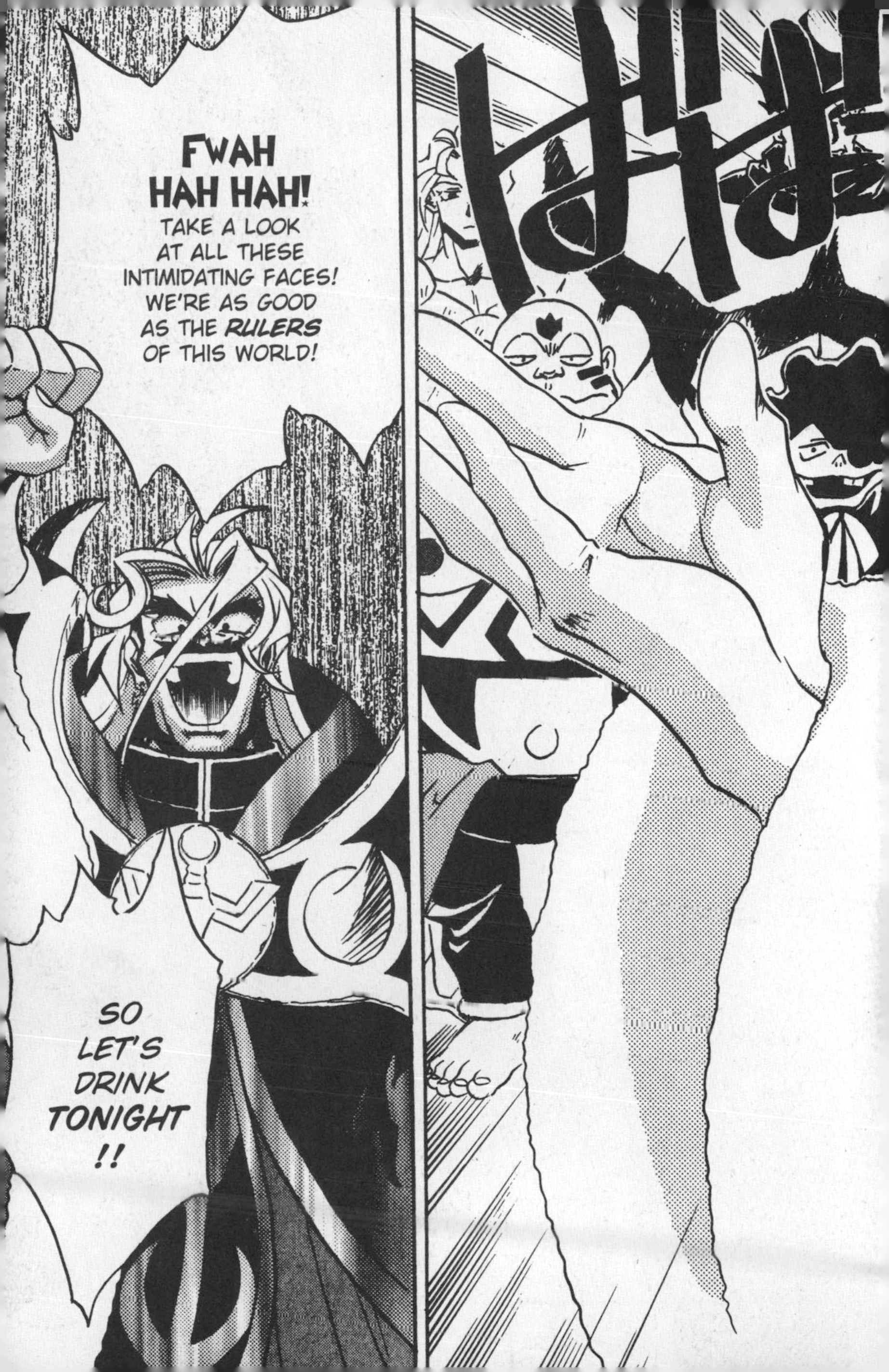
FWAH HAH HAH! TAKE A LOOK AT ALL THESE INTIMIDATING FACES! WE'RE AS GOOD AS THE *RULERS* OF THIS WORLD!
SO LET'S DRINK TONIGHT !!

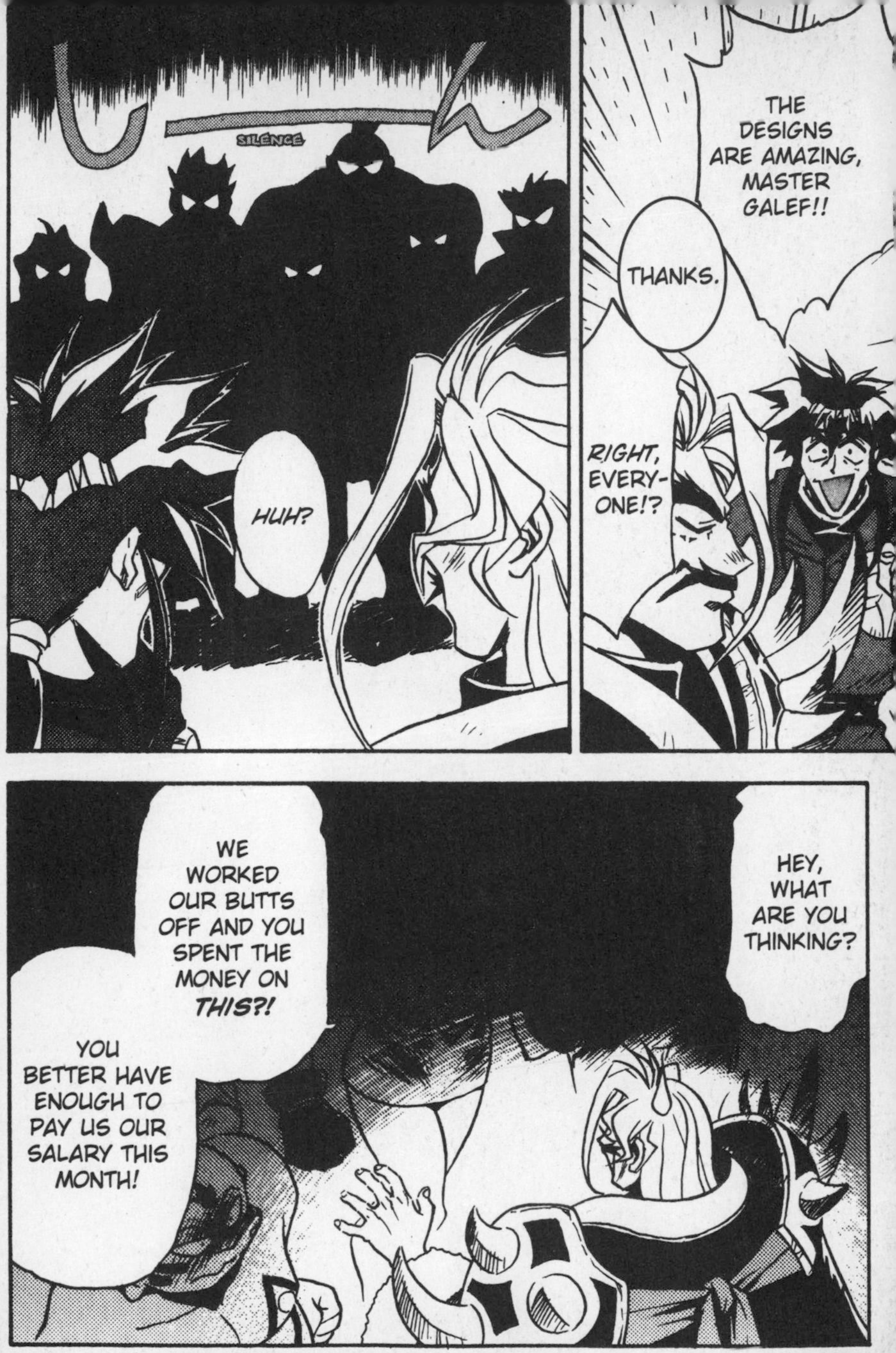
THE DESIGNS ARE AMAZING, MASTER GALEF!!
THANKS.
RIGHT, EVERY-ONE!?
SILENCE
HUH?
HEY, WHAT ARE YOU THINKING?
WE WORKED OUR BUTTS OFF AND YOU SPENT THE MONEY ON THIS?!
YOU BETTER HAVE ENOUGH TO PAY US OUR SALARY THIS MONTH!

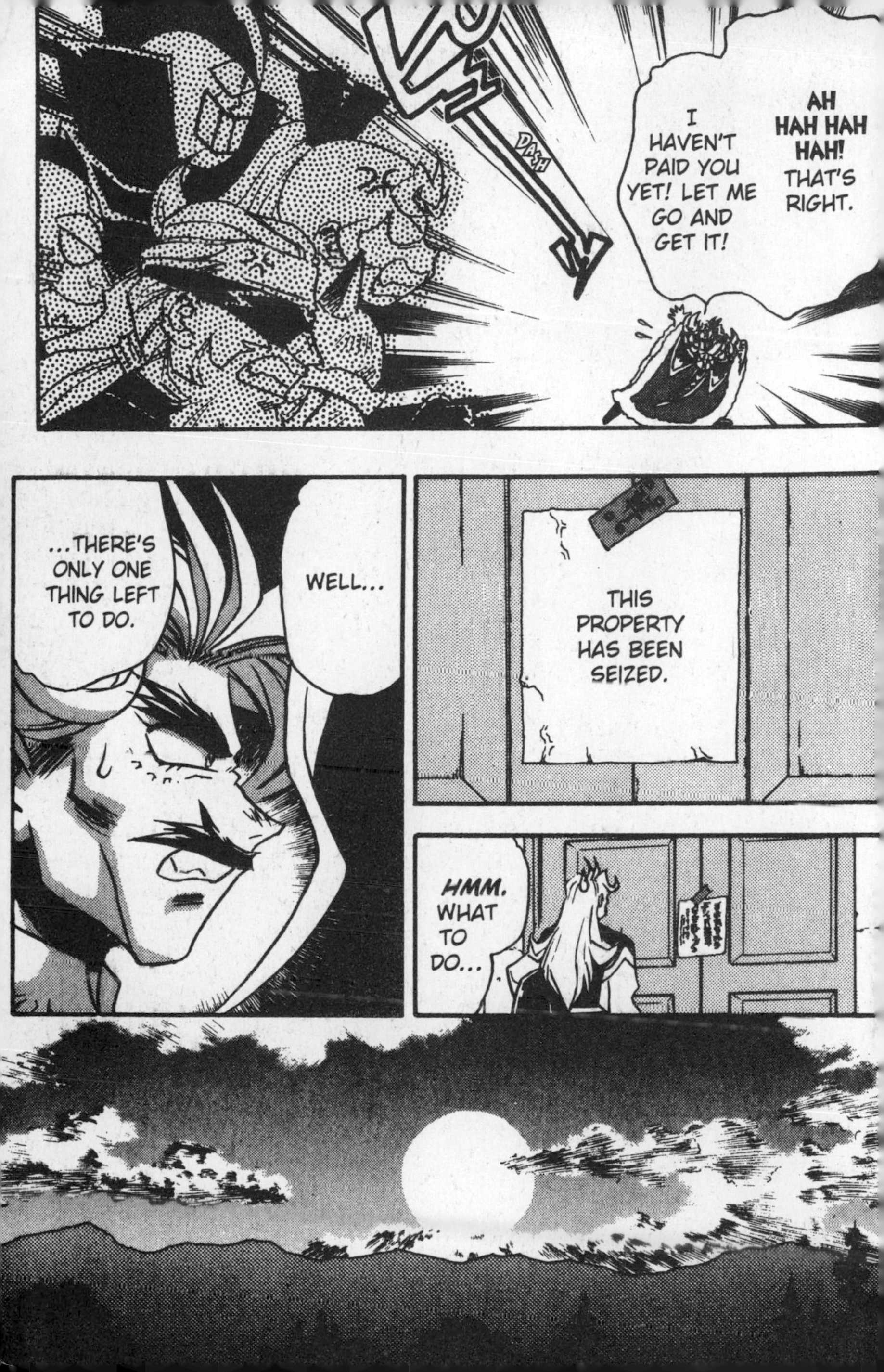
AH HAH HAH HAH! THAT'S RIGHT.
I HAVEN'T PAID YOU YET! LET ME GO AND GET IT!
DASH
THIS PROPERTY HAS BEEN SEIZED.
HMM. WHAT TO DO...
WELL...
...THERE'S ONLY ONE THING LEFT TO DO.

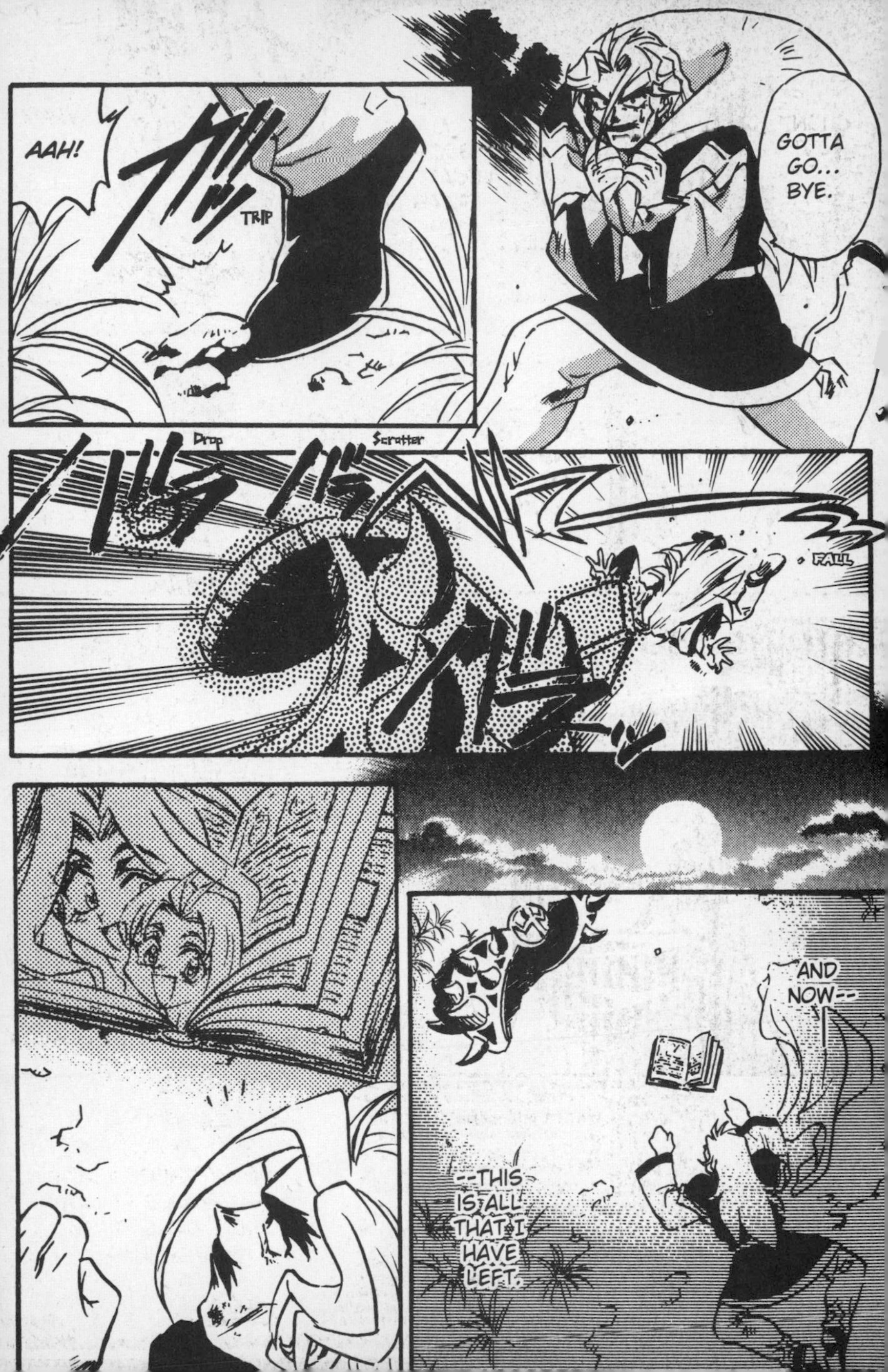
GOTTA GO... BYE.
AAH!
TRIP
FALL
Scratter
Drop
AND NOW--
--THIS IS ALL THAT I HAVE LEFT.

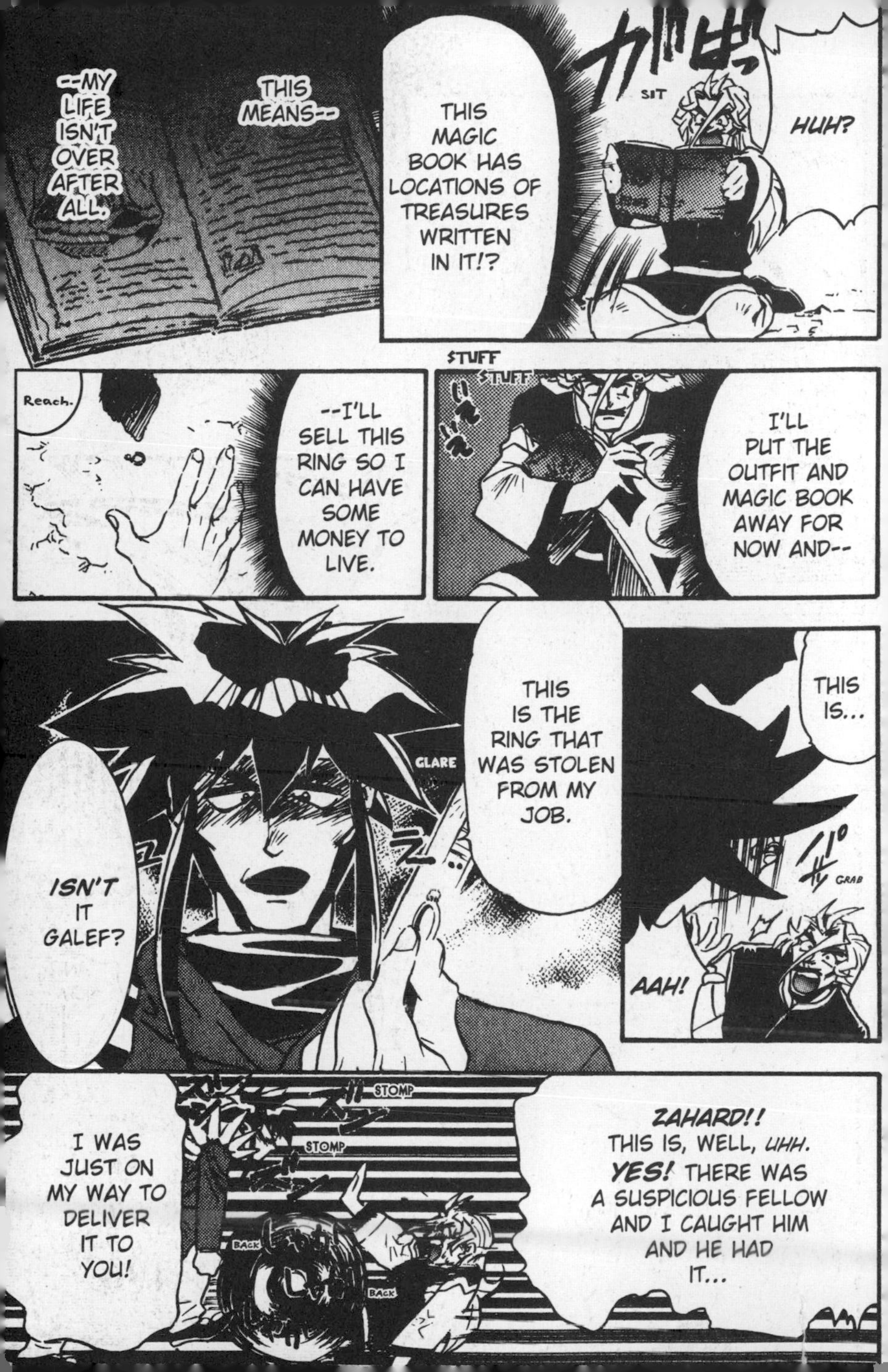
HUH?
SIT
THIS MAGIC BOOK HAS LOCATIONS OF TREASURES WRITTEN IN IT!?
THIS MEANS--
--MY LIFE ISN'T OVER AFTER ALL.
I'LL PUT THE OUTFIT AND MAGIC BOOK AWAY FOR NOW AND--
STUFF
STUFF
--I'LL SELL THIS RING SO I CAN HAVE SOME MONEY TO LIVE.
Reach.
GRAB
AAH!
THIS IS...
THIS IS THE RING THAT WAS STOLEN FROM MY JOB.
GLARE
ISN'T IT GALEF?
ZAHARD!! THIS IS, WELL, UHH. YES! THERE WAS A SUSPICIOUS FELLOW AND I CAUGHT HIM AND HE HAD IT...
STOMP
STOMP
BACK
BACK
I WAS JUST ON MY WAY TO DELIVER IT TO YOU!

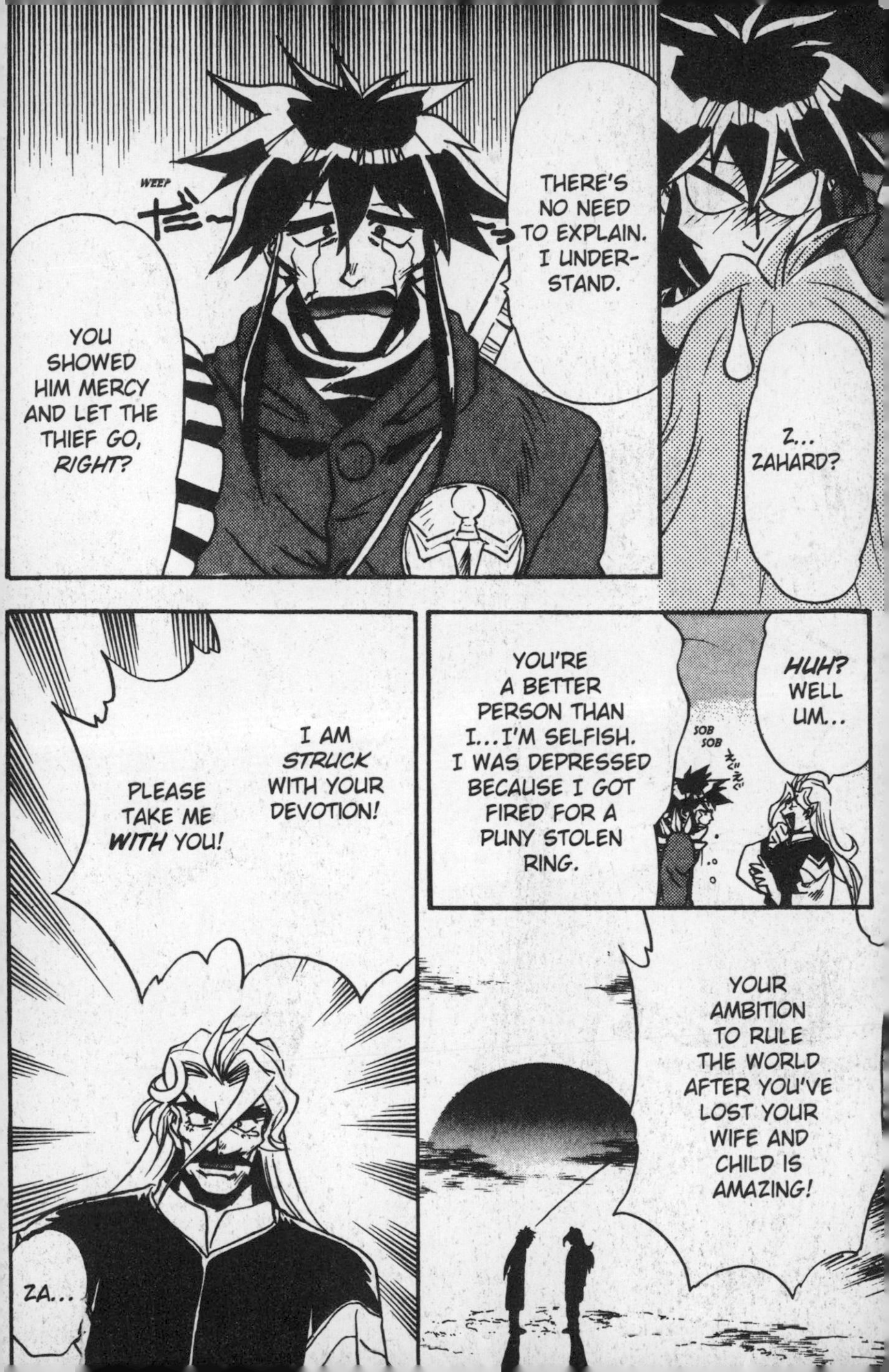
Z... ZAHARD?
THERE'S NO NEED TO EXPLAIN. I UNDERSTAND.
WEEP
YOU SHOWED HIM MERCY AND LET THE THIEF GO, *RIGHT?*
HUH? WELL UM...
SOB SOB
YOU'RE A BETTER PERSON THAN I...I'M SELFISH. I WAS DEPRESSED BECAUSE I GOT FIRED FOR A PUNY STOLEN RING.
YOUR AMBITION TO RULE THE WORLD AFTER YOU'VE LOST YOUR WIFE AND CHILD IS AMAZING!
I AM *STRUCK* WITH YOUR DEVOTION!
PLEASE TAKE ME *WITH* YOU!
ZA...

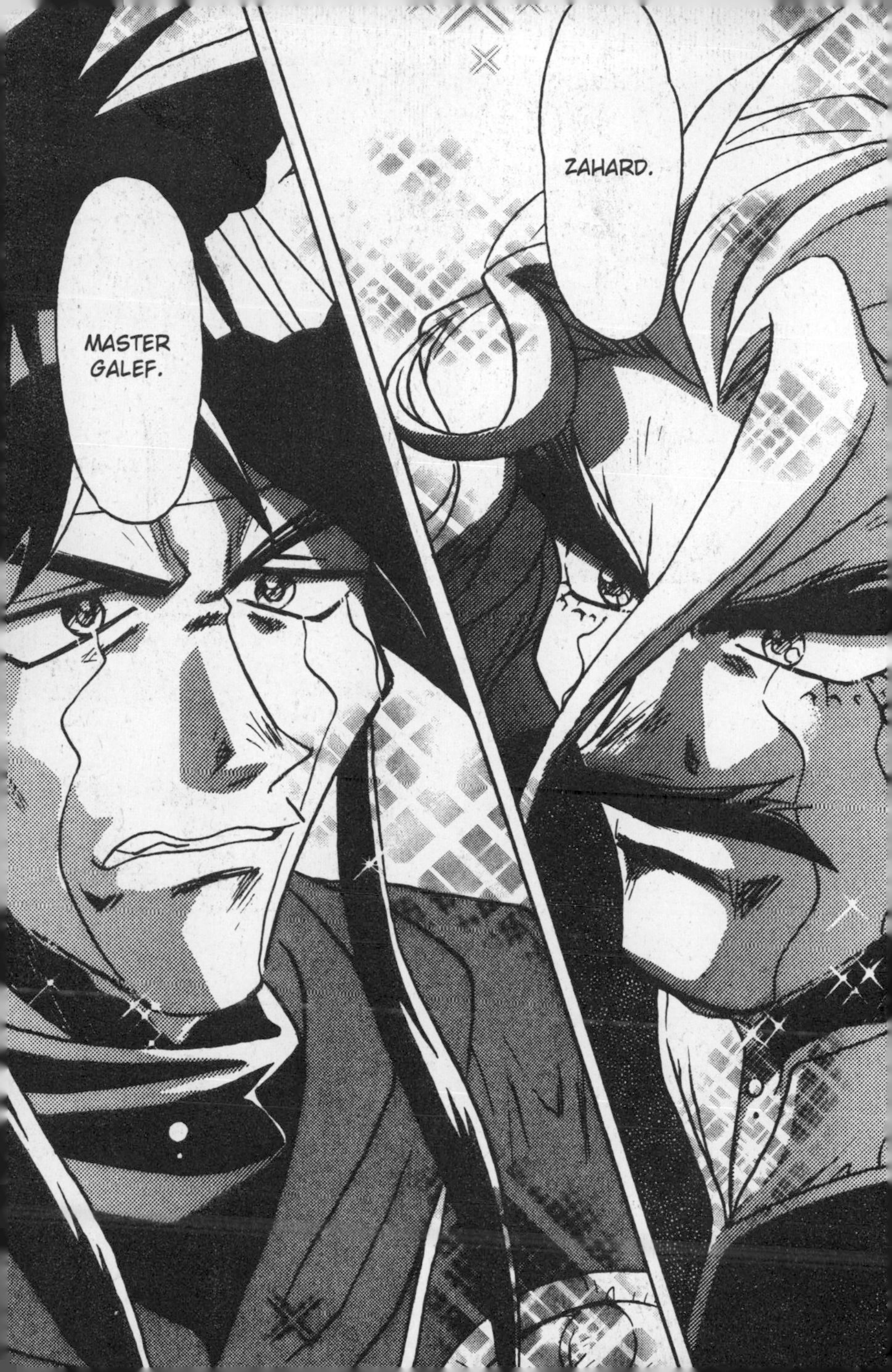
ZAHARD.
MASTER GALEF.

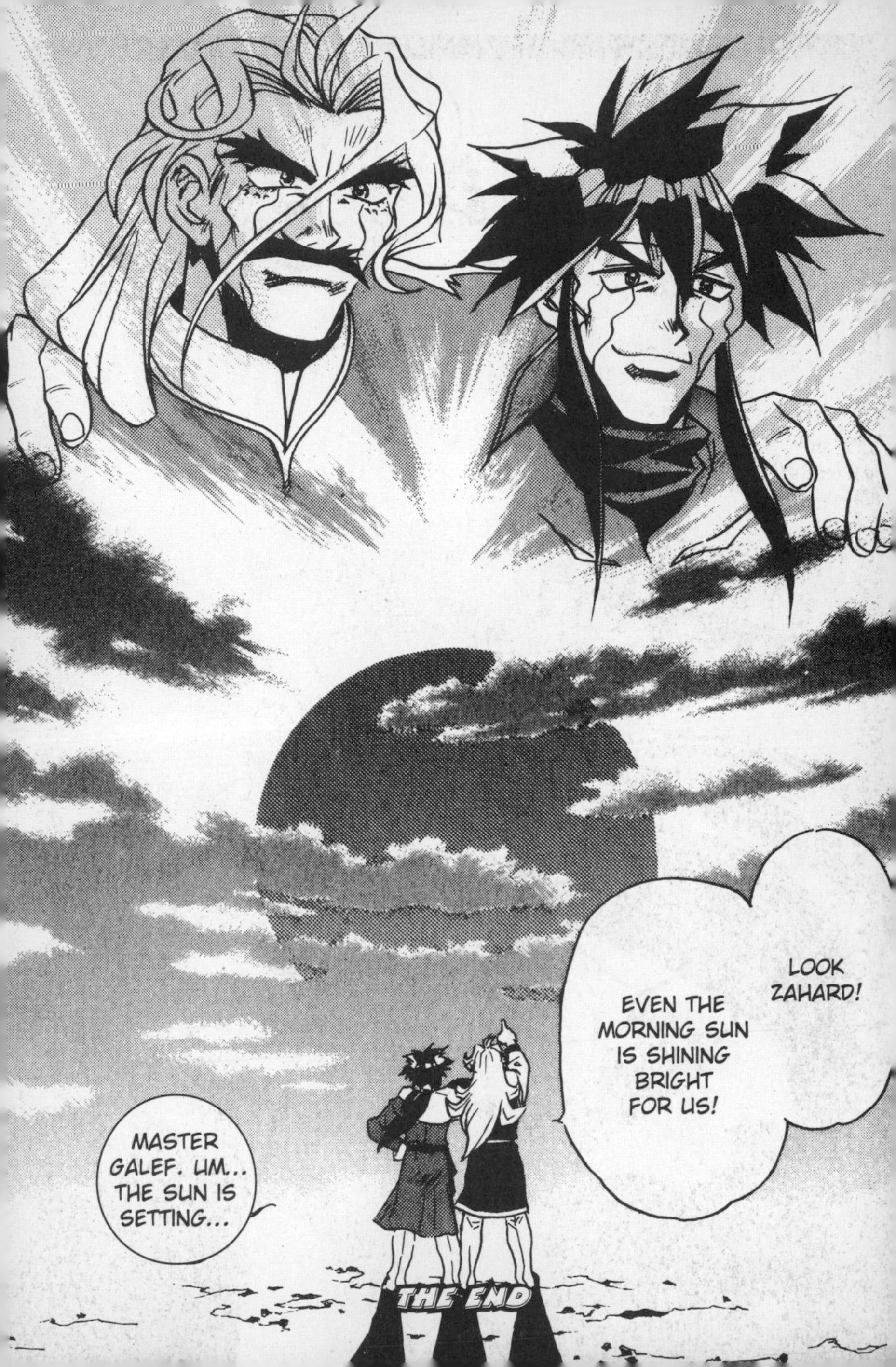
LOOK ZAHARD!
EVEN THE MORNING SUN IS SHINING BRIGHT FOR US!
MASTER GALEF. UM... THE SUN IS SETTING...
THE END

Creator Biographies

Hajime Kanzaka was born in Hyogo-ken Perfecture. He debuted doing doujunshi (fan-based manga) and is now an explosively popular manga and anime creator. *Slayers* began as a series of novels written by Mr. Kanzaka, and spawned a number of popular animated movies, television series, and role playing video games. He also created *Lost Universe*.

Hajime Kanzaka

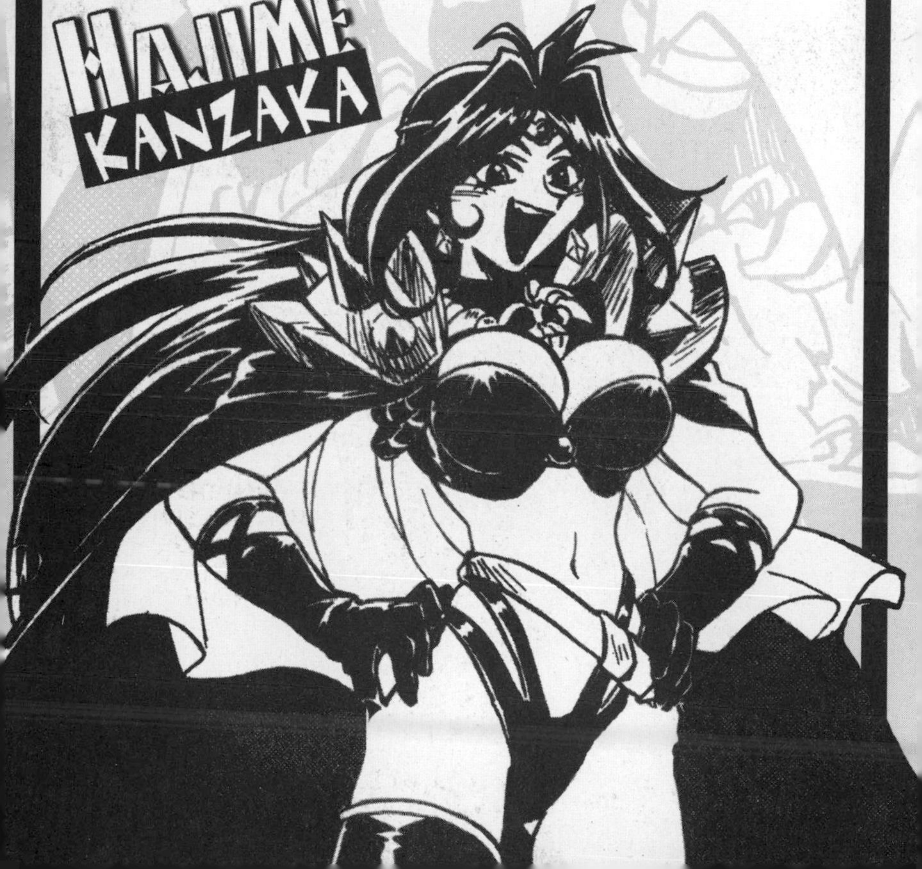

SHOKO YOSHINAKA

Shoko Yoshinaka is the artist of *Slayers Super-Explosive Demon Story* and *Lost Universe*. She was also the lead character designer for the *Lost Universe* anime.

"Everybody should have at least one person who they want to be like. This kind of person is valuable because he/she will serve as an example of how not to behave. But you'd better be careful not to have too much hate for them, because you become a person you don't want to be. We human beings are creatures who must love ourselves more than anything else."

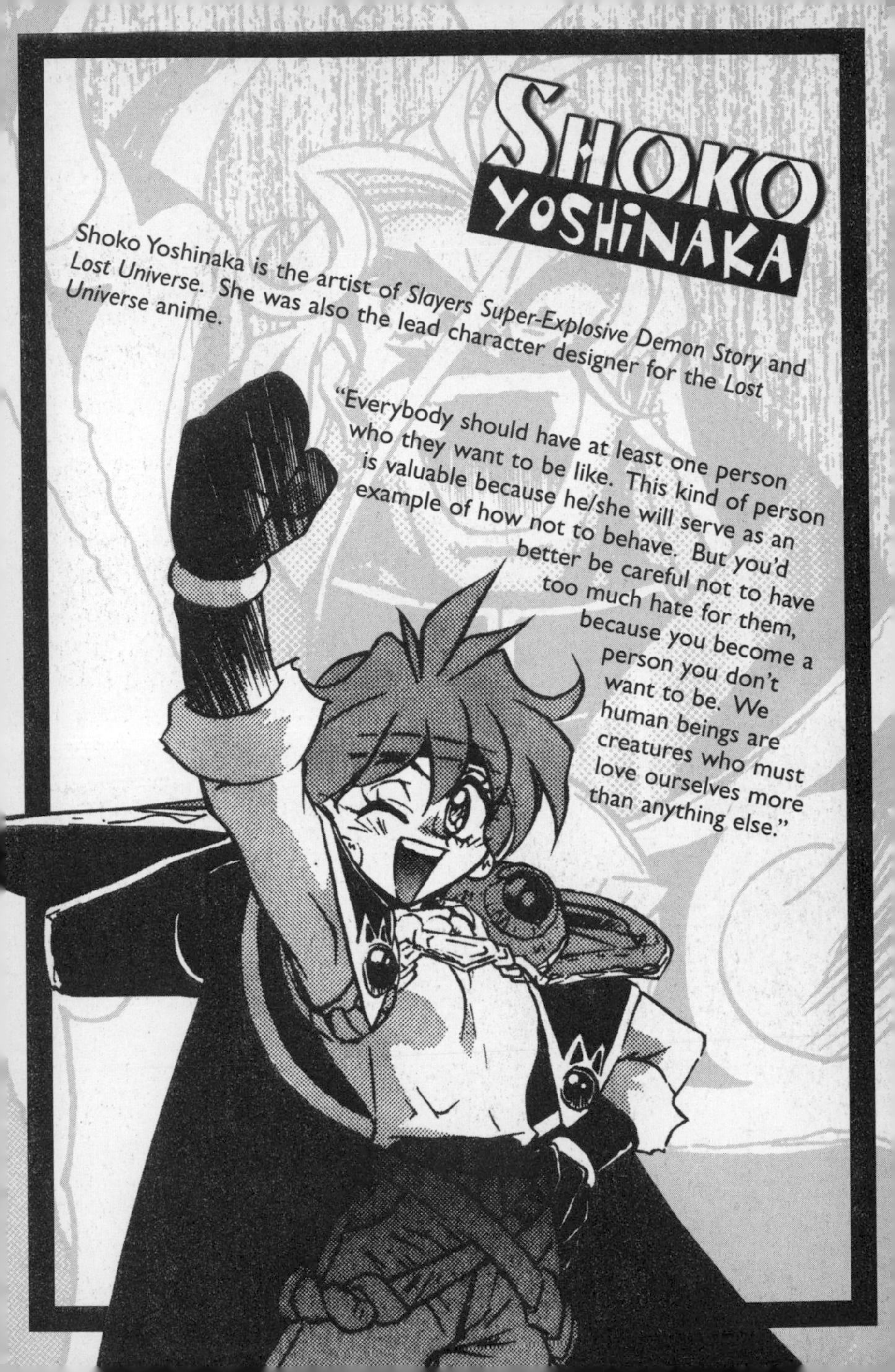

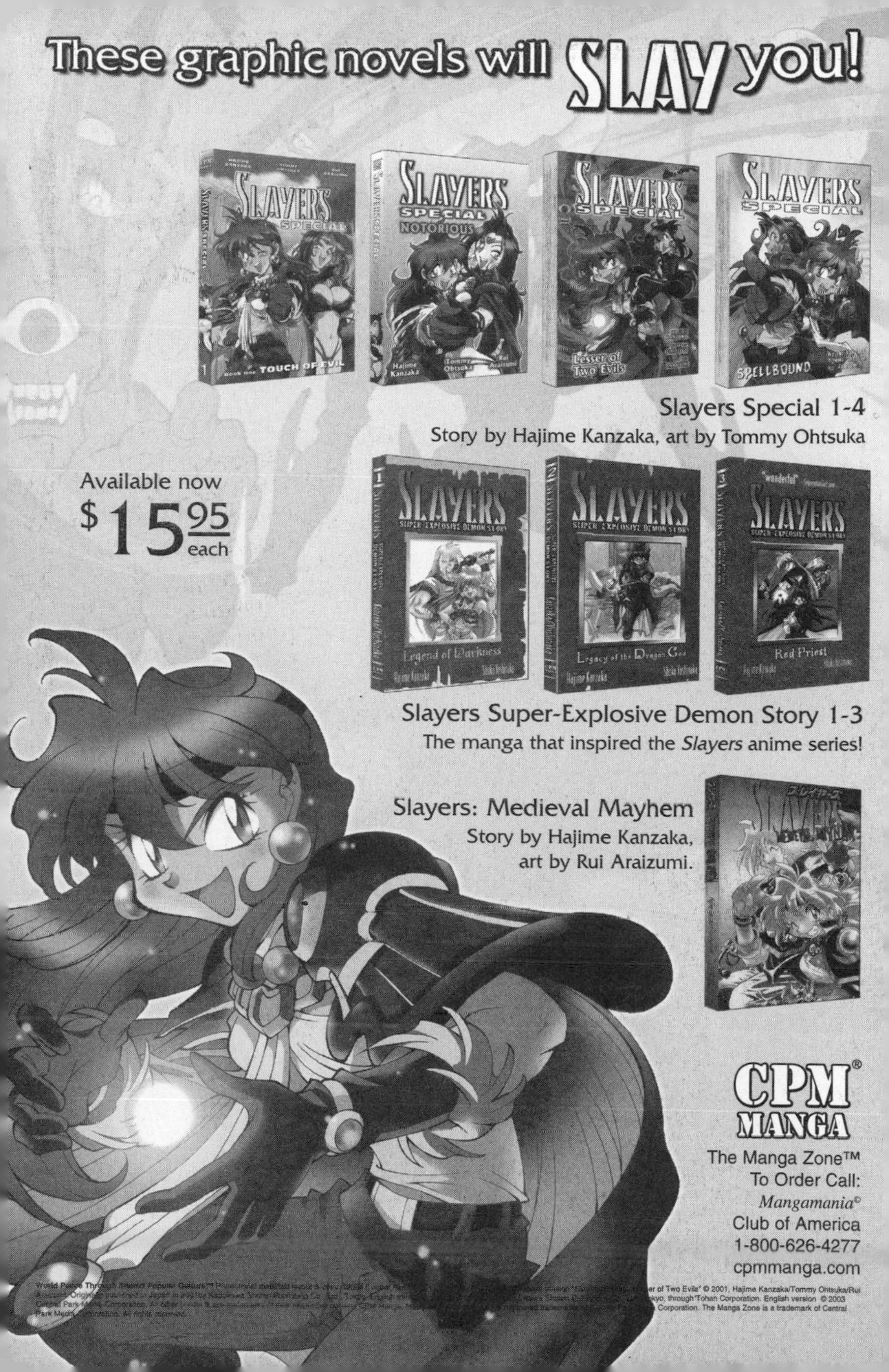

These graphic novels will SLAY you!
Slayers Special 1-4
Story by Hajime Kanzaka, art by Tommy Ohtsuka
Available now
$15.95 each
Slayers Super-Explosive Demon Story 1-3
The manga that inspired the Slayers anime series!
Slayers: Medieval Mayhem
Story by Hajime Kanzaka,
art by Rui Araizumi.
CPM® MANGA
The Manga Zone™
To Order Call:
Mangamania©
Club of America
1-800-626-4277
cpmmanga.com

You've never seen *The Slayers* anime? Then take an

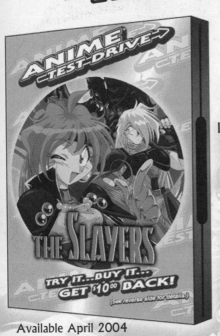

Try it...Buy it...
GET $10.00 BACK!

The Slayers Anime Test Drive DVD includes the first 2 episodes + over 45 minutes of cool anime trailers!

If you buy the corresponding box set at a great low price, you'll get $10.00 back!

(Mail-in rebate coupon included with every *Anime Test Drive DVD*)

$7.99 DVD

Available April 2004

"More anime for your buck"
-*Wizard Magazine*

CENTRAL PARK MEDIA®
The Anime Zone™
To Order Call:
Mangamania® Club of America
1-800-626-4277
centralparkmedia.com
software-sculptors.com

SOFTWARE SCULPTORS®

Box set includes episodes 1-26 of the original *Slayers* series!

4-disc set
$89.99

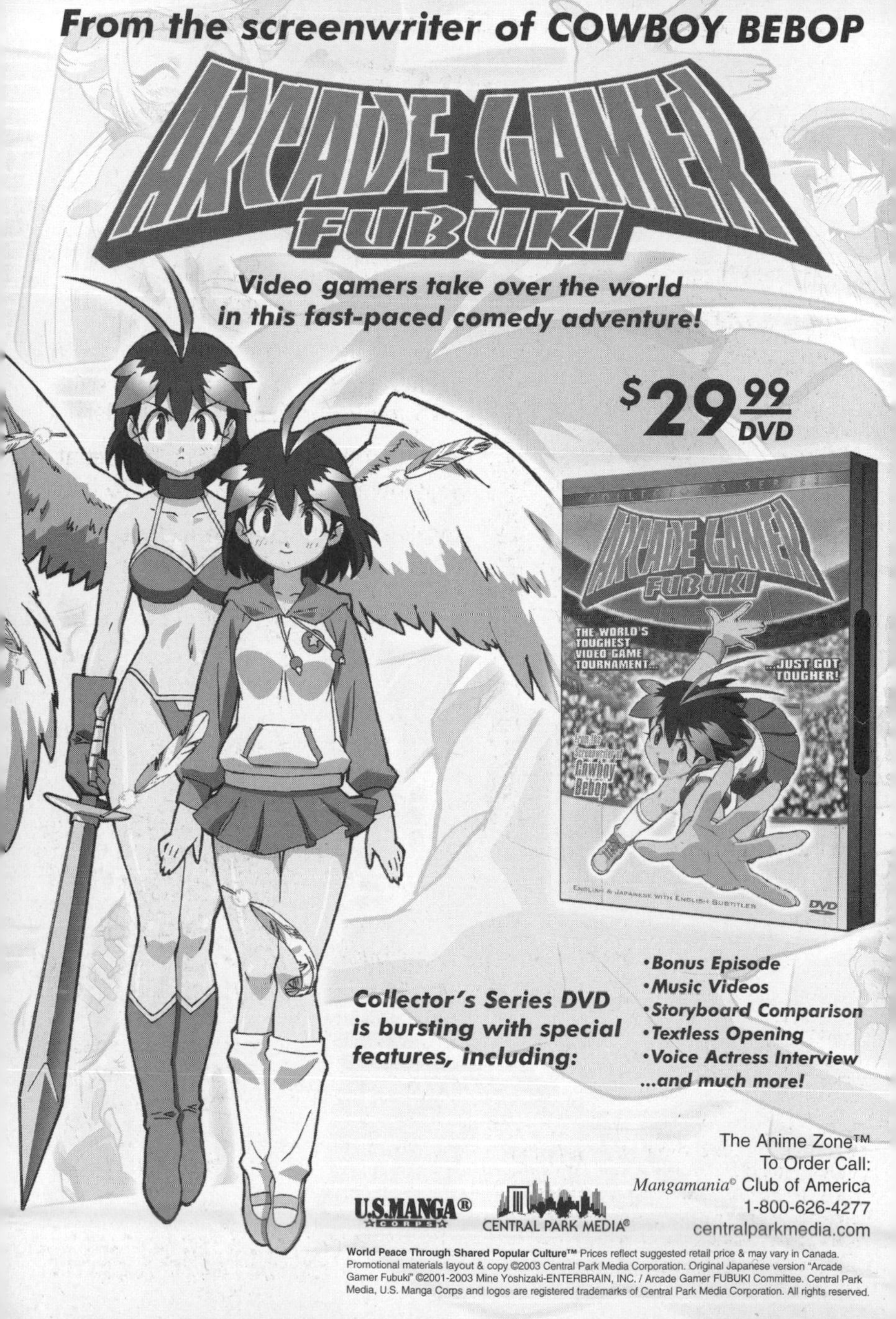
From the screenwriter of COWBOY BEBOP
ARCADE GAMER FUBUKI
Video gamers take over the world
in this fast-paced comedy adventure!
$29.99 DVD
ARCADE GAMER FUBUKI
THE WORLD'S TOUGHEST VIDEO GAME TOURNAMENT...
...JUST GOT TOUGHER!
From the Screenwriter of Cowboy Bebop
ENGLISH & JAPANESE WITH ENGLISH SUBTITLES
DVD
Collector's Series DVD
is bursting with special
features, including:
•Bonus Episode
•Music Videos
•Storyboard Comparison
•Textless Opening
•Voice Actress Interview
...and much more!
The Anime Zone™
To Order Call:
Mangamania© Club of America
1-800-626-4277
centralparkmedia.com
U.S.MANGA® CORPS
CENTRAL PARK MEDIA®
World Peace Through Shared Popular Culture™ Prices reflect suggested retail price & may vary in Canada.
Promotional materials layout & copy ©2003 Central Park Media Corporation. Original Japanese version "Arcade Gamer Fubuki" ©2001-2003 Mine Yoshizaki-ENTERBRAIN, INC. / Arcade Gamer FUBUKI Committee. Central Park Media, U.S. Manga Corps and logos are registered trademarks of Central Park Media Corporation. All rights reserved.

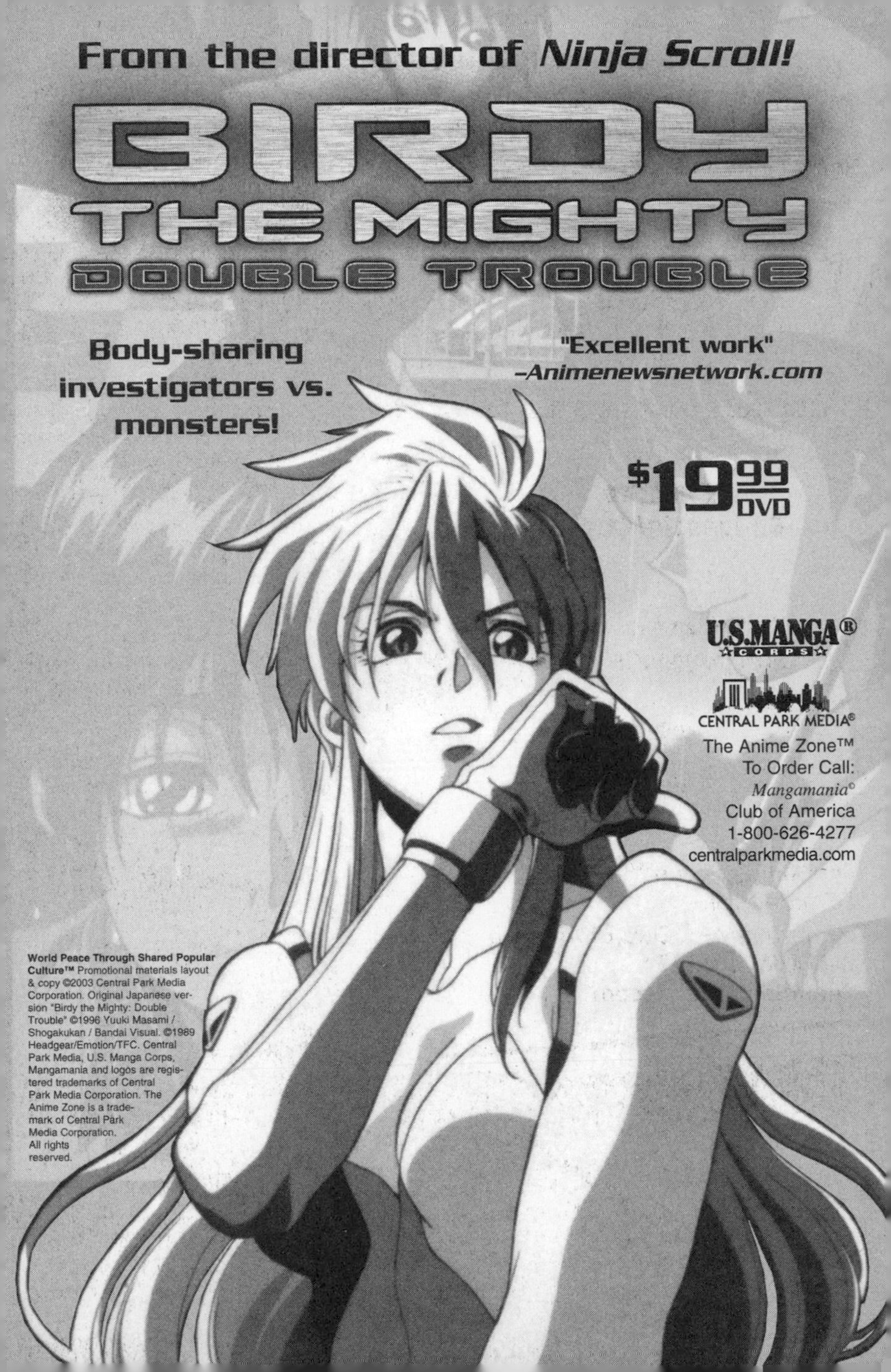

From the director of Ninja Scroll!
BIRDY THE MIGHTY
DOUBLE TROUBLE
Body-sharing investigators vs. monsters!
"Excellent work" –Animenewsnetwork.com
$19.99 DVD
U.S.MANGA® CORPS
CENTRAL PARK MEDIA®
The Anime Zone™
To Order Call:
Mangamania©
Club of America
1-800-626-4277
centralparkmedia.com
World Peace Through Shared Popular Culture™ Promotional materials layout & copy ©2003 Central Park Media Corporation. Original Japanese version "Birdy the Mighty: Double Trouble" ©1996 Yuuki Masami / Shogakukan / Bandai Visual. ©1989 Headgear/Emotion/TFC. Central Park Media, U.S. Manga Corps, Mangamania and logos are registered trademarks of Central Park Media Corporation. The Anime Zone is a trademark of Central Park Media Corporation. All rights reserved.

Classic Manga
The Right Size, The Right Price

$9.99 each

Call Me Princess

Popcorn Romance

Aquarium

Three great shoujo titles from
Tomoko Taniguchi (Available now!)

Nadesico
Book 1

Dark Angel
Book 1

Two great sci-fi titles from
Kia Asamiya (Available now!)

The Manga Zone™
To order call:
Mangamania® Club of America
1-800-626-4277
cpmmanga.com

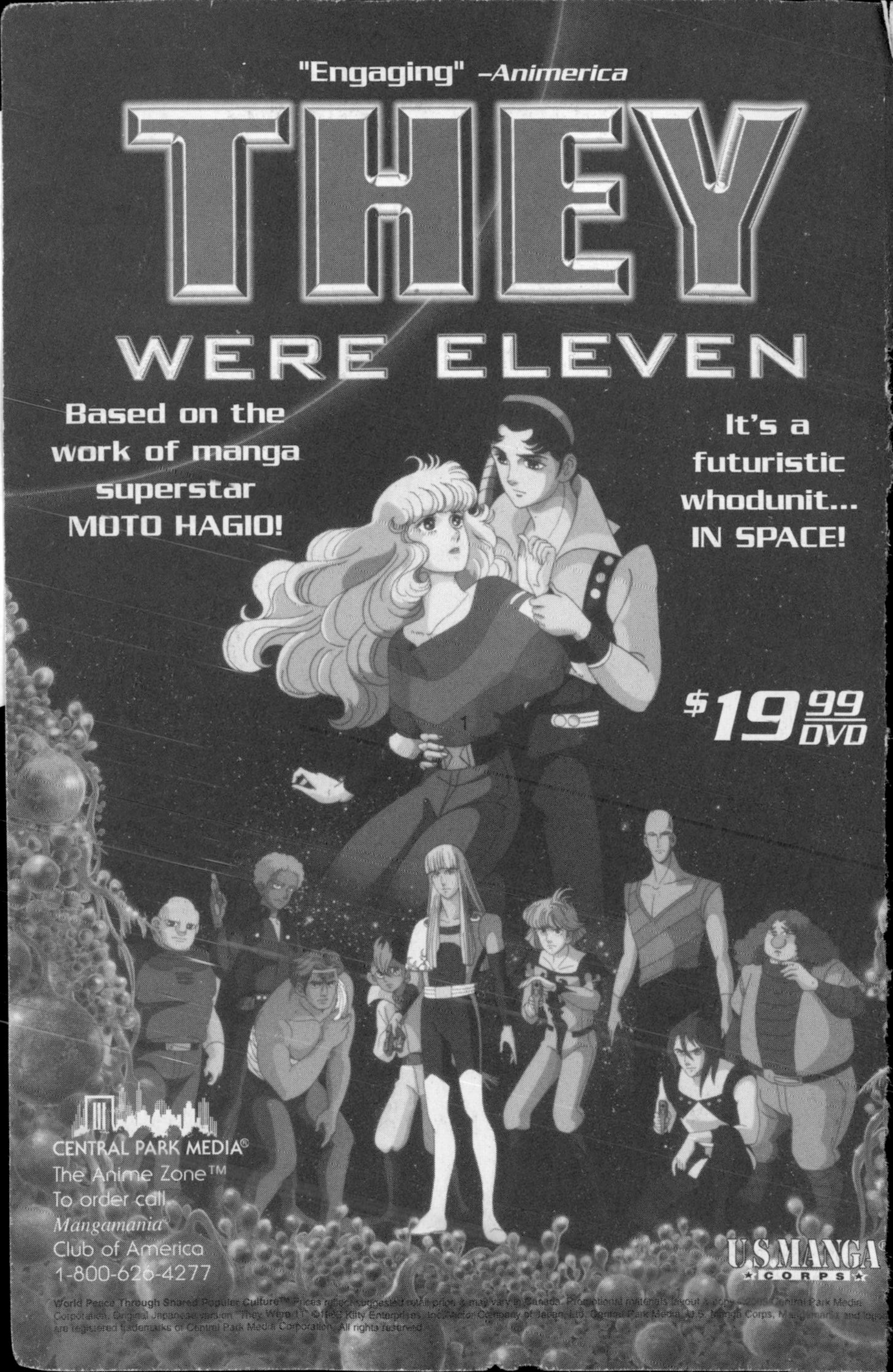
"Engaging" –Animerica
THEY
WERE ELEVEN
Based on the work of manga superstar MOTO HAGIO!
It's a futuristic whodunit... IN SPACE!
$19.99 DVD
CENTRAL PARK MEDIA®
The Anime Zone™
To order call
Mangamania
Club of America
1-800-626-4277
U.S. MANGA® CORPS
World Peace Through Shared Popular Culture™
All rights reserved

This sign reads "

S

THIS IS THE LA
OF THE BOOK! DON
RUIN THE ENDING
FOR YOURSELF.
This book is printed in the
original Japanese format,
which means that it reads
from right to left
(example on right).

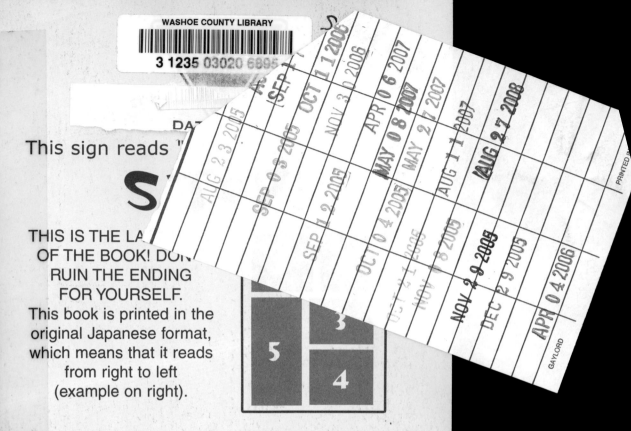

You'll find that all CPM Manga books that are part of our Original
Manga line are published in this format. The original artwork
and sound effects are presented just like they were in Japan so
you can enjoy the comic the way the creators intended.

This format was chosen by YOU, the fans. We conducted a
survey and found that the overwhelming majority of fans prefer
their manga in this format.